Return With Honor

RETURN WITH HONOR

by

GEORGE E. DAY
Colonel
U.S. Air Force (Ret.)

CHAMPLIN MUSEUM PRESS
MESA, ARIZONA

COPYRIGHT © 1989 BY GEORGE E. DAY
REGISTRATION NUMBER TXG 393-999

ALL RIGHTS RESERVED. NO PART OF THIS BOOK MAY BE REPRODUCED IN ANY FORM OR BY ANY ELECTRONIC OR MECHANICAL MEANS INCLUDING INFORMATION STORAGE AND RETRIEVAL SYSTEMS WITHOUT PERMISSION IN WRITING FROM THE PUBLISHER, EXCEPT BY A REVIEWER WHO MAY QUOTE BRIEF PASSAGES IN A REVIEW.

FIRST EDITION

LIBRARY OF CONGRESS CATALOGING - IN - PUBLICATION DATA

Day, George E., 1925 -
Return With Honor

1. Vietnamese Conflict, 1961 - 1975 — Prisoners and prisons, North Vietnamese. 2. Vietnamese Conflict, 1961 - 1975 — Personal narratives, American. 3. Day, George E. 4. Prisoners of war — United States —Biography. 5. Prisoners of war — Vietnam — Biography. I. Title.

DS559.5.D38   1990   959.704'37 — dc20   90-23566
ISBN 0-912173-16-5   CIP

Cover illustration by Jack Fellows, ASAA

Published by
Champlin Fighter Museum Press
Mesa, Arizona

PRINTED IN THE UNITED STATES OF AMERICA

DEDICATION

For the Viking who waited and fought her way for my release. To my son Steve, who at age eleven had to become a man; and who became a good man. My son George Jr., twin daughters Sandra and Sonja too young to understand but waited patiently.

To all of those people who remembered me, who prayed for me, and who wore P. O. W. bracelets.

For President Richard M. Nixon and those brave aircrews who laid their life on the line during Linebacker I and II and proved that the U.S. could bomb Hanoi back into the Stone Age in ten days . . . and who did it for my freedom.

To my departed comrades who did not die in vain . . . but in their steadfastness helped to cripple the rotten evil of Communism . . . which now in 1990 lurches into the sewer from whence it came.

And to "MISTY."

TABLE OF CONTENTS

	PREFACE	ix
	FORWARD	xi
1	ESCAPE!	1
2	ACROSS THE RIVER	20
3	MISTY	40
4	ON THE GROUND	51
5	BEHIND THE BAMBOO CURTAIN	59
6	THE BLOODY SHOE MARCH	63
7	CRIPPLED FOR MY FAITH	70
8	THE HANOI HILTON, 1967	79
9	THE PLANTATION, 1968	103
10	THE ZOO, APRIL, 1968	123
11	THE ZOO, DECEMBER, 1968	139
12	CRUCIFIXION	156
13	HEARTBREAK HOTEL	182
14	THE SHORT REUNION	194
15	BANISHED TO SKID ROW	210
16	NO O.K. CORRAL	229
17	THE END COMETH	243
18	OUT OF THE DARKNESS	248
19	OUT OF THE MALEBOLGE	252
20	CALIFORNIA, HERE I COME	254
	EPILOGUE - 1989	256
	ABOUT THE AUTHOR	258

Preface

This is a true story. It is my view and does not pretend to be an official history. It does not represent the political views of every POW, the Air Force, Department of Defense, or the United States Government.

This book is dedicated to my wife, Doris, who waited and waged her war for my return . . .

To those POWs' wives who shamed their government into the right response . . .

To the brave Americans who gave their lives in the Vietnam War, and most particularly to those men of courage who died on the cruel cement floor of "New Guy Village," for simply trying to return with honor.

Lastly, this book is written that there be no excuse for history repeating itself in fighting a war we do not intend to win, or fighting it in a way that the soldier is not permitted to win.

The concept of undeclared war for the United States is a failure, and permits our internal and external enemies to destroy us from within it, as they did from 1965-1975, by dividing us and setting our people against one another.

The North Vietnamese Communists stated that they would win the Vietnam War on the streets of San Francisco and New York City, and they found a lot of Americans to help them.

In a declared war, you can hang the rotten bastards — which generally silences them!

This book came into being in 1973 when I made a series of tapes for Ken Tomlinson of *Reader's Digest*. Ken was a coauthor of the splendid, comprehensive story of Americans imprisoned in Hanoi, entitled *POW*. Those tapes were reduced to writing as my freshest recollections of that awful time, and I mailed my manuscript to the Air Force for approval of publication.

The Air Force objected to my comments on President Lyndon Johnson, etc. I was still in uniform as a colonel and pilot, and had some hopes about my future as a fighter commander, and about getting promoted. I knew that I had "the right stuff," but that does not necessarily mean a promotion.

I felt strongly that I could not collect an Air Force check and publish a story my employer objected to . . . so I put the book away. When I failed to achieve my job and promotion goals, I retired early and dug out the book again.

"Reg" Davis pressed me to get this book published after a couple of rejections, one of which noted the story was "too Red, White and Blue, too long, too opinionated . . . and about Vietnam!" Those words about the book are mostly true! But the pointy-heads who hated the Vietnam War in those days cannot print enough stories and film enough movies about "Nam" in the late 1980s and 1990s!

Reg Davis and Susan Nixon of Phoenix cut the book down to size and smoothed out some rough spots. *Return With Honor* would not have gotten into print by Champlin Press without them. Thanks to Reg Davis for arranging and coordinating the publishing of this manuscript. Lastly, Barrett Tillman made the final editorial fixes. Thanks to all!

Colonel Bud Day, USAF(Ret)
Shalimar, Florida

Foreword

My involvement in *Return With Honor*, unknown to me at the time, began in 1968. My impeccable record of attendance at "happy hour" stood me well with the pilots of an F-4 Phantom training wing in Tucson, Arizona. I was loyal to those many occasions and was accepted as a welcomed guest by a wonderful host — the U.S. Air Force.

Stories were constantly bantered about in the "PR Bar." Often they dealt with certain pilots' exploits in Vietnam, as well as some of their own heroics. As it is in war, some of their friends never returned and had been killed or were now missing in action or were known prisoners.

The Friday afternoon golf game, followed by an "elbow-bending" event, soon graduated to a regularly-scheduled affair. I became a trusted friend and confidant of many pilots. Their need to speak to someone other than the military piqued my keen and honest interest, as did my need to hear them. The result was many treasured stories and relationships.

As a civilian trying to grapple with and understand what was happening in Southeast Asia, I was taught in a brief period a truthful, concise course in the real story about our presence in Vietnam.

The story of Colonel George E. Day was brought to my attention by Captain Mac McHugh. Mac flew secret "Misty FAC" missions in a squadron "Bud" Day had commanded at Phu Cat Air Base, South Vietnam. McHugh had provided cover for Bud until dark after the CO's shootdown. Bud's was a story of august proportions, and its dimensions have never changed.

I met Colonel Day at Phoenix, Arizona, in February 1974 when he was traveling throughout the U.S., speaking of his POW experiences. However, it was not until 1980 that I expressed a prodigious interest in developing his story into a movie or TV miniseries as well as assisting in publishing his book. NBC approved the story as a miniseries in 1986, but it was later cancelled due to the so called "sensitivity" of the subject matter.

Return With Honor is not an all-encompassing sociological, philosophical or moralistic study of prisoners of war. It is, however, a story of one man's personal tribulation about his capture, escape, recapture and incarceration. Mainly it deals with triumph and survival of the human spirit under inhumane and brutal conditions during the Vietnam War. This is a story of a genuine hero, in the same cut as those he followed in World War I, World War II, Korea and the Vietnam Conflict.

George E. Day rose from humble beginnings to become America's most-decorated military hero since General Douglas MacArthur. Of his 70 medals, over 50 were won under combat conditions. Day's love and faith in God, his fellow prisoners, his country and his love of family provided a powerful, winning combination. A strong parallel exists between World War I and the Vietnam conflict — both were totally wasteful, bringing political confusion at staggering costs and no puposeful outcome.

The men who endured the worst of WWI were forever distinguished from their fellow men. Similarly, the experiences Day had been through were so colossal, so far in contrast from anyone who had not been through the same experience, that it is impossible to share that experience in a real sense. The Vietnam POW had a different war than any other soldier. Even those taken captive early had a very different experience than those captured later.

This book portrays those experiences that will forever differentiate Day from his fellowmen. He had to conceal the top-secret "Misty" missions, his success in killing 143 Viet Cong on a single mission, and the massive destruction he had personally wrought upon the North Vietnamese.

Thus, Bud's book depicts a heady contrast. It is totally authentic, telling the truth and pulling no punches. It describes the will that refused to accept defeat; the man who refused to quit; the simple love and care for one another in order to survive. The character of the men who fought this war was foreign to the character of the men who sent them.

As POWs, all had lost their power of choice. Freedom brings choice. Now, that freedom had been abruptly and forcibly taken from them. Freedom is always expensive. Their captors were men of enraged and twisted minds. They directed their anger with exacting brutality. War requires the full measure of every man, as it did for Bud Day. His is a thoughtful, penetrating story of war's experience into hellish depths.

Bud depended heavily on his wife, Dorie. Though correspondence was almost nonexistent, his fantasies, planning and learning kept his survival instinct teeming. Day could sense the enormous courage and support of his wife in standing firm and resolute in her purpose while he was gone.

Yet Day suffered the backlash of his own integrity. In North Vietnam's prisons, injuries and disease often went untreated. There was deliberate starvation, torture and murder amid survival and sometimes humor. The American POW experience in Vietnam now is part of our military

FORWARD

heritage. We, as Americans, ought to know how Day and other prisoners endured in those camps — how they lived and how many of them died, and especially how they were treated by the enemy.

The Medal of Honor, our nation's highest award for bravery, is presented by the President in the name of Congress for "conspicuous gallantry and intrepidity at the risk of life, above and beyond the call of duty." On March 4, 1976, President Gerald R. Ford awarded the Medal of Honor to Colonel George E. Day.

Bud was cited for his epic escape attempt in August 1967, and for nearly six years of maximum resistance and stalwart leadership despite horrendous injuries and many bouts of severe torture.

The Vietnam War was not as much a blight on America as it was a direct reflection on America's unqualified leadership. Ordinary Americans just mourned their dead and cared for the scarred. The aftermath resulted from ignorant, inept policy makers and political impotency. The cost of these decisions was enormous. The Vietnam War was an appalling political botch.

It would appear that once the United States became committed, even to an undeclared war, we had the military strength, manpower, money and superior equipment to have concluded it quickly in a conventional way, as President Nixon proved during the 1972 Christmas period of Operation Linebacker II.

As the second conflict our nation has entered without victory as an objective, Vietnam was doomed for devastating results. The undeclared status usually destroys the primary goal of war — to control, gain power over, occupy or to win quickly, while losing as little as possible. The government imposed incredible handicaps on our fighting men. Thus, the war was a tragedy for the United States; it fragmented our people, causing many to question their faith in America. The effect upon Indochina still is seen two decades later.

The enemy achieved what they expected — conquest of their neighbor. And America found again that there is no glory in restraint. We moved a lot of men around, killed about a million of the enemy, lost over 58,000 of our own, bewildered some 300,000 families who are still attempting to come to terms with those events. America spent billions waging this conflict and in the end we gave away billions in planes, equipment, supplies and even air bases. The enemy of course accepted.

One last provoking thought. Was it necessary for America to lose our last two "police actions"? If so, why? Many options were available to this country. If war had been declared, unity would have prevailed. Our countrys enormous military power could then have yielded victory; quickly, effectively and with finality. Who benefited from these failures at the expense of Americans' blood, money and prestige?

This book tells a sometimes depressing story, but one full of courage and truth. It was a glorious, shining moment when Bud Day returned, as it was for all returning POWs.

The 4th Allied POW Wing was formally established in Hoa Lo Prison, Hanoi, North Vietnam. The wing motto became:

"Return with honor."

This is Bud Day's story; one of love, of undaunted courage, of honor and integrity.

Reginald Davis
Phoenix, Arizona
April 1990

CHAPTER ONE

Escape!

From the moment I was captured on August 26, 1967, I thought of little except escape. My mind frantically considered dozens of schemes and discarded each as too risky or harebrained. With three fractures of my right arm, a badly-wrenched knee and a damaged eye, even the most optimistic Air Force fighter pilot had to admit that chances for escape were low.

However, the gullibility of my Communist guard was encouraging. The young irregular could not have been more than fifteen years old. Despite his instructions to sit sphinx-like outside the hole in the ground where I was being held prisoner, he became more careless each day. He spent more and more time talking with a friend on the dusty road several yards away.

By faking internal injuries and pretending I couldn't even move, I had convinced him that I posed no escape threat. He swallowed my act so completely that he began leaning his rifle against the entrance to my bunker to engage me in sign-language conversation.

In one of these "conversations," he unwittingly told me that the moment had come for desperate measures. He entered the hole to bind my legs with cheap clothesline. After drawing the outline of a jeep on the clay wall, he said, "Hanoi!" His message was clear.

It is an unwritten rule of the battlefield that the best chance for escape lies in the first days after capture, while in the custody of untrained guards and outside the walls of an organized prison. Now, only one week after my F-100F had been shot down, the best escape conditions were in this primitive area of rice paddies. The only impediments to escape were my injuries, the lack of shoes, and the possibility of a bullet in the back if I made the attempt.

I knew I was about 18 miles north of the DMZ — the "demilitarized zone" between North and South Vietnam. Even in my condition, I thought I could make it in three nights. I could ford the Ben Hai River and walk through the DMZ to a South Vietnamese town. It would take a week at the outside.

Any escape plan had to take into account my wife, Doris, and our four children, all waiting for me in Arizona and a sobering restraint to ill-considered ventures. What reasonable man wants to make his wife a widow and leave his children fatherless?

Life as an Air Force major, jet pilot and squadron commander was sweet. Travel, excitement, challenge, and comradeship were part of my rich rewards. I didn't want to blow a good thing by volunteering for a bullet in the back.

I considered my alternatives. The previous day, I had hung by the feet like a side of butchered beef for many hours because I refused to answer my captor's questions. I knew that treatment was only the prelude. There would be prison in Hanoi. I was aware that my friend, Colonel Robbie Risner, and many other pilots had suffered through barbarous marches in that city. Nor was I looking forward to the long, arduous journey to the capital with propaganda parades through every village.

So far, my North Vietnamese captors had exposed me to the same cruelties and disregard for human decency that U.S. prisoners had suffered at the hands of the Chinese and North Koreans years earlier. Remembering the forty percent death rate of Korean prisoners, and the cruel, manipulative brainwashing they endured, the notion of going to a Communist prison was not enticing. Perhaps a bullet in the back would be preferable to being alive in Hanoi.

I was also concerned about my duty as an officer of the United States Air Force. God, honor, and country were the cornerstones of my philosophy. Not only common sense, but our Military Code of Conduct required that escape take priority over personal fears and concerns. My government did not expect me to be a kamikaze, but it did expect me to exploit any reasonable opportunity. Thanks to the carelessness of my guard, that opportunity was mine.

My plan was both simple and audacious. Like the master escapist, Houdini, I was going to disappear before the very eyes of my captor. First, I had to untie the cheap garden rope that bound me. Next, I'd wriggle out of the hole with a minimum of movement to avoid that bullet in the back. Finally, I had to choose the right blend of darkness, guard distraction, and timing. I could not escape too late in the evening, or it would be impossible to make my way through the paddies into the protection of the jungle, several miles away.

As dusk fell, my guard ambled lazily to join his rifle-carrying friend on the dirt road and began a playful, noisy conversation. The perfect moment had arrived. My frightened lips formed a silent prayer. "Help me, Father!"

When my guard headed for the road, I started untying. I was frustrated and nervous, my fingers clumsy, but at last I was free of the ropes. I scooped up my canteen of water and eased to the off side of the hole. The sky was a friendly blue-gray. The guard stood relaxed, his back to me.

I took a deep breath, said another short prayer, and slid out of the hole. There was no shout of alarm from the guard. No gunfire, no sharp crack of a rifle or searing pain!

I slid around the side of the mound. So far, so good. Luck was with me. I eased up on my feet behind the mound, out of sight of the two guards, and stole over the bank of the rice paddy.

My stomach tightened as I listened for a shot or a shout, but it was deathly still. I climbed over the paddy. As my foot hit the slick, silty bottom, I fell clumsily into the shallow water, smashing my broken arm on the ground. The pain was excruciating, and I had to grind my teeth to avoid screaming.

I swallowed the groans and listened, sure this clumsy trick had cost me my life. I eased up on to my knees, gingerly, but in the silence every move I made sounded like an earthquake to me. I kept listening. Nothing! Not a sound! Could I be this lucky?

Sweet Jesus, I'm alive and free! I looked up at God and thanked Him. Stars twinkled like little diamonds. The Milky Way pointed a neon arrow toward freedom.

Day One - September 2, 1967

Navigating was no problem. A huge thunderstorm lit the area frequently. By bearing slightly to the left of the storm, I would arrive at the tip of the woods projecting into the alluvial plain at the base of a huge mountain, just north of Khe Sanh in South Vietnam.

I listened for the sounds of discovery once more before sneaking silently down the paddy. I feared that the guard might have looked into the hole and lit a cigarette lighter or held up a small kerosene lamp to see if I was there, as he sometimes did. I was ultra tense, walking slowly because of my injuries and my fear of discovery.

I had traveled perhaps two miles through the dikes and canals of the paddy system when the night erupted with frightening sounds. Gongs clanged. Whistles blew. Flashlights began to flicker. My captors had discovered that I was missing.

My pace quickened. I shivered as I thought of the consequences of being recaptured and returned to the camp. It would make Dante's Inferno seem like nursery school.

A short while later I heard some noise to my right, and I wondered if the camp had a telephone system to the outposts. That proved to be a poor guess, but it served to accelerate my pace. I tried not to panic, or move any faster than safe under the circumstances, but I felt a desperate urgency.

Now they knew I had escaped. The die was cast!

My experience in flying over this terrain had been deceptive. From the air, it looked almost level, fairly dry, with only medium forestation. In the darkness, that same ground had become a difficult new world. It was slippery, uneven, brutal, punishing, and more barren than I had suspected.

I had anticipated only rice paddies between my "hole" and the small woods that was my goal. Instead, I found myself on firm ground that might have been used for grazing. It was fairly irregular and very, very difficult to travel. The pain in my knee caused monumental trouble with walking. It was torture even to move my leg. My arm throbbed like sin and I hobbled in a state of near shock.

Lightning from the friendly storm seemed to illuminate a path, and the thunder distracted me from the pain. My hopes buoyed. With a little luck and a cool head, God willing, I felt I had a pretty good chance of getting out of North Vietnam and making it to the South. After all, the big step was over. I was free!

Only a few weeks before, Navy Lieutenant Dieter Dengler had been rescued out of Laos. I had read his escape debriefing two weeks before my own capture. I knew if my break were successful, I would be the first man to escape from North Vietnam.

If it worked, I'd soon see my wife in Honolulu. If it failed, I might not see her for . . . how long? Who could tell? Some men had already been prisoners for years.

For now, I had to concentrate on the present, not the future. The simple task of walking was nearly impossible because my broken arm kept me from moving with the dexterity that I needed. My injured eye affected my depth perception, and the ground never seemed the right distance from my face. I kept expecting to fall or lose my balance.

Still, another mile passed and an overwhelming sense of exhilaration and self-satisfaction bubbled up in me, particularly since I knew that they knew I was gone. I savored the triumph of getting out of the hole without getting shot. My scheme had been well planned and well executed up to this point. I felt encouraged by a new sense of confidence.

The score: Yanks - 1; V.C. - 0!

Day Two - September 3, 1967

As dawn approached, I saw with relief that my navigation had been good. My landmark jutted out about where I had visualized it. I could see that I could make it before daybreak, but without time to spare since the Vietnamese are early risers.

Ahead, I saw what looked like a forest. As I came within range of the trees, however, I saw they were disappointingly thin. Staying there through the day would be risky.

I surveyed the area. My only choices were to remain where I was or to enter the limited cover of the trees. While I was debating which way to move, I saw straight ahead, and to the south, a fairly good-sized lake. It was a substantial barrier, and I had to decide whether to circle it to the left or to the right.

I studied the terrain and decided my best bet would be to go around the left side of the lake, that being the most direct course. Suddenly, I heard a whistling, high-pitched, almost shrieking noise. I sensed that it was an aerodynamic sound, something moving through the air. Even with sixteen years as a pilot, I had never heard anything quite like it. Then a long string of bombs began exploding along the left side of the lake ... exactly down the path I had selected as my future course!

The first bombs hit about a mile from me, but as the next ones churned the ground, the explosions seemed to be "walking" toward me. They augered holes in the ground about thirty feet apart, like punctures from a giant corn planter. I realized it was a B-52 strike. More than 100 bombs exploded one by one along a furrow almost a mile long.

The noise was deafening, explosions going on minute after minute. They were throwing tons of mud, dirt, and rocks about, but I felt strangely detached. There was an amusing irony in it. "To live by the bomb, to die by the bomb." Poetic justice?

As quickly as it started, the blizzard of destruction halted barely half a mile from me. Later, I realized that the B-52s had struck gun concentrations near the lake.

My fatigued body begged for sleep. My arm throbbed. My leg and feet vibrated with pain. It is hard to do written justice to the problem of being without shoes. Walking the entire night had extracted a heavy toll from my shoeless feet.

It was about 6 a.m. and the gun emplacements which hadn't been damaged by the air strike began to fire and continued for most of the day. I bedded down in the densest brush I could find.

Mere yards away, numerous children were moving about. Vietnamese adults were busy carrying meals to the soldiers manning the guns. Luckily, the adults were not searching for me and my puny cover was adequate. My body was tense, demanding sleep to ease the fatigue. I was afraid I would start snoring and betray my hideout. I wanted no part of imprisonment again! Freedom was too sweet to be captured on my first day out. Sleep could wait.

I planned my route for the evening, opting to depart through the recently bombed area. Because of the possibility of unexploded bombs, it wasn't the safest area, but it was on my course. I hoped that common sense would keep the Vietnamese away.

I wanted desperately to get moving, and I planned to travel all night. The day was dreadful, in that twilight zone between conscious and unconscious. I was in limbo, fighting sleep and waiting for the soothing touch of darkness.

The canteen gave me comfort, still full of the water I had carried out. I sipped a little, budgeting it carefully. As dusk fell, the people in the gun positions began abandoning them and returning to their homes. I envied them the luxury of bed. The children disappeared.

Dusk melted into the mouth of another beautiful night. The sky was very dark and the stars extremely bright. It was encouraging to see my own friendly Milky Way. It was going to be a great night to navigate. The shield of full darkness fell, and with six or seven miles travelled thus far, I had many miles left to cover.

In the area where the bombs had landed, I came in contact with enormous, rough clods and surprisingly sharp melted rocks formed by the explosions. There is a sub-strata of sand, a low-grade limestone, about six or seven feet below the topsoil in Vietnam. As a bomb blast goes off, it excavates the subsoil and fuses the sand and soft rock into a glassy obstacle course, very sharp and irregular.

Walking was difficult, almost impossible. My leg had stiffened and the pain slowed my progress. I had to pick my way through the burned dirt piles, rubble, rocks and clods thrown up from the holes. It was a job for a much more nimble man than I was and my shoeless feet became a shredded, bloody mass.

I forded a shallow river, trying to keep my injured arm dry. I remembered the jungle rot that had been the plague of World War II G.I.s in Southeast Asia. An ounce of prevention was important.

Heavy tropical rain began to fall and I searched for a large, heavy bush that would offer a measure of protection. Lightning in Vietnam, and the ensuing thunder, are fantastic. Wet, chilled, and injured, in the lonely darkness of a thunderstorm, it was comforting to have God.

I tried to keep my cast dry, but couldn't. I reluctantly accepted the cold drenching, since I couldn't vote on it. Finally, the rain eased off, but the clouds remained. I stood up, looked around a little, and speculated on where I wanted to go. It was too dark to make any meaningful decisions. I decided to wait for a clear sky.

I knew I had to avoid making any panic moves that would be self-defeating. Borrowing the best bush I could find, I laid down and dozed off. The mosquitoes were thick and noisy, but I was so tired that I could have slept through just about anything.

ESCAPE!

Day Three - September 4, 1967

I was only partially awake when I was raised up off the ground and thrown violently sideways! A bomb, a rocket, a shell . . . something had exploded very close to me. I began vomiting violently. With ears ringing, I lay in a daze. I tried to understand what had happened, but I couldn't organize my thoughts. The physical shock from the blast wiped out my power to recall the event itself.

Nausea unlike any I'd ever known before compounded my pain. I vomited repeatedly. The convulsions were intolerable, but I continued to retch long after my stomach was empty.

I needed thicker cover. As I tried to stand and walk, I was overcome by dizziness. Off balance, ears still ringing, I was forced to crawl like an animal into the brush. I tried a couple of sips of water, knowing I would be dehydrated soon at the rate I was vomiting. The water acted like a match in oxygen. It triggered another spasm of vomiting.

It seemed that the only option was to lie down, try to rest, and see what nature could do. My ears were still ringing as I collapsed in troubled sleep.

When dawn finally came, I felt like I'd been hit by a truck. I've had some bad mornings in my day, but never a headache like this, the granddaddy of all skullbusters.

"Count your blessings," I thought. "It isn't all bad. At least you're out of the 'hole' and free."

The day broke beautifully . . . a gorgeous sky, light, pretty, blue. Although I felt awful, I was glad, and more than a little surprised to be alive. I had lost a night of travel, I hurt terribly, but I was alive!

I had to wait out the entire day. Each time I tried to stand erect, I was overcome with nausea and dizziness. From the dried crusts of blood on my face, I knew both my nose and ears had been bleeding. Since my ears were ringing, I knew my eardrums had ruptured. I was too exhausted to care. When the alternative is death, injury has its appeal.

As I was to learn in years to come, God designed our bodies to do a great deal of self repair. All I needed was rest and some sleep.

Day Four - September 5, 1967

I woke again to a lovely morning with a near cloudless sky. A beautiful orange sun was burning an apple-sized bite out of the horizon to the east. My stomach growled slightly, reminding me that in two days I had not even thought about food.

On this fourth morning, I sipped hesitantly from the canteen, expecting the worst. My lips were hard, my mouth and throat parched, and I was convinced I must have a light fever. The water felt cool, soothing, almost tasty to my fuzzy tongue. The nausea failed to reappear, but was replaced by a slight queasiness.

I checked my urine and it was bright yellow. My vital body fluids were pumping overboard. I washed another tiny taste of water around in my dry mouth and didn't vomit.

It seemed that today could be a walking day. Assuming that the sun rose in the east, even in a Communist country, I had a good "terrain fix" on due south. The brush was well suited to cover my travel if I walked in a crouch to conceal my five-foot, nine-inch frame.

Fatigue overwhelmed willpower, and after a few steps my legs folded. I had to sit down. Warm, feverish flashes gave way to self pity. I was carrying the burdens of the world. I couldn't dispel the thought that I had probably botched my great chance to make good the escape. Lines from Shakespeare popped into my mind:

> "When in disgrace with fortune and men's eyes
> I all alone beweep my outcast state
> And trouble deaf heaven with my bootless cries
> And look upon myself and curse my fate
> And wish me like to one more rich in hope . . ."

I certainly felt outcast and in disgrace with fortune. No one could deny I was "bootless!" Yet some other part of my mind protested these negative thoughts. Self pity had never been my bag, and I had always been contemptuous of such attitudes. If I had subscribed to "can't do," I'd still be a high school dropout working on an assembly line.

I got up and forced my feet to move, but as day aged into afternoon, it became more and more difficult to keep going. I was so distracted by my physical condition, I had not been looking for the enemy, or taking any sensible action to stay concealed. I realized I was out of control, like a horse with the "blind staggers," simply lunging along.

I was concerned that my mind was wandering, lacking continuity of thought. It replayed episodic flashbacks of unrelated events with frightening frequency. School, flying, hunting, camping, music, poetry. I wondered how near I was to insanity.

Nagging pain in my lower right leg made me aware that I had a problem. During a rest period I found a huge, angry red spot with a bloody, scabbed area in the center. Could I have been injured in the recent blast explosions, and not even known it?

I told myself, "Surely I would have felt it. It's out of the question for me to have taken a hit and not know it!" Despite that summary dismissal, the calf was enlarged and tender. It was clear that I had a new problem . . . shrapnel in my leg.

ESCAPE!

The day was a bonanza for water. A fairly large banana tree had water trapped in its leaves. I refilled my canteen again by manipulating the leaves so the water could run into its small opening. It was fresh, probably yesterday's rain.

Once again I realized I had not been concerned about food. My nausea had vanished to obscurity. As I discovered that I felt much better, my morale began to soar.

"Hell, I survived the explosions. It has to be all downhill from here. I'm going to make it!"

The thought of freedom pushed my optimism a notch higher. What a thrill it would be to hear and see an F-100F, my "Misty." What a coup it would be if my own people could somehow help me in this escape!

Right now it was breakfast, brief, and pre-launch time at Phu Cat. I idly wondered who had taken my job. By now Bill Douglass had rotated home. One, even several, of my Mistys could be flying over North Vietnam at this exact moment.

Back at Phu Cat, someone was packing my personal effects to mail home. Someone was reading the letters from my wife, Doris, and wrapping my plaques to be mailed.

What about Doris, whom I affectionately call the Viking? What had she heard of my shootdown? What did she tell four small children about the fact that they might no longer have a father?

Gathering both my thoughts and energy, I assessed the problem of staying free. The pain in my leg was increasing and triggered the fear that I might lose my ability to walk. I estimated my position at 15 to 20 miles from the Ben Hai River and the "neutral" area — the Demilitarized Zone between North and South Vietnam.

A compelling urgency nagged me to get to the river as soon as possible. I hoped that the probability of capture was lower there. At least it would get me away from the villages that dotted the countryside.

I expected the intensity of the V.C. activity to be lower on the south side of the river. I didn't have much of a reserve left to run on. It was clear that I would either start getting hungry soon, or I would drop from lack of energy.

I didn't know how long I could exist without food. I estimated no more than eight to ten days. Quite suddenly it occurred to me that in all my traveling I had not seen a single bird or animal. That food source was denied me.

Strange-looking, stubby trees appeared late in the day. Four or five feet tall, jagged, broken, burned and mauled from the ordnance that ripped through them, it appeared as though an angry Colossus had passed by. Remnants of napalm cans, an aircraft drop tank, and other signs of violence were visible in all directions.

Boxes of mortar rounds with Czech markings lay forgotten on the ground, including a box with seven or eight rounds left. On this day, I had to climb through a trench where, in the past, a corpse had laid rotting. That hideous pervasive stench was unmistakable.

Day Five - September 6, 1967

The following morning, I looked up at God and found myself rested. The sky was beautiful again, another lovely day, balmy and cool. I anxiously examined my right leg where swelling was now a major concern. It seemed to be holding its own.

I was north of a jungle area I had to get through. I decided to play it by the book, stay in the brush to the side of the trail and see if I could make it to the river. The ringing in my ears was no longer the piercing screech of the past few days. Although occasional dizziness lingered, nausea had lessened and water didn't cause vomiting.

A good-sized ground swell presented a view of a prominent rise that I named "Porkchop Hill." I took a fix on it, locked it into my memory, and decided that this was the time to make haste.

"Like the Allied army heading for the Rhine," I thought. The best way to evade the enemy who walked the trails was to stay off the path myself.

With my surroundings covered by brush, thin trees, mesquite, and healthy bushes, I was convinced that I could get off the trails and navigate, although it would be slower. Off-the-trail travel proved a pipe dream; a great theory, but unworkable. Whoever had written the manual suggesting it in the jungle had never tried it here.

I began to pray more fervently, and it embarrassed me that my interest in prayer was increasing. I felt like a hypocrite, since my recent actions didn't match my religious fervor. I felt guilty for using God only when the chips were down. Even so, I told myself it had to be better to pray than not to pray, and I started a prayer of thanksgiving. I was thankful that I'd gotten out of the camp, that I was moving along well, and, particularly, that I had escaped death in the explosion two days before.

All things considered, I had a good chance of reaching Da Nang Air Base in a few days, getting a new cast on my arm. From my present position I was only an hour away by plane. After Da Nang was home and family.

I found that by concentrating I could hear the Viking's voice and see her face. I remembered some of her endearing phrases and felt a warmth of spirit in the fantasy that I was somehow in communication with her. I remembered her warm arms on our last night together in Phoenix, and how I could always sense her steps when she approached.

I thought of my son, George, pleased and excited in his first cowboy boots. I recalled the thrilled shrieks of the twins as we streaked down a hill on our bobsled. There was Steve, smiling over his first pan of bacon and eggs in the pine forest.

I began making promises to myself about things we would buy and do. A larger boat would be a great way to lock the family together. Travel! How sweet it would be for my children to see the world as I had seen it.

Snapping back to my wilderness surroundings, I knew that those plans were possible if, and *only* if, the escape were completed. The first order of business was to make the escape work.

I pointed myself toward the southeast, by estimation straight to Dong Ha and freedom! My plan fell through with unexpected rapidity. A heavily forested area forced me to consider the obvious. I couldn't walk through the stone wall of dense jungle.

In spite of the techniques taught in survival school, my attempts to penetrate the underbrush were fruitless. It was far too tough, the trees were too thick, and the jungle canopy cut off all reference points for navigation fixes. There was no way I could travel through the jungle without a compass, and no way that I could walk, except on the trails.

It was something like being placed in a pitch black closet, turned several times, and then being asked to find south. I had to rely on instinct, make judgments, and guess. I picked a trail and hoped for the best.

It took a long time to get through the heavy jungle, using less caution than usual. I was determined to get within striking distance of the Ben Hai that night. Late afternoon, as the sun began to hide in the west, I had an opportunity to assess my progress.

Standing on a knoll with a commanding view of Porkchop Hill, I looked at the sun, faced the south, estimated my distance to the hill, and compared it to my position that morning.

I could have cried. Porkchop Hill was definitely farther away now than it had been when I started! I had lost at least two or three miles. The only explanation was that I had walked in a circle. Curses ripped from my disappointed mouth.

"It's time to reassess what I've been doing," I told myself. "Dammit! There's only one way I can make it. The 'V' are moving north-south and those will be the wider, hard-worn trails. I'm going to walk them. I'll have to accept whatever navigation errors this causes. I'll cage these errors in the mental computer and keep a general idea of the course across the ground," I planned. "I'll make corrections at the end of the trail, instead of accomodating all day long."

My physical condition was demoralizing. Both legs were nearly unusable, sore, unsteady, almost palsy-like. My feet were battered and each cut was swollen, the raw edges pursed outward like a set of Ubangi lips. I didn't understand why, but either the soil or the brush had a peculiar toxic effect on each wound. I needed more foot problems like I needed appendicitis!

The skin on my forehead was burned and filthy. The stink of my unwashed body disgusted me. The idea of a shower was appealing, and particularly sweet was the thought of soaking my sore feet in hot water.

My trousers had been reduced from rags to a breech clout. Held together only by the backing on the waistband, the fly and pockets, they no longer offerred the faintest protection. My shirt was in equally poor condition, shredded by the brush and thorns. I realized I had made the full circle. I came into the world bare and again I was bare. But I was also *free* bare, which had to be the best kind!

The day was not a total disaster. Fortune smiled on me faintly as I came to a bush with a slightly purplish berry. Though not a color recommended by survival instructors, I sampled one to see if they were safe to eat.

There were very few ripe berries on any of the bushes. There were so many explosions convulsing and rattling the earth that the ripe ones were knocked off by the shockwaves. The ones I found were disappointingly small, perhaps two-thirds the diameter of a man's little finger. They were similar to a blueberry in shape, and less flavorful than a mulberry. My mouth watered with anticipation! After days of abstinence, the lightly sugared berries tingled my taste buds.

My prayers for food had been answered, but this discovery was a curse as well. It triggered off a preoccupation with food, compulsive and overwhelming. I found myself staring fixedly at every light green bush that came into view. Berries became the new beacon of my existence. In my searchings that day, I discovered only five or six ripe berries, after examining several hundred under-ripe ones.

Surprisingly, there were no serious symptoms of nausea. I tasted additional berries, and was overcome by the delicacy of the tasty blend of sugar and berry acid. It was a rare treat, recalling to mind exotic foods of days gone by: Mahi Mahi, lobster, clam chowder, Andulusian cream sherry, Georgia paper shell pecans, mallard, the breast of pheasant.

It was time to pray and mentally debrief the day's events. Debriefing was a ritual from my fighter pilot training. Every aspect of a flight was discussed in order to improve future performance.

All in all, the day had been pathetic. I felt dejected again, remorseful and angry. I was running out of stamina. I knew there were not many days like this left, since my physical condition could only become worse.

I would have to spend more time and effort looking for food to build up my energy. I had to be alert for opportunities to catch frogs, which were plentiful.

Like a bolt from the blue, it occurred to me that while I'd been thinking and planning, I'd heard many gun positions firing from the south. That was the answer! I'd be on the lookout for a friendly gun position in South Vietnam. I slipped off the side of the trail, found a good bush, and laid down for a good night's sleep.

Day Six - September 7, 1976

As dawn broke on the sixth morning, I looked up at God's clear sky. I dashed a little water in my face and it was refreshing.

"To be alive, how sweet it is! My cup runneth over," I mused. "I'm really a lucky man."

Water was still no problem. Small streams criss-crossed my route, many running clear and almost virgin pure. Tree stumps and banana trees held plentiful stores.

It was good to be five-nine and a wiry 150 pounds. "Lean and mean" is A-OK. Before shootdown I could do 25 one-armed push-ups with either hand. Even though I'd been damaged, I still felt strong and determined, without serious ill effects from lack of food.

There was an angry lump around the scab on my right leg, reminding me of a walnut tucked under the skin. I was so scratched up that I couldn't see whether or not I had a blood-poison streak.

I eased off the trail. The reduced visibility and the noise of a light rain made walking too dangerous. As I crouched under a friendly bush, I heard and saw a Vietnamese. A small sheet of green plastic was draped over his shoulders like a shawl, turning the rain aside. His head was covered with a steel helmet, painted a dark camouflage brown, and he carried a rifle partly slung across his shoulders, protruding from the piece of plastic. His feet sported the typical rubber tire thongs and were unusually noisy as he slopped down the trail.

Although this was my first brush with an NVA soldier in the jungle, I was to come to know their habit patterns very well; their dress, actions and movements. They were as careless as if they were in their own village, and exercised no caution.

When the rain shut off, I eased onto the trail and inched my way down into the valley.

In a small marshy area I saw a large frog. More and more frogs appeared and leaped into two small, shallow pools of water. I stood ankle-deep in the pools and tried to catch them, but they were too quick. Finally, I caught a large one. It was my chance to taste raw frog.

Back in the 1930s, college boys swallowed live goldfish, and it had become a nationwide fad. Here was a once-in-a-lifetime chance to make my mark on history. Taking the frog by his back feet, I stretched his legs out, opened my mouth and slipped him in. I took a couple of big hard chewing bites and swallowed. I had to talk fast and furious to sell myself on the idea. Raw frogs will not win a Duncan Hines award!

The energy from froggie was going to get me home, so I went after another. I skidded and slipped clumsily, and they eluded me easily. Had I been more mobile, it would have been possible to survive on frogs alone, as I saw hundreds of them in the next few days.

As I skirted some trees and bushes, I noticed a single fruit that resembled a tangerine, with a fine textured skin, obviously of the citrus family. I peeled it in anticipation of a tasty, juicy morsel. Much to my surprise, it was totally different from American citrus. Under the skin was a thick layer of pulp, delightfully sweet and sticky, like marmalade. I ate it quickly. The center was three rock-hard segments with natural divisions like an orange. It was Balefruit—an orange with the world's largest seed!

From a high ridge, I took a fix on the south and then turned around. Happily, I could see Porkchop Hill to the north. By George, I'd moved forward!

Today, and in the course of each day to come, I was within earshot, or sight, of several guns firing from the south. Frequently I could see or hear incoming rounds landing near me. There was evidence of shelling everywhere. Broken and maimed trees, gouges, and shell holes dotted the landscape. Aircraft roared and zoomed over the DMZ. Most were F-8s, A-4s, or F-4s, which I assumed were Marine aircraft operating from Chu Lai or Da Nang.

From my flights in this area, I felt that I was close to a large white house on the north side of the Ben Hai River. It sat majestically to the west of the so-called Freedom Bridge. Somewhere southeast of my position was a built-up area. I saw a huge, red North Vietnamese flag flying in that direction during the afternoon. I expected the village to be southeast of my knoll. It was more nearly due south, proving that I was substantially farther to the east than I wanted to be.

In the afternoon, I saw another Vietnamese, then two of them together. I began to wonder if they were U.S. Marines. Their uniforms were familiar to me, grayish green, unlike the dark forest green of the Vietnamese uniforms I had been seeing. My first impulse was to whistle to them, but discretion was the better part of valor. I couldn't believe there were any Americans operating this far north. I watched them, thinking they might be scouts of a larger unit. They passed out of sight, never to be seen again.

I came to a huge area that looked like a photograph of the moon. There were hundreds of bomb craters, one after another. It was awesome; most holes were filled with a very deep blue-green water, a strange contrast to the bright red soil.

My courage waned at the sight of the millions of tiny sharp sand, glass, and rock fragments which would slice my feet to ribbons again, and leave me without a shred of concealment. By the end of my crossing, I was so lame I could hardly take the last steps to get through. When I stopped on the south side of the "moon" and rested, my morale began to climb. It had been a great day! I was never to see Porkchop Hill again, and I counted my blessings, forming some long prayers. "Thank you, God, for my good progress and navigation."

I was on another elation jag, high as a wino on a quart of port. Not a doubt now that, with a few breaks, I'd be home free. I pictured what was going to happen next.

I'd cross the river and the DMZ. There would be a road and a gun position, or maybe a truck. I let my mind outline the picture. A truck would come roaring up the road, a bunch of armed GIs on it, and I'd slip out of the brush with my hand in the air, showing them the cast on my arm so they wouldn't shoot me on the spot. Even though I didn't have any identification, I'd show them my flying school class ring, and I'd be an identified American.

Then would come the hospital at Da Nang, having my arm and leg taken care of. Following a hot bath and clean uniform, I'd have jet transport to Pearl Harbor and a reunion with Doris. I let thoughts of her take over: that beautiful smile, and her loving, pleasant laugh. I could hear her voice saying things as only she can say them. She was there with me — I could hear her so plainly.

Unhappily, real-world time returned. I finished my prayers and slept.

Day Seven - September 8, 1967

This day was going to be a hard one. The terrain was "some kind of tough," very irregular, with super trees to the south. To get through there and up the other side, then over to the river was to be one of the truly great acts of this drama.

As I started down the bank, just my weight on my feet brought excruciating pain. I picked a trail with a southerly heading, and immediately lost track of the sun. I carried on, followed the trail, and hoped that it continued to the south, which it did.

The valley was another "moon" village of gaping craters and thinned-out trees. The sky was filled with air activity to the south and west. An O-1 spotter plane buzzed and sputtered, marking targets with smoke rockets for the many A-4s, F-4s and F-8s making bombing passes at the ground.

The O-1 that I'd heard two or three times during the morning finally popped into view. He was pointed in my general direction, flying slightly toward me. Flying low and slow, the spotter looked more like a toy than a war plane. He was perhaps a mile and three-quarters away. Making a turn, he headed to the west and dropped out of sight behind the horizon. This gave me hope that at the right place and time, I might attract the attention of a spotter plane.

Right over the bluff and down the hill had to be the Ben Hai River. I figured I must be due north of Dong Ha, South Vietnam. At the end of a long hard day, I could see the trees along the river.

My feet hurt unbearably. It took every ounce of mental ability to force my legs to move. I became so preoccupied with picking and choosing where my sore feet would touch the ground, and thinking about my empty stomach, that I could not daydream, nor could I remember to watch for the enemy.

Food obsessively sapped my waning self control. I found myself staring at the brush, dawdling and stalling, partially out of control. I kept jerking myself up with inspiring pep talks.

"Get a move on. You can't search every bush for a few puny berries."

By diligent scrounging, I found eight to ten delicious berries. This miniscule bit of food was like a banquet. I drank as many canteens of water as I could hold, but water does not satisfy hunger. My urine was now running clear. A little food, some water, and lots of determination would carry the day!

As I got to a ridge on the downhill side, I could see the big old plantation house. It seemed to pop out of the greenery, just as I imagined "Tara" from *Gone With the Wind*. There it reigned in stark white splendor, its red tile roof muted in the dusk.

The old house warmed my heart. It was as antebellum as Montgomery, Alabama in 1855, and looked like my territory. I made my way down the hill, physically and mentally elated. The journey had come off like a hole-in-one on the golf course.

I mentally patted myself on the back. My navigation had been accurate and satisfying, except for the big circle. The trail dead-ended on the shore of the Ben Hai River where it cried muddy tears from west to east.

As I approached the house, heavy dusk mantled the river bottom in purple shades of evening. I rounded a slight turn in the trail and three "V" filed straight toward me. Luckily, I was well concealed against the brush and they were neither vigilant nor aware. They proceeded a few steps in my direction, made a 90° turn to the east, and paralleled the river bank.

Soon I recognized the familiar noises of a camp. Machettes whacked and chopped, cooking smells tantalized my nose, and laughter floated on the breeze. Having no other outlets, their principal time killer was horseplay. A poorly trained lot, they were totally lacking in the noise discipline that is an integral part of American combat training.

Their boisterous, careless clowning left them pathetically vulnerable to surprise attack. What was more pathetic was that, despite the great power of the U.S. and our long history of commando actions during World War II, a totally unimaginative command in Saigon and our even more inept commander-in-chief were fighting the war solely on enemy terms. Little wonder the enemy felt secure.

My heart longed for a closer look at the big white house, but the brush was too thin for safe maneuvering. My existing cover failed to conceal adequately, but it was safer than running into security guards or outposts. It was time to bed down and review plans for getting across the river.

Freedom was only a few yards and hours away. It was a challenge to curb my mounting excitement. I planned for a 3:30 A.M. wake-up by my mental alarm clock. Then, moving to the west of the big house, I'd find some driftwood for flotation across the river. I needed to be across and into the brush on the south side before the "V" in camp came alive. I believed the river current would not be swift, and I planned to be across well before floating abreast of the big house. The Ben Hai is a major river, comparable to the Missouri near St. Joseph.

Darkness swallowed me. In accordance with the pecking order, first the gnats chewed me, only to be overpowered by the roaring clouds of mosquitoes. As I thought about the next day, it was easy to soar into pipe dreams. Things were going so perfectly that I owed a prayer of thanks.

I marvelled at the wonder of having my prayers answered. How lucky I was to have God. How lucky just to be alive! My excitement built until I wanted to jump up and cheer.

My elation was stabbed by sudden, stark cold terror. The familiar sound of an inbound artillery shell pierced the black silence and it was close! I knew with frightening certainty it would land within lethal range. Each type of shell has a distinct sound, and with practice, one can become expert in predicting the impact point. This one whined toward me like an arrow fired at my heart.

I mashed my awkward body into the earth, wishing I were a mole or an earthworm. The shell thumped into the soft dirt some 75 yards in front of me. First it shivered the earth, lightened the black night with orange glow, and then uttered an earsplitting, BLAM! Shell fragments spun and tore at the arms and bodies of the low-standing bushes.

The impact of the first round was barely absorbed when another roared menacingly inbound. Vaguely I was aware of the "V" screaming and jabbering in the void to my left. Listening, I predicted this one would land in that direction. I realized this was harassment and interdiction fire. Each incoming round would impact a few yards from the previous rounds.

If the next one "walked" about 70 yards to the north, it would be goodbye for George Day, ex-Air Force major! The round impacted short and well to my left, so far away that it barely rattled the ground.

While there was no satisfaction in being shelled, there was great comfort in knowing that a particular shell would not be the one to fragment my body into a cloud of bloody particles. A desperate urgency welled inside my skull to do something, to stop this, somehow to stay alive, to survive. Fortunately, my brain over-ruled such ill-conceived notions and my body pressed and squeezed itself into the earth. My ear now tuned to another round pointing to my right. It impacted well short and the blast effect was minimal, but the noise of the explosion boggled my mind and vibrated the membranes of my ear like a tuning fork.

Mud and dirt subsided from the third round as the fourth one knifed inward. Again, it was coming straight at me. My stomach churned and I prayed as I waited for the strike. It impacted near me — a dud. I lay in disbelief, unable to understand that it had not exploded. My disbelieving ears tracked an additional nine rounds, every one of which was a dud.

My mind grasped the fact that some turncoat gunner was sabotaging these rounds by not fuzing them properly. He was probably a Viet Cong sympathizer on the payroll of the South Vietnamese Army.

Unanswered questions swirled in my mind. Questions every man faced with eternity may contemplate. Can this be real? Am I actually on this lunatic stage? Or am I the audience? Is there any meaning to it all?

This week's events had been like the tortured dreams of a drunk drying out. Am I the walking parallel of that demented soul who inserts a single round into a revolver, spins the cylinder, and with closed eyes and white knuckled fingers squeezes the trigger, uncertain whether he hopes to hear a harmless click, or . . .?

I have no control over these events. Why does death call my name? Has God predestined me to live? Or is there some quirk of fate such as high winds that deflect the missiles? Is it merely luck that my tired and battered feet did not carry me closer to some impact point?

Caution told me the duds had been fired with a delayed fuze, and would explode in minutes, or hours. Past experience said no. Small-calibre rounds had an instantaneous fuze which exploded upon contact. I was confident none of these rounds would explode, and none did.

It was not easy to sleep with the charge of adrenalin I had. I offered another round of prayers, knowing I had already blocked every line to God with the prayers and petitions of the last few minutes.

I discovered that heretofore I only thought that I knew something about mosquitoes. This was the big league. They met some disappointments, however. My forehead, exposed skin, eyelids, and ears were simply one crusty scab. Every inch of me was either so sunburned, scabbed up, or so filthy that there wasn't a lot these vampires could bite. The dreadful din of the swarms that tried to fly into my ears, jockeying and fighting for landing rights, was as annoying as the bites. Because of the combination of noise and adrenalin, sleep was slower in coming than any previous night.

My mental alarm clock fired off with precision. As I sat rubbing the sleep from my eyes, my ears detected the sound of falling bombs. As the noise increased, I realized these bombs were going to be bloody close. They were!

"Sweet Jesus," said my head, "here we go again. Hey, Lord, what are you so mad about? I'm your friend!"

As I squeezed against the earth once more, bombs began to rain dead center on the Viet Cong camp. They "walked" away from me, west to east. BLAM! BOOM! KERTHUMP! The ground vibrated in agony and shock waves from the almost continual blast that cut through the early morning silence.

Pieces of shrapnel, mud, and trees were hurled about like pebbles from the hand of a giant. They whined, whizzed, and buzzed above me. I rejoiced that I was at least a quarter of a mile from the holocaust. Huge fires burned as bright orange, ammunition instantly torched and exploded.

Approximately every fifteenth or twentieth bomb went off in an air burst, 40 or 50 feet above the ground, and lighted the area, deafening the ears. The effect of these air bursts was devastating. People in the target area were being rained on by blast effect, steel, and fire. It was far more effective than ordinary ground bursts. There was no doubt that the bombers had a good target since fires from fuel and explosions of ammunition continued long after the bombs ceased falling. At least three full aircraft loads of bombs, not less than 200, smashed into the shore of the river.

I was relieved that I was not under the storm and its cloud of death. "Thank God!" I said. "I guess You can't be too mad at me. In fact, You must like me quite a bit!"

I remembered Viking's comment after I survived my no-chute bailout, "He has to be saving you for something. One day, you will know what."

There could not have been a better diversion to cover my movements. The surviving "V," if any, were going to have some sore heads. They would be dazed, excited, and busy. If there were sentries posted at "Tara," they would have rushed to the carnage of the camp.

I passed "Tara" with disappointment, feeling a strong bond of affection for this single vestige of civilization in a prehistoric jungle. The resemblance to the legendary home of Scarlett O'Hara was poignant. It *was* the mansion, exactly as I had pictured it in 1940 when I read the book.

A certain sorrow nagged me at the notion of passing without examining the magnificent veranda, circular staircase, and cut-glass chandelier. I put the fancies behind me and continued my journey.

CHAPTER TWO

Across the River
Day Eight - September 9, 1967

I slipped undetected past the front of the old house and onto the river bank, my eyes searching the dark underbrush for pieces of wood to use as water-wings. Luck was with me. I found fat pieces of bamboo ideally suited for support.

For camouflage, I searched for small bushes I could pull down. There was no shortage of bushes, but they were tougher than a one-armed cripple. Finally, taking down a couple of puny scrubs, I was ready for the water. I hoped that the branches would break up my silhouette and make me look like a bit of floating brush.

The river bank was frightening, falling nearly straight down to water level. "Good Lord," I wondered, "can't anything be easy on this trip?"

I searched frantically along the shore for a sloping bank where I could walk or slide into the water, but there was none. Somehow, I had to get into the water with minimum injury to my arm, with my pieces of bamboo, and without losing my canteen. Time was running out as the faint first light of the rising sun painted gray circles to the east.

Jamming a float pole into the water, I discovered that the river bottom had a steep slope, immediately becoming four or five feet deep. It was impossible to position myself for an easy entrance into the water, and being as agile as a four-day-old corpse did not improve things. Clawing and flailing clumsily at the bank, I fell into the stream like a broken log. I found myself standing in water up to my chin. My largest bush floated rapidly away in the current. The speed of the water was perhaps eight knots, far more than I had expected. It was swifter than the Missouri, which I knew so well from my boyhood.

My single puny bush was poor camouflage. I maneuvered both bamboo poles into position and slipped my broken arm over them, pressing my chest onto the ridge. They provided more buoyancy than I needed, floating me like a small child on a large plastic raft. With a good arm and two legs to use for paddling and steering, I popped out into the current.

ACROSS THE RIVER

Immediately, I was disturbed by my rapid progress downstream. I began a spirited paddling as I angled for the distant shore. I sensed that the current would dump me against the far shore much farther down than I had estimated. It was not going to be easy to get out of the river, since the bank rose like a cliff above the water.

To my horror, as I passed the big house, I caught sight of a rifle-carrying VC standing on the landing. He stared curiously at me in the dim light, not knowing what to make of what he saw. He inclined the rifle slightly toward me, then became undecided. Surprisingly, he failed to identify me in the dim light, probably figuring that I was a piece of driftwood or a pile of trash. Perhaps the bombs had boggled his mind. I'll always believe that the B-52 raid was a blessing for me.

As I rapidly drifted out of rifle range, I breathed a sigh of relief. The line between life and death, success and failure seemed so tenuous that I was becoming a stronger and stronger believer in predestination, or kismet, or pure luck — or the watchful hand of my God.

The old "Freedom Bridge," so called by the Vietnamese who had escaped from the North with the arrival of the Communists, was only minutes downstream in this swift current. Sure death had to lurk at it's foot in the person of the troops who camped near the approaches. I had to get out of the water, but the question was, HOW? How would I scale the steep banks?

Dame Fortune smiled brightly over my shoulder and solved my problem with the same deft hand that had spared my life so miraculously in the past. A deep crevice came into view, cut beautifully out of the south bank, as if I had special ordered it.

A huge dead carp, bloated and putrefying, bobbled lazily in the backwater of a jumble of broken logs that thrust into the river. Seizing hold of one, I pulled myself stealthily into the draw, which was washed out right down to the very water's edge.

I scanned the north bank of the river warily, but saw no one. Easing on to the soft muddy bank, I noticed that the water had washed my cast a snowy white, which I quickly smeared with mud. I sneaked my way up the bank, trying hard to become invisible and fully expecting to hear a shot fired.

The crevice had been created by a river boat or an aircraft firing an explosive straight into a gun position that had once squatted sturdily in the bank. From the angle of the crater, it seemed more likely that a gunner on a river boat had plugged the round in as if it had eyes, dead center into the gun position.

The gun pit was now a dilapidated pile of rubble. Several badly-scarred logs poked crazily into the water. They appeared to be heavy, dense-grained logs, possibly teak, and highly reminiscent of the Japanese fortifications during WW II on Tarawa.

The round had been a "daisy cutter," and a strong putrid stink of death clung to the hole. A small folding-stock automatic rifle lay on the ground. There was another old rifle of European design, possibly Czech or Russian. With its broken stock, it looked crippled and ineffective.

Still another rifle barrel and a piece of the broken stock lay there, along with several thousand rounds of .30-caliber ammunition. It was linked in a cheap canvas belt unlike anything I had ever seen. Because American ammunition linking for automatic weapons is done with metal, I had difficulty visualizing how one of these belts, which looked as though they were made for a machine gun, would have been fed into the weapon.

It occurred to me that I might make a pair of shoes from the canvas belting. After selecting a couple of pieces, I wrapped my feet and fashioned a pair of very crude sandals.

The automatic rifle was loaded and in fair condition. It had probably been blown out of some VC's hand. I picked it up and examined it, then rejected the idea of carrying the extra weight. My skinny body was more than I could handle.

My morale was up. Way, way up! It was a beautiful morning, beginning to burn golden dawn. I looked at the terrain in front of me. I thought of the Hemingway story, *Across the River and Into the Trees.* Yes, Ernest, I've crossed my river. Now I'm going into the trees.

The brush was much thinner here. It seemed that if I continued straight, it ought to be plain and easy walking.

More than ever I was feeling the impact of starvation. My attention was easily diverted. My eyes stared distractedly at the maze of light-green bushes. There were thousands of them, and my confused brain had trouble selecting which bush to examine for berries. I grew more obsessed each passing hour with the idea of finding food.

My stomach complained so desperately that I made an attempt to tear down a small banana tree which I knew had a starchy nutritious heart in the stalk. After hours of dismantling the tree, I found a little pithy tube in the direct center.

My net product was disappointing, a tiny piece between two and a half and three inches long; at the very largest end, about twice the size of a lead pencil. When my teeth sank into it, it was tasteless, simply exciting my taste buds and raising my hunger consciousness to a higher level. I raised my canteen and drank deeply. The water filled my stomach, but both my brain and stomach agreed that it was a lousy substitute for food.

I hadn't moved more than 25 or 50 yards when I came to an enormous cache of discarded G.I. food rations. Evidence of their menu lay accusingly on the ground - ham and lima beans, turkey, pudding, cookies, and pork and beans. These were unmistakably U.S. combat rations. There had been a patrol, possibly South Vietnamese, probably U.S. Marines, sitting right here! By the good condition of the paper packages, it was clear that it had been recently.

I was positive that somewhere in this large pile of cartons there was something fit to eat. And though there was plenty of food, it was all spoiled. The discipline of these troops had been very good. They had taken every can of food they didn't eat and bayonetted the can. In this climate, the food inside had become almost instantly rotten.

While it was heartbreaking for me, I felt a certain pride that they hadn't left anything for the enemy to subsist on. Some squad leader had been doing his job well. This was the kind of Marine Corps I remembered from my days as a Leatherneck Private.

I'd eaten identical rations when I pulled flight alert out of Tuy Hoa. It amused me to notice that what they had left behind had not been popular with fighter pilots either!

There were also cans of mosquito repellent. I'd had no idea there were this many cans of it in the world! It was an unnecessary luxury for me. I had my own built in variety . . . a mixture of scab, stink, and filth.

Concealment became my most serious problem. It required moving from bush to bush and tree to tree. The idea of moving only at night was appealing, but was unreasonable when compared to the loss of a full day of walking.

Further into the DMZ, I knew there lay a flat, scraped-out area cleared by bulldozers. I remembered intelligence briefings of huge mine fields located there. Having seen several mine casualties in the past, I didn't want my own leg blown off. Therefore, I had to enter this area in the daytime and under the best conditions. So, even though I was in relatively open country right now, I had to vote down walking at night.

I came across the highly decomposed carcass of a water buffalo, the Vietnamese "tractor." There were no carrion or scavengers, not even a buzzard! In this violent area, all wildlife had disappeared, leaving the land to the VC, insects, and a hungry American escapee.

As I came to the side of a trail, I saw, or perhaps more correctly, sensed a party of VC. About a dozen of them popped into sight. This was the standard size group and I saw many of them while in the DMZ. They were moving south, following a hard-packed path which went straight down to "I" Corps, the most northern area in South Vietnam.

They were loaded down like pack mules and about sixty-five yards away. Each man carried a large canvas back pack, with a bouquet of broken limbs and greenery stuck into their packs, covering their helmets and shoulders. They were camouflaged as well or better than any soldiers I had seen in my 25-year career.

I knew they were carrying heavy loads. I had carried them myself as a Marine, and I knew the position that one had to take. Each of them leaned well forward, head down, staring at the trail. They couldn't look around and maintain their balance, a good deal for me.

I reflected that it was a long way from Prague, Moscow, or East Berlin for these mortar shells, bullets, and grenades. It took a lot of little men taking little steps to move these war materials from Communist-land to a free country.

I relished the thought of how perfectly simple it could have been to take out that whole squad with a grenade or automatic weapon. I'd have dropped every one of them in their tracks before they knew what hit them. I knew intuitively that their packs were full of ammo or mortar rounds, which would have helped blow them apart. Their total lack of security was surprising. Having been an infantryman, I knew what it took to stay alive.

I had seen these VC because I was looking for them. Movement stands out immediately in the forest. In the jungle you seldom see people, you see movement or color. They were camouflaged so well that, had they been standing still, I would never have seen them.

I was convinced that all of them were green troops, just cannon fodder, waiting for their place to die. This was true of almost all of the thirty groups that I saw. These were more of the so-called "Southerners" whom David Halberstam, CBS News, and the host of other anti-administration critics continually praised and lauded as South Vietnamese revolutionaries. It was another successful snow job by the Communists.

I debated bursting across the trail, figuring that the "V" were clear and I wouldn't have any problem. Suddenly, only a few yards away appeared a second group. More "people rising up!" They were right behind the first group, looking the same, dressed in new dark-green fatigues. Some of them wore white tennis shoes and some had nearly new camouflaged shoes.

My mouth went dry and my heart pounded. I froze in the brush and their tennis shoes slapped the trail only inches from my head. If one had looked to his left, he couldn't have missed seeing me, for there was no way I could move deeper into cover.

Several of them were carrying mortar stakes, a faded white stick with red elevation markings. Two or three of them looked about 14 or 15 years old, perhaps younger, and were slightly bigger than my 11-year-old son. There was not a wrinkle on their faces, very tender, young boys. They, too, were loaded with mortar ammo, supplies, and horse collars filled with dry rice.

Later that day, when the patrols had passed, I captured another small frog and wolfed him down. A disgusting way for a gentleman to subsist, but all in all, it had been a good day. My progress had been slow, but there was no other way. I was now in "neutral" territory, although it was typical of Communist "neutrality." I hoped that with some luck, the going from this point would be far easier than in the past.

I finally parked for the night, and as I tried to say my prayers, I realized that I was getting disconnected. I couldn't concentrate on anything. My prayer started like a sputtering cold engine and then faded off into limbo land. Attempts to finish were unsuccessful. Finally I dozed off without mentally debriefing the day or completing my prayers. When I woke in the morning, I tried to think my situation out.

Day Nine - September 10, 1967

I awoke later than normal and the sun was much higher and brighter than usual. To compensate for my weakened condition, my body demanded more sleep. It was reassuring to know that my mind understood why my body was taking more time to recharge. My hunger-tortured thoughts urged me to get something to appease my stomach.

The overpoweringly lush beauty of the day imprinted itself on my mind. I wondered, "How can it be so beautiful, yet so dangerously unfriendly? Why is everything trying to kill me: jungle, bombs, gooks, airplanes, starvation. Why?"

The ever-near threat of death, coupled with my diminishing ability to react quickly and correctly increased my fear of making some monumental error. The pressure not to do anything wrong was nagging and oppressive.

I was fairly certain that I wanted to proceed slightly to the southwest. It would take at least another two, perhaps three days to get close to Dong Ha. If I ran into some unusually adverse terrain, it could be longer.

From this morning on, many of the details are fuzzy. I began losing track of time. My brain jumped track from one thing to another completely unrelated thought.

One of the more exaggerated cases of this was the presence of a very loud voice speaking in English. The voice sounded familiar. Suddenly I realized that it was my voice and I was talking to God. I had been thinking about my navigation problem and what to do next. Now, I was telling Him how grateful I was for His help, the fact that I had gone in the right direction, and was still thinking. This voice plagued me continually. If something stimulating occurred, it could hold my interest, but only briefly.

The tempo of air action picked up. Many of the Skyhawks, Phantoms, and Bird Dogs I had seen previously in the distance were very close; some overhead. Air strikes were going in around me, into the jungle. I could hear the bombs explode, some within perhaps three quarters of a mile, others farther away.

I found myself up on top of a ridge looking down into a valley, having moved out of the easy smooth traveling terrain that flowed south of the Ben

Hai. I had to take a course far off my desired path. A heavily-bombed area lay in the bottom center of the valley. I worked my way tortuously down the hillside.

Remaining on the trail, I was certain I would run into a group of Vietnamese coming north. This, in fact, was never to be the case. Out of the total 33 groups I saw, only one was heading north.

Moving downhill was dreadful. My right leg had swollen enormously, the calf twice its normal size, and hard as a rock. Each step was excruciating; it felt as though something in the wound was rasping like a file. Red and angry as it was, there was no sign of pus under the scab.

I had just arrived at the bombed out area when I heard an O-1 spotter aircraft. As he approached, I could tell he was very near. The canopy of the trees was so heavy that it was impossible to see him. In fact, daylight barely flickered through the limbs.

My mind jumped its tracks again and at that moment it occurred to me that for all the comments about the hot steaming, sweltering jungle that I'd heard, it was neither hot, nor steaming. It was quite cool, not unpleasant.

I continued walking, very excited as I thought of the possibilities that could arise if the Bird Dog should see me. My adrenelin began to pump. Because his engine was so audible, he had to be circling his O-1 overhead looking for someone, and that someone wasn't me. I had to believe that there was a concentration of enemy troops nearby. Otherwise, he wouldn't be circling over the area.

I felt an overpowering demand to start running, as impossible as that would have been. It was highly probable that if I could get into the cleared-out area, I could make myself visible to the pilot of the low flying O-1. If he could see VC, he could also see me. He circled overhead at about 1,000 feet, and under the right circumstances he would see me very easily.

I got into a perfect area within minutes, but I couldn't hear the O-1. He was working and circling nearby. I was standing on the lip of a bomb crater in plain view when I heard him again. He was approaching from the southwest, coming slightly from my right and heading almost directly toward me. He was flying a path which made it possible for him to look down into both parts of the valley. Now I was certain he was looking for VC. He came almost perfectly head on, in a slightly angling left turn. It appeared that he would go almost directly over me!

I saw a large shiny aluminum piece of napalm tank which was perfect for signaling. I hobbled over to it as quickly as I could, seized it, got back onto the lip of the crater, and frantically waved the piece of aluminum. It became sickeningly clear that if he continued the turn, he would blank me out completely with the bottom of the plane. There was no way he would see me.

ACROSS THE RIVER

If he had offset another 50 or 75 yards in either direction, there is an outstanding possibility he would have seen me. He continued the turn around to the left and wound up on a heading of due west. I knew that he had seen some sign of Commies, because of the way in which he circled and searched.

Something had him excited. He turned back in my direction. I waved the aluminum like a windmill in the western Kansas wind, signaling wildly, praying for recognition. He set up a racetrack pattern and began homing in on me again.

If lightning never strikes twice, you could not prove it by me, for his second pass across me followed exactly the same course as the first! I couldn't believe it. "What the hell, God?" I thought. "I'm doing my part. If someone up there likes me, he must be pretty mad at me today!"

The odds against such a pass in combat were incredibly high, since smart pilots avoid flying over the same area twice in a row. Therefore, something must be just west of me which was attracting his attention so markedly that he'd set up an identical pass. I listened very closely, certain that I'd hear some rifle fire as the VC shot at him.

I was dejected and crestfallen after the second pass, and I had the sinking feeling that when he departed and continued to the west, he had not seen what he wanted to see and would not be coming back. I was right.

With great anticipation, I waited there for an hour or two longer. My mind raced through the possibility of a helicopter rescue. How sweet it would be! Finally, I recognized that he was gone and would not be back.

Among the several low points during my escape and evasion, this was the most demoralizing. I was within five or ten seconds flying time of having been observed by friendly forces. I knew that I was within easy helicopter range of Hue (30 minutes), and "no sweat" helicopter range of Dong Ha or Khe Sahn (15 minutes), so my failure to be seen was eyewatering. I felt physically sick, and tears of self-pity welled into my eyes. I eased off the dirt pile, stared at the sky, and, to borrow a line from my favorite poet, Shakespeare, "Bewept my Outcast State."

There was no point in waiting any longer. The chance of the aircraft returning was a million to one, so I tried to head south. As soon as I moved out of the clear area, I was back into the triple-canopied jungle and squeezed back onto the trail. The trails did not seem to go in any direction that I wanted. Like a roulette player, I had to hope I picked one that would take me southbound.

I sat down and mentally debated my options. I tried to reason out the "what if I go left?" My thinking process was ineffective and unresponsive. I was too demoralized.

Going left and to the east, I came to another large group of green-leafed, bushy friends with the little blue berries. I found six or eight berries. These were the greenest that I had picked, but they were better than nothing. My thoughts were so gluttonous that there was little pleasure in them.

There was a small trickle of water coming down the center of the trail, which fell gently out of the heavy valley. The trail was fairly wide, and short green grass on either side blended into scrub brush. The light scrub gradually tapered up into higher and higher trees, first the double and then the triple canopy. Stepping through this very shallow and narrow stream, my feet were comforted by the water.

I debated whether or not to fill my canteen. It was almost full, but the water below felt cool and looked clean. I took some long draughts from my canteen, and dipped it down into the water.

Just as I bent over, I saw a land crab about three feet away. He was the size of a silver dollar, round, thick, healthy, and fat. "Hot damn," said my mind. "More chow!" I screwed the lid on my canteen very quickly and stepped gingerly toward him.

As I knelt to capture him, I heard a sound that petrified me. A machete was hitting a piece of wood, not more than 15 or 20 feet away. I was terrified to move my head! I eased my head up slightly and searched to the left. My eyes were staring straight at the back of a Vietnamese with a machete in his hand, chopping away at a small tree. I had located the VC that the O-1 had been searching for.

I was so paralyzed with fear that I forgot my treasure, the crab, and crawled off the trail on my hands and knees, angling right to the closest bushes. I felt like the cue ball on a pool table again. The Vietnamese did not turn around. I breathed a silent prayer of thanks and melted into the low brush on the right side of the trail.

My heart and adrenalin were both pumping at maximum rate and my hand shook with fright. I hadn't been off the trail for more than 15 or 20 seconds, when from my right, up the hill came more Vietnamese, chattering and yukking it up like bluejays on a spring day.

Again, I tried hard to become invisible. I sat quietly in very poor concealment, squeezing myself as best I could into a small bush, relying on their neglect to avoid discovery. I was able to see their legs and tennis shoes moving around. I had walked smack dab into the center of a VC camp! "This is our lucky day!" said my brain sarcastically.

I was sitting four or five feet off the trail. Within a few seconds I heard more machetes hacking away. There were enemy troops on both sides of the trail. They had dug themselves some ambush emplacements behind me, to the side, and in front of me.

"This is really neat," I thought. "I have them cornered!" They were set up in a deployed ambush camp typical of their combat teams. I really wanted to take a better look at what they were doing, but prudence dictated otherwise.

I rested there, listening to camp noises, until 12:00 or 12:30, when I became aware of the silence. Although my head was working very, very poorly, it was obvious that it was siesta time. Siesta time is like the office coffee break in the U.S. Never in history have the workers missed a coffee break, and the same is true for siesta. Every self-respecting Vietnamese was lying down for his daily nap. Siesta normally ran from 11:30 to 1:30. Considering this, I said to myself, "What a great time to bug out!"

I sneaked out on the trail, took a look in both directions, knelt and listened for perhaps five minutes, and heard nothing. Not even a snore!

I started up the hill, faintly expecting to hear a shot, or a shout. Instead... nothing! I walked straight out of the camp. Happiness is a sleeping VC.

I went up an extremely steep hill, more difficult than it looked from below. It was absolute torture. My strength was minimal, my arm began to throb, my legs ached, and my feet burned. I was having intermittent mental delusions. I would start talking to Viking or friends or God. I cursed out loud at my difficulties and then hated my mouth and throat for moving.

With all of the energy I could muster, I concentrated on maintaining my tenuous hold on sanity. I tried desperately to listen for signs of danger, but my mind completely jumped track, defied reality, and embraced some strange, unexplainable subjects.

I was back in Sunday School at Riverside Methodist Church in Sioux City, Iowa. I was talking with my delightful old teacher, Mrs. Cameron. We pupils always raised such a fuss when we were due to pass to the next grade, the church administration simply passed Mrs. Cameron along with us. I talked with her and she answered.

Another time I was in a boat with Doris. We were fishing for crappie, and I became impatient with putting minnows on her hook. She kept me so busy baiting the hook that I could not fish.

My thoughts hopscotched from church, to wife, to pain, despair, future, past, hunger, happiness, or regret in a fragmented, fractured pattern. Any semblance of full control of my faculties was evaporating into a jumble of incompetence. I continued frightening myself with involuntary sentences that boiled from my clumbsy, mumbling, uncooperative mouth.

I moved laboriously up the hill, frightening myself with another boisterous outburst, and leaped with fear as a large gun fired nearby. Between blasts, I detected the sound of people coming down the trail toward me. By the time my numb mind reacted, I could only crash off the trail and fall into the brush, making no attempt to be quiet.

Within seconds, a pair of VC came down the path. Their tennis shoes slapped the bare dirt trail. Slap, slap, heels touching the ground first, followed by the soles slapping noisily. Their voices were piercingly loud in the stark stillness of the jungle. Looking sideways through the foliage, I watched their faded trouser legs pass out of view. Fortune smiled again. Another horseshoe used up! Could there be any left?

Recollection and comprehension became chameleon-like vagaries resembling a poorly-tuned radio station . . . sometimes playing clearly, then fuzzily, or totally off frequency. Thoughts and things came . . . and happened, frequently with no clear break in between them . . . bobbing in and out of reality like the float on a fishing line.

More dangerous contacts with the VC. Mosquitoes in clouds like the locust swarms of antiquity. A built-up hooch in the deep jungle. I touched it before recognizing it as an object of danger.

Uncontrolled noises bubbling ungoverned from my lips and directed at God, man, beast, self, past or future. Prayers had no end, for the distance from beginning to end was unachievable. Sleep became so intertwined with consciousness that the separation died like a dried pumpkin vine at the onset of frost.

Suddenly, and clearly, a beautiful green verdant valley popped into sharp focus. The stream that split the valley was not visible, but the tree line and growth pattern of the vegetation testified to its existence. The overflow from the river had purged a wide area of the valley with its drowning powers of death. Huge grassy areas fringed the tree line, making approach to the water hazardous.

Though my acuity was diminished, the obvious danger of this area flashed through my head like a warning light on a tall television antenna. It was necessary to get into the woods.

"Woods . . . ," my mind said. "Whose woods are these?"

"I think I know."

"Know what" a voice asked.

"The woods are lovely,
  dark and deep
  But I have promises to keep,"

"And miles to go before I sleep," another voice replied.

"Promises to keep. You bet you have promises to keep. You've got to get on the ball if you are going to meet Doris in Honolulu in a few days," said my conscience.

I started pep-talking myself. "C'mon, boy! Let's get up to the task here. You've got to concentrate! If you have any more of these stupid lapses, some VC will get you. If you don't get with it, it's going to be too bad for you!"

Nothing could have been more prophetic than these thoughts. When "Lucid" was in charge, he was still effective. The impact of the lecture was useful, for in just a few minutes I detected some motion. As I took cover by the trail, another dozen-man patrol nearly overran me. Adrenaline was pumping again and I realized that without measurable improvement, there wasn't going to be any airplane ride back to Hawaii. There wasn't going to be any meeting with the Viking on Waikiki beach under the huge banyan tree. Life was going to be recapture, prison, or death.

My mind obstinately refused to plan a way across the river below. Instead, it recalled yesterday's heavy gunfire from the south. My thoughts played with the idea of finding a gun site. I remembered that I had thought a gun position could be my salvation.

Almost as if I had ordered it, a gun suddenly began firing. It was loud, and it was damned close. Lucidity insisted that the search for a gun site be the prime objective.

I saw an O-1 spotter plane appear, rising over the tops of some trees a good distance away. I knew immediately that this airplane was on takeoff. I estimated his distance at about five miles. That airfield had to be around Con Thien, perhaps another dirt strip between Quang Tri City and Dong Ha. "I must be well into South Vietnam," I thought.

I turned to study the area surrounding the river. I couldn't see a better place to cross it than right where I was. There was a heavy tree line on the south side. If I went to my left or my right very far, I would cross over open land. I decided my best bet would be to "bull it" across right here. "Fortune favors the bold!"

The vegetation I had seen from the north side turned out to be a huge cultivated banana forest. It was old, obviously an area where some villages had been located. There was no village in sight, but as I sneaked along on the right-hand (west) side of the trail, I saw a shelter. It was a typical banana leaf hooch. Shortly, I saw quite an old man, probably in his early seventies, very stocky, extremely beefy for a "V."

I watched him puttering around, maintained good cover, and eased past him unobserved. No sooner had I cleared him, than I saw additional trouble in the form of three very young boys in irregular force uniforms. They were carrying old bolt-action rifles, and were proceeding northeast.

I did not know my position. I could be well into South Vietnam and these boys might be South Vietnamese. I could not be sure.

On my left was a large open banana orchard. To the right was a rather scraggly intermittent orchard interspersed with a lot of small shade trees. Getting into heavier cover was essential. As I walked, I heard the *whop, whop* of a helicopter.

About a mile and a half in front of me, in the exact area that I thought the gunfire had come from, I saw two Marine Corps choppers. Both were large. One of them was holding high, flying at about 2,000 feet. The other was clearly going to ease in, settle down and land. They removed any doubt about being in South Vietnam.

"Choppers, choppers . . . this is it!"

There was no question but that I'd found the gun. I could immediately picture the whole thing in my mind's eye. My thoughts unfolded the sequence . . . two choppers, one of them a gunship, the other a supply bird. It was airlifting ammo into the gun, bringing water, food, medicine and supplies. It became absolutely clear to me!

The chopper was holding high to provide fire support in case the Communist troops try to bushwhack them. I could see it so clearly! Some superhuman primeval instinct seized control of my bloody, torn feet and began to drive me rapidly onward, but I could see it would be impossible to make the area before dark.

Dusk, mild and warm was falling. As evening's gray mantle spread, it became harder to see the chopper. The *whop, whop* of the blades pierced the jungle silence. In a matter of minutes, that chopper would have to lift off! There was no way to make the area by nightfall, but I thought, in consolation, it would be a "piece of cake" to make it in the morning! I had tuned back in.

My brain was in control again. I thought to myself, "There's no problem. All that's required is to locate the gun position! Next, I must make certain that I don't walk into a mine field around the guns. I'll look it over very carefully, making some nice smooth, calculated moves. If I don't get a leg blown off by a mine, or take a Marine Corps .30-caliber bullet, I'll be home free. That nice clean cast, operating room, doctor, friends at Da Nang, an airplane to Honolulu, all are right here in the palm of my hand. 'Viking' and 'thy sweet love remembered, such wealth brings . . . ' How sweet it is!"

It was just a matter of hours now. Play it cool. Think things out well. "Home free, baby!"

I hurried in the direction of the landing site in an impatient trotting crouch, when I suddenly popped out onto a 180-degree loop in a small stream. I found myself looking straight at the posterior of an enemy soldier, bent over washing his clothes in the muddy water. His attention was fixed on his chores. A brand-new Chinese AK-47 rifle was on the bank about four or five steps closer to me than to him. I debated what to do.

I was really in a bind! I would have to ease around him very quietly. Or, I could race him for the gun and kill him. A poor idea since he was sure to be one of several.

The area was so sparsely forested that if I made a move backward, it would be as dangerous as moving forward. There was an equal risk of him seeing my movement either way. If I stayed where I was, it was guaranteed that as soon as he turned around, or as soon as he came to pick up his rifle, he would have to see me.

I was trapped out on the pool table again! I opted for the old motto, "Fortune favors the Bold."

I walked past him, moving very slowly, very carefully, from bush to bush. In about five to eight minutes I had circumvented him. Mercy! The tension rippled the hair on the back of my neck and nervous sweat dripped off my body in tiny rivers.

Suddenly I was in cover where I could get down into a low profile and simply walk away. By this time it was almost dead dark. I had to find a hotel for the night. Relief flooded over me. Wow! Was I elated? Was I in luck? I did not have a solitary extraneous thought. Something inside me was working again with new strength. I went through my prayers and sorted my thoughts. What a day! How many things to be thankful for! The end - how near it was, the long-sought end of this desperate journey. How sweet the thought. Sweet Jesus, but this had been a hairy day!

As I lay down, I tuned in to the Viking. I heard her voice come through very clearly. I concentrated on the pleasant time we were going to have in a few days, just the Viking and I. Tomorrow I would be back at Da Nang. In three or four days I would be in Honolulu, under the comforting arms of my favorite banyan tree.

I had lost track of the days. I believed that it was Friday and that this was the 12th or 13th of September. I thought I'd been out 12, 13, or 14 days. My movement today had been the poorest of any day. Even though I was exhausted, my brain would not turn off.

Day Ten - September 11, 1967
The Last Day

In the morning it was overcast, the first and only day I awakened to find the weather dull. I sat up, had a good shot of water from my canteen, and mapped out my plans.

I looked at the area where I wanted to go. Now that daylight traced its brightness on the jungle floor, I could see a fairly solid wall of trees running roughly east-west. Off to the right, thrusting back into the dense richness of the jungle, was a long spear-like, grassy plain. It stabbed the woods like a huge wedge driven deep into the trees.

On this knoll was heavy, coarse grass, about three feet tall. The knoll sloped slightly and I could picture the scene perfectly in my mind.

"Friendlies" were set up in a "big gun" position. They were Marine Corps! They had their weapons dug in with some good fields of interlocking fire. They had the high ground. Anybody who wanted to move up and attack them would be shot by their defensive fire.

Strangely enough, the gun had not fired today. Nevertheless, I chose to believe it was a battery of 155mm rifles. I looked around carefully, scouting the area. My position was exposed.

I could see why there were so many enemy troops in this area. They were either preparing an attack on the position, or they were here to ambush supply lines.

As I continued through the grass at the edge of the knoll, I began to lose confidence. I did not pick up the profile I had expected. There was nothing resembling a gun position. There were no humps or mounds on the plain, characteristic of a big gun, or batteries of guns, and the collateral supporting positions. I had even pictured some sandbagged lookout towers. I could see none of these things here.

I had a sinking feeling of disaster and impending doom. Had I made a mistake? I kept telling myself I couldn't be wrong! I traversed the entire length of the peninsula.

I had incorrectly evaluated the situation. The choppers might have been there to pick up a patrol. They were not supplying a gun, for there was no gun. Great Scott! Yesterday, I may have missed a pickup by 30 minutes. Only 30 minutes! How can everything go so wrong?

The gun I had been hearing for days was not firing this morning. Why? Where was it? Was this another goof-up like the big circle I walked? Had I only imagined I heard a gun? Why hadn't I been there earlier, in time to meet the chopper?

My morale fell like a landslide. I went over my miserable physical condition. I had lost 20 or 25 pounds. My arms were thin and my stomach was drawn up to nothing. My puny arms and spindly legs were scratched, injured or broken. I didn't have much more strength and I was almost at the end of my tether.

If I were going to make it at all, it would have to be today or tomorrow. I was on the verge of collapse, my mental processes were marginal and getting worse.

I regressed into old bad habits. Standing in the brush directly on the north edge of the peninsula, I debated whether to go west or east. There was no going south. It had to be right or left.

If I went left, I would be more exposed to the VC I had just walked through than if I went to the right. On the other hand, I knew nothing about the area to the right.

If I went to the right, it would be more circuitous. I debated. Do I have the strength to go to the right? Is the chance of trying to walk to the left worth it? If I go to the right, will I have the strength to make it?

After losing track of my thoughts many times, I finally told myself aloud, "I flat don't have the strength. I've got to go left. If I make it at all,

I've got to make it going back through this area where I've had the contact."

Suddenly, I discovered I had wandered to the ruins of destroyed village. Not an object was standing. It had been abandoned quite some time before. Old trash, junk, and broken trinkets littered the ground. There were little pieces of poor-quality pottery. My brain took charge again.

"You damned fool! What are you thinking of, standing here, looking at this junk? If you scoop up the entire pile, it would be worth half a cent. How can you stupidly risk being captured?"

With this exhortation, my feet started moving again. I followed the trail flowing from the village where a funnel shaped entrance knifed into the trees. The jungle was heavy, two-canopy growth. The trail cut through it initially on a heading of 130 degrees toward the southeast. Not too bad! It maintained the direction I wanted to go.

I knew from my view of the spotter plane, hearing the friendly guns, and helicopters, that I was in freedom's front yard. All I had to do was find the old homestead. I prayed that it wasn't a needle in a haystack.

About 25 or 30 yards into the jungle, I heard a shout behind me. My head jerked around in dismay and my stomach churned with apprehension. Very close to the demolished village, I saw two young Vietnamese. I looked at them over my shoulder, not knowing whether to run, or stay. Are they north or south "V?" I tried to figure it out.

For a moment, I was unable to tell. Suddenly it dawned on me that the rifles they carried were AK-47s.

One of them said what sounded to me like, "Hey, boy." I later found out it was an expression in Vietnamese, "Ay doi," which means, roughly translated, "Hey, you," or "Hey, buddy, let me have your attention."

When I realized they were North Vietnamese, I calculated my chances of making it into the jungle. Maybe they couldn't hit me if they fired! I decided I had to run. It was either that, or surrender. I hadn't come this far to surrender to these little sons-of-bitches! "Run, run!" screamed my brain.

Gunfire began to my left and from behind. I tried to weave, but I was as agile as an elephant. About 10 or 15 yards from the dead edge of the jungle, I was struck by bullets in the left thigh and the left hand. I was nearly felled by the bullet's entrance into my leg, burning a numbing, searing fire. I managed to struggle on into the jungle trailing a stream of blood behind me.

I dodged under the brush, the heaviest I could find. I could hear the boys racing up behind me, their shoes slapping the ground. Immediately a long heavy string of automatic fire rattled through the bushes right over my head! I heard the bullets snapping off twigs and burying themselves in the trees.

I heard them talking, calling back and forth to each other. I twisted my head around and was startled to see the pupil of this fellow's eye as he crouched about three feet away. He did not see me!

This one had instructed the other man to make a circle around and then walk toward him. He fired a couple of rounds into the air. I could hear the other Vietnamese stomping around through the brush.

A couple of minutes went by and I could hear the second Vietnamese moving in my direction. The man I was watching shouted instructions. His eyes burned through the brush as he continued talking. The man who made the circle appeared suddenly a foot or two from my side. He stood there talking. He was apparently looking past me. Suddenly, his gaze fell on me. He gave me a kick, and shouted at his friend.

I was recaptured! It was the blackest moment of my life.

The two "V" were overjoyed. As a couple of young boys might be inclined to do, they literally danced with joy. Had I not been so crestfallen, it would have amused me.

I'd estimated that they were 15 to 17 years old, both looking incredibly young, fragile, and deceptively spindly. Their curiosity was unveiled and unashamed. I was intrigued by their deep interest. It reminded me of the fashion that Japanese school children had stared at me 15 years previously. I doubted that either of them had ever seen a Caucasian in the flesh.

They were genuinely alarmed at the bleeding hole in my leg and one of them attempted to provide some assistance, trying to get me up on my feet. In their youthful ignorance, they wanted me to march away!

After second thoughts about my ability to move, the smaller one of the two handed his rifle to the other boy, ran off, and came back shortly with another Vietnamese. The younger man and the new arrival put their arms around me and attempted to help me walk away.

I'd been captured by some members of the same group of people I had evaded the day before, perhaps even the man washing clothes. I was later told that I had been taken two miles from the Marine Corps camp of Con Thien, perhaps six or eight miles south of the DMZ.

My treatment by the combat Viet Cong was far better than any I had received from non-combat troops. An older man, ruddy faced, beefy, tall, and obviously part caucasian, approached me. He immediately asked me my name in French.

I responded, *"Je m'appelle Georges Jour,"* meaning, "I call myself George Day."

He asked, "Where did you come from?"

I replied, *"Je response avec nom et nombre."* I answered with name and number.

He said, "How do you spell your last name?"

ACROSS THE RIVER

I told him, *"Jour."* Day.

He disappeared over the ridge into an area where I suspected a radio transmitter was located. I think that he made an inquiry to the North about me, because he came back in a few minutes and stared at me with unconcealed curiosity.

Treatment was brusque and business-like, rather than the brutality I had experienced in parades through the villages during my previous capture. A young soldier produced a rounded ball of rice about the size of a baseball. Holding it out to me, he asked in sign language if I wanted some. I gave a vigorous, "yes," and thought it a testimony to human decency that the same people who had tried to kill me were now trying to feed me.

He sliced off a piece just as one would slice an apple, and handed it to me. It was unflavored and unsalted, but to say it was delicious is an understatement.

Almost immediately I felt my strength returning. The young man cut off three or four small slices, then brought a small sardine can containing some high-powered, foul fishy smelling sauce. He asked if I wanted some of this and I gave another emphatic, "yes."

The meat had been removed from the sauce and the grease remained. It was dreadful, stinky, and not a long way from raw frog. Nevertheless, I intended to eat anything that my stomach would accept.

He cut off another slice of rice and poured the horrid grease on top of it. Mentally, I held my nose as I chewed and swallowed.

A medic appeared to examine my finger. The bullet had gone through the end joint on the ring finger of my left hand, making a clean hole where it entered and a gory mess where it exited. The fingertip remained attached only by some tenuous threads of skin and meat.

The medic indicated that he would like to treat my thumb and finger and I agreed. He liberally sprinkled both wounds with sulpha powder, then wrapped both tightly. He did not splint the finger, relying only on the bandage.

Next came the serious problem of the large hole in my thigh. The AK-47 round had splattered the flesh into a gaping raw hole. He was convinced that a foreign object was lodged in the meat and kept pressing the area around the wound with his fingers.

The medic disappeared and returned with metal and bamboo probes. He took the metal probe, the smaller of the two, and poked it down into the wound, which was about the size of a 50-cent piece and bleeding profusely.

It burned like a hot fire and I bolted up and thrashed around violently, frightening the medic. He leaped back out of the way and called some friends. Shaking his finger at me to caution me not to resist, he made signs to show that he had to do something to me.

The second attempt was more painful than the first. It was like having an appendix removed without the benefit of anesthetic. I leaped into the air and knocked him aside.

Giving up, he disappeared again and came back with a morphine syrette which he stabbed into my leg. Once more he started probing. By now a river of blood was pouring from the wound. Moments later, he showed me a little thing which he indicated had come out of my leg. I couldn't make out what it was. I think he simply fished out a piece of meat, or a piece of gristle, or he picked up a bloody pebble. Although it looked like the old "save face" game to me, I was to find that he was the best medic I would encounter in North Vietnam.

Shortly, Red Face came back and asked me if I wanted something to drink. When I said, "yes," he asked me if I'd had anything to eat. Again, I told him, "yes." But when he wanted to know if I'd had enough, I told him, "no."

He asked, "How long has it been since you've had anything to eat?"

I told him I thought it had been about two weeks.

He said, "We will give you food later, but now you can have something to drink." He brought some freshly boiled water which was cloudy and heavily silt-laden. I suspected it came from the same stream where I'd seen the "V" washing clothes.

The medic came back and poured sulpha powder into the wound on my leg, and put on a walking bandage. This youngster had a lot of experience with flesh wounds and his work was expertly done.

Fatigued, in deep pain, I lay like a wounded animal and rested for about 20 minutes, until Red Face showed up again. He had five larger Vietnamese with him, two of them carrying a fat bamboo tube perhaps seven feet long. Suspended from it was a net sling attached to a pole. They made motions for me to get in the sling and put a blindfold over my eyes. Whenever I moved it to look around, I earned a hard lick on the head.

It was essential to stay oriented, because I was determined to escape again if I could, and I continued adjusting the bandage. There was no brutality for trivia. When they told me to do something, they expected me to do it. Non-compliance resulted in serious retaliatory violence.

My two bearers started off at a shuffling dog trot, and I sank deep into depression. My distress and remorse became more and more intense. All of my good planning and hard, exhausting travel were for nothing. I had been so close to freedom. Now each arm and leg was broken, shot up or injured. For what? I could expect jungle rot under the cast on my arm, blood poisoning was highly probable, and my life expectancy could hardly be lower.

I ripped off a couple of dozen disappointed curses to myself and lay there crushed and broken spirited. If I'd only gone right instead of left. If only the spotter plane . . . if only the chopper had turned right.

With heavy heart I realized that my super luck had finally run out. "Lord, every extremity is damaged. I'll die of neglect, for sure," I thought.

What had I really accomplished? How in the world had I gotten into this position? My thoughts drifted back to the events leading up to my last flight.

CHAPTER THREE

Misty

When the buzzer on my handheld radio awakened me, it was a dark gray morning, the 26th of August, 1967, at Phu Cat Air Base, South Vietnam. Sleepily, I searched for the light. The faintly stale odor of scotch rose from the half-empty glass by the bed. Despite average work days sixteen to eighteen hours, including six or seven hours of combat missions in the F-100, I was having trouble sleeping. I was still groggy as I "Rogered" the second call from the duty officer, Captain Charlie Neel.

"What's the weather in North Vietnam?" I asked.

"Looks great!" he answered optimistically. "Maybe you'll have a good day."

Charlie probably predicted that the Edsel would be a safe long-range investment. This was definitely not going to turn out to be a good day.

The call sign of my unit was "Misty," which was my favorite song. We flew Forward Air Control missions, and we were dubbed the Super-FACs, since we flew F-100F Super Sabres (or the "Hun" as we affectionately called them) into North Vietnam. Our jets were the counterparts of the tiny propeller-driven spotter aircraft which flew in South Vietnam, searching for targets.

I felt tired and my eyes burned. Tired or not, it was time to go to work. "Work" took us where enemy guns rested in hostile silence awaiting our arrival. Every day we made the rendezvous. My airplanes roamed the lower part of North Vietnam looking for trucks, missiles, and other military targets.

We Mistys spent more time each day getting shot at than any other pilots in North Vietnam. Our job was to find fleeting targets, mark them with smoke rockets and get the fighter-bombers on the scene to strike them. This transferred much of the risk from the fighter-bombers to my Sabres, and greatly reduced the loss of F-4 Phantoms and F-105 Thunderchiefs, the workhorse fighter-bombers in my area. It also improved the quality of targeting and the amount of damage we inflicted on the Communists.

MISTY

I put my feet on the floor and stared at my flying suits, hanging like two empty gray scarecrows. One name tag read George E. Day, U.S. Air Force, in camouflage black on gray-green. Black embroidered major's leaves adorned the shoulders. One flying suit was faded, with a set of Air Force wings topped by a star, indicating I was a senior pilot.

In two weeks I would be a command pilot after 15 years as a rated pilot. By then, I would have acquired more than 5,000 hours of military flying. With 4,500 hours of jet time, I was one of the most experienced fighter pilots in Vietnam.

I slipped into the faded flying suit and felt again the glow of pride as a tactical fighter pilot and commander of a hand-picked fighter unit. I'd worn this uniform in Japan, Korea, England, Africa, Germany, and Greece.

I wondered if there would ever be a day when I would not consider the tactical fighter pilot the best of professions. My wife, Doris, to whom I had been married 18 years, frequently kidded me about my love affair with fighter flying.

Picking up the portable two-way radio which was my 24-hour-a-day link with the 37th Tactical Fighter Wing command post, I stepped out into the cool darkness to wake up the "dawn patrol." I hammered on doors until I got responses from Major Bill Douglass, my operations officer, and Captain Dick Cunningham, one of my squadron pilots. As I opened the mess hall door, the wing commander, Colonel Ed Schneider, greeted me cheerfully with his good-natured smile.

Breakfast was field ration food. It was not great, but it was improving. A combat pilot could be fed at any time of the day or night, and the kitchen folks were trying hard.

I washed down my dried egg omelet with hot, sweet tea and drove to wing headquarters. The building was new, cheap, temporary and clean. Misty offices were on the second floor where we occupied about one-third of the space, adjoining the wing intelligence office.

It was still pitch black as I turned the key to my office area. The rooms glistened with newness since the base had been open only a few weeks and the pervasive Vietnamese mud had not worked its way this far yet.

Bill Douglass and Ray Bevivino had selected the strikes for the day and flagged the target maps with large adhesive paper arrows. I compared them with my intelligence map which showed areas of high flak density.

There were thousands of highly-mobile Russian, Czech, and Chinese guns in North Vietnam. Usually we discovered they had been moved when we were fired upon from a new location. Then we noted the new locations on our maps and tried to stay out of range, if conditions permitted. Somehow, conditions seldom permitted.

RETURN WITH HONOR

I was studying the target map when my intelligence officer, Lieutenant Ray Bevivino, appeared at my side.

"Good morning, Major," he said cheerfully. Ray believed that this was his personal war and he could end it if he worked hard enough. He studied me apprehensively, expecting me to give him hell for being there so early. When I had left for bed the previous evening, he had still been working on the intelligence summary. I decided to say nothing.

The calendar read August 26, 1967. Major Bill Douglass and Captain Dick Cunningham were to launch the first sortie at 0455 and return to Phu Cat by 1225, God willing. I was on the afternoon flyng schedule with Captain Corwin Kippenham from Amana, Iowa.

Dawn was beginning to break when I drove Douglass and Cunningham to the Misty ramp where the F-100Fs squatted. It was too early for light conversation. Bill and Dick climbed clumsily out of the truck, looking like men from another world.

Each man wore a beige survival vest full of signaling devices, radio gear, pistol, miscellaneous food, knife, compass and other items. A large, long backpack parachute was slung over their shoulders. Their legs were encased in dark-gray "G" suits whose pockets were full of maps, water in baby bottles for survival, a sewed-on knife and case, and a survival radio. Each carried a white plastic jet helmet in one hand and cameras, water bottles and knee boards in the other. The weight of this equipment was perhaps as much as a small man.

They struggled up the ladder of 951, an F-100F two-seated fighter which I had on loan from the 31st Tactical Fighter Wing at Tuy Hoa, South Vietnam. I had requested this particular "Hun" by tail number. I had flown it a number of times when I was assigned to the 31st Wing, and I loved it.

Fighter planes are a little like cars and women. They all do about the same job, and look somewhat the same, but each performs with significant differences. Number 951 was a special performer. It had been my first choice when word came down from the 7th Air Force at Saigon that I could choose from all the birds in Vietnam.

I stood watching Douglass through the start and taxi procedures, and I slowly followed him to the arming area near the takeoff end of the runway. There one of our "gun plumbers," whose job was to arm the rocket pods and guns, completed his checks in the half haze of dawn.

The Super Sabre eased onto the runway and clamped the brakes down firmly. As the engine accelerated, the nose of 951 lowered like a bull readying for the charge. It rolled forward a few feet. The afterburner exploded and a twenty-foot tail of blue-white flame pierced the early morning greyness, ripping the silence apart. The Sabre roared off to the north.

I was filled with the unexplainable awe I always feel when I see fighters flying or "Old Glory" waving in the breeze. When I first heard that someone had labeled horse racing the "sport of kings," I knew he had never flown a fighter.

As the fiery tail of the "Douglass comet" disappeared, I turned the truck back toward my room. I felt a strong compulsion to get a short tape-recorded message off to my wife and children.

Doris was waiting for me in Arizona. I had nicknamed her "Viking" because, with her Norweigian looks, strong courageous face, ice-blue eyes and dazzling smile, that's what she reminded me of. We had been childless until we began adopting children.

Steve had been the first, adopted in Germany. He had just turned eleven, and was tall, blonde and blue-eyed. He was the only one mature enough yet for the special bond between father and son. He had climbed over and in my jet trainers and fighters. We had flown light planes together; hunted geese on North Landing River in Virginia; hunted ducks and fished for bass in Currituck Sound and at Nags Head; shot pheasant in Iowa and Nebraska.

Steve had always been a quiet, deep boy who amused himself very easily and was extremely unemotional. When I left Luke Air Force Base near my home in Glendale, Arizona, for Vietnam, he had suddenly burst into tears, shaking and sobbing. Viking and I had both been amazed. I had reflected on that tender scene many, many times, realizing how much this dear son was concerned for me.

Six years after Steve, we added a Californian to our family when I carried George, Jr. back to St. Louis. He was dark-haired, brown-eyed, and four years old. He was the brightest and most serious of the four children.

In New York we had adopted blonde, blue-eyed twins, Sandra and Sonja. They were two now and we were amused at how much adopted children frequently resemble their adoptive parents as much as natural children.

Our past year in New York had been our first real "together" year. Sledding and ice-skating are great family builders, and there is nothing like camping cookouts on the piney banks of the St. Lawrence River to weld family unity. I hoped I would survive this combat tour to continue raising my nice kids.

My assignment to Misty had greatly increased my risk. Flying fighter-bombers against ground targets in South Vietnam was vastly different from flying against targets in North Vietnam.

The risk in North Vietnam was so high, a pilot was required to fly only 100 missions. The pilot who flew against targets in the South had to fly combat for one year, regardless of the number of missions. It was not uncommon for the pilot in the South to fly over 350 missions during one year, as the loss rate was much lower.

I remembered a letter I'd received from Krop Kropenick, a close and respected friend with a distinguished combat record in World War II, Korea, and now Vietnam. "My recommendation is, don't come over here, not unless they change the rules, pull the plug and go out to win."

However, I hadn't been able to vote on whether to go to Vietnam or not. I had volunteered for combat in Vietnam as I had in World War II and Korea. My requests for combat were turned down until the military started running out of bodies. With my extensive training, I felt a strong sense of duty. If my country and fellow pilots were fighting, I ought to be fighting.

Robbie Risner, Jim Kasler, Jim Hiteshew, Norm Gaddis, Hervey Stockman, and a host of comrades from previous squadrons had been downed by enemy fire. They were either listed as missing, or were now residents of the "Hanoi Hilton." One of my closest friends had not returned from his first combat mission. Thoughts of their fate, the infamous Hanoi March of July 6, 1966, and the fact that there seemed no end in sight to this war ran through my mind often.

Still, I could never quite picture myself in their position. Being shot down seemed a little too unreal to dwell on. More importantly, flying against North Vietnam was satisfying.

Bombing targets in the South was frustrating, like tweaking the end of the tentacle of an octopus. Most of the targets were insignificant, described by pilots as "turning jungle into toothpicks."

Targets in the North were more obvious and significant. If you struck a truck and saw it burn, it was tangible. When you blew up a missile, a little flash of pride welled up in your heart. It was a simple matter of job satisfaction. You could see *results* in the North.

We were also proud to be flying Misty. Fighters liked working with us, since we always had a lucrative target for them. We put the pilot in on target with minimum exposure, marking it with a smoke rocket, observing the bomb drop, and advising him of his strike results.

This was not the simple "civil war" described by Communist apologists and the biased American press. This war ran on trucks, ammo, guns and fuel supplied by the Soviet Union, Albania, Cuba, China, North Korea, East Germany, and all the Communist Bloc countries. Every bullet, rifle, truck, gallon of gas, missile, aspirin, and bandage were part of the world Communist war on tiny South Vietnam. If this never-ending flow of material, which entered at the port of Haiphong and poured down the dirt roads into South Vietnam, Laos, Cambodia, and Thailand, could be cut off, those who kept the war going would be in a bad way.

In addition to fighting the whole Communist Bloc, we had against us the America-hating Cora Weiss, Jane Fonda, and the left-wing fringes of the United States. All of us in the Misty program, and most other fighter pilots, also understood that the war was being fought in the most inefficient and expensive way.

The obvious solution was to seal off the port of Haiphong and the railroads in the same manner that we sealed off the European and African ports in World War II. We knew this had been proposed many times by our military leaders, but our political leaders chose to pursue instead a policy of gradual escalation. The policy employed in Vietnam was well described as "throwing a bound man into the mouth of a tiger" and asking him to emerge victorious. The November 1967 *Air Force Magazine* described our dilemma in these words, "The Vietnam question is... the least susceptible to solution of any national issue...

"What bothers us is the *missing element* in what we read and what we hear - *a sense of history*... U.S. involvement in Vietnam took the turn it did when U.S. military policy was openly announced as one of 'flexible response,' the philosophy so persuasively advanced by General Maxwell Taylor in his book *The Uncertain Trumpet*, and so eagerly adopted by President Kennedy and his advisors... The flaw in the concept of flexible response lies not in its flexibility, but in its rigidity. After all, the U.S. has responded with a high degree of military flexibility to a string of crises over the past twenty years... the public articulation of flexible response... and the implementing of flexible response as a kind of creeping escalation... caused the real mischief. The U.S. told the opposition exactly how it would respond to future overt aggressions... the U.S. proclaimed policy was begging to be tested. Tested it has been, and found wanting."

So it was that the military fought the war of an industrial giant against a piss-ant with both arms tied behind our backs, frustrated and fuming over senseless strategies that violated every basic rule of war. Any plebe at the Military Academy could produce a better solution to the Vietnam War than Lyndon Johnson and the arrogant, strange Robert MacNamara and Dean Rusk. History *must* always ask the question, "Why?"

Back in my room, I picked up the mike on the tape recorder and looked at my calendar. Wednesday, September 13, 1967, was heavily marked and only 19 days away. On that Wednesday I was to meet my wife in Honolulu to spend my one week of rest and relaxation.

I voiced a short letter to Doris and the children, one of two I made that morning. Later, and frequently, I would ask myself what compelled me to cut two tape letters in one day, the only time during this war that I had done so.

But, then, everything about this day was a little different. I went to the aircraft with Captain C. N. Kippenham, who had flown O-1s at Khe Sahn prior to becoming a Misty. Today was his checkout flight. He was flying from the front seat for the first time.

I checked all my gear into the back seat. I'd be riding the back 'hole' as instructor pilot when we were out of the combat area. Once into North Vietnam, I would become a forward air controller and the eyes of my headquarters.

As I was seated in the airplane, getting strapped in and squared away, I noticed an airplane from 7th Air Force taxiing toward the revetments where my birds were parked. This particular small jet transport was called Scatback, and there seemed to be an unusual amount of interest in it.

I speculated on whether it might be our boss, General Spike Momyer, Commander of the 7th Air Force at Saigon. Spike's nickname was the "bird killer," earned for having fired so many Air Force colonels.

When General Momyer visited a base, he got attention, particularly from colonels. When senior generals visited, we always wanted to have our "ducks in a row." I had briefed Momyer on two occasions, and I was tremendously impressed by how quickly he could grasp the gut issues in a complex briefing.

Misty was my first combat command. It was the first time in my Air Force career that I was totally and fully responsible for every achievement or failure for my dozen aircraft, my 300 plus people, and for combat accomplishment. I felt well prepared for my job, with 72 combat missions in the "Hun" in South Vietnam, and 65 more over North Vietnam. With 2,000-plus hours in the "Hun," I had more flying time than almost any American flying commander of World War II.

A vehicle came straight from Scatback to my airplane. A young airman got out, holding a huge picture, obviously an intelligence photo. A photo interpreter showed up and briefed me on a stunning new development. I now understood the interest showed in the Scatback's arrival.

The photo was high quality and showed an SA-2 surface-to-air missile (SAM) site with a radar van and three missiles. They were located in a fruit orchard west-southwest of a well-known landmark in North Vietnam, Fingers Lake. This site was very close to the DMZ and presented just the kind of threat we could not tolerate.

Seventh Air Force had analyzed this photo and wanted to put a strike on it as soon as possible. It was the classical deployment of the SA-2, and it confirmed the worst of our fears.

At this time, B-52s were bombing only along the DMZ due to political restraints. The SA-2 was a Russian missile, the same type that defended Moscow. The Russians would be most interested in knowing if their missiles would stop the best U.S. bomber.

I studied every detail of the picture, as well as other intelligence information on coordinates, flak, etc. I was sure I would be able to find the target, even though it was difficult to find well-camouflaged positions on the ground. While the camera does it quite well, the naked eye is frequently fooled and can easily miss what the camera finds.

I knew the SAM site location, generally west of the small Fingers Lake. It was about 30 miles due north of the friendly Dong Ha Tacan, a navigation facility in South Vietnam. Dong Ha was one of the major military installations south of the DMZ to the west of Quang Tri City. The lake stood out very well. I knew the entire "Route Pack I" area of southernmost North Vietnam like my own back yard.

"Kip" cranked up the airplane, and we took off from Phu Cat. As we flew north, I was impressed with the good pattern of roads and heavy truck traffic in South Vietnam. This, along with the industrial smoke and evidence of production, were a fantastic contrast to the stark bleakness of North Vietnam. I wondered if the villages in the north were as primitive as those in the south. I was touched by the beauty of the white sand beaches which rival those in northwest Florida.

Our flight plan was to take us past Chu Lai, Da Nang and follow the coast northward for about 280 miles. We were to probe this SAM site from the east, on a northwest heading. Our first plan was to make an angling pass across the target on a heading of 300 degrees at about 450 knots, and approximately 3,000 feet altitude.

Our high speed kept our exposure to flak at a minimum. Every second saved was that much less time that the enemy could shoot at us, and around a target like this, they would shoot quite a bit. Also, we would be over the Tonkin Gulf as much as possible, over the target for the minimum amount of time, and finish the pass over some rugged karst.

Like many things in Vietnam, karst is something straight out of prehistoric times. It's a series of low mountainous formations, whitish in color, probably limestone, which resemble upside-down icicles. The terrain was so rugged the North Vietnamese could not use it.

We flew 50 minutes to our turn point on the coast, then dropped down low for our run inbound. The target area stood out well, but as I had expected, it was superbly camouflaged. The Communists were masters at camouflage, forcing great numbers of people into work efforts. As a result, their positions were hard to find.

They began shooting at us long before we reached the target. The flak was a shower of explosions. They had seen us coming because we had to be above the smallarms fire. A rifle bullet smashes a jet like a sledge hammer. Even though some surprise was lost on this kind of high pass, the reduced loss rate justified the tactic. To my disgust, we did not see the target.

We continued across the karst toward the Laos border and then headed northeast toward targets "Up North." Because of heavy flak and the high probability of shootdown, we did not circle or make consecutive passes over hot targets. This was a very hot target!

We had a strike to put in west of Dong Hoi, and met our fighters there. Our white phosphorous smoke rocket pinpointed the target for the bombers. It was a truck park and storage area that we had staked out from the previous day's work. After the bomb run and the smoke and dust cleared away, we photographed and assessed the damage, passing this info to the strike aircraft.

Diminished fuel made it necessary to leave the target area and head for a flying tanker. One of the interesting aspects of our mission was the double, occasionally triple, in-flight refuelings. We would exchange our daily joke with the big flying tankers. They always asked "Fill it up? Regular or ethyl?" The answer didn't matter. They simply wanted to help us.

Misty missions were probably the longest, most fatiguing missions flown in North Vietnam. The exposure of Misty aircraft was evidenced by our loss rate of 42% for the first six months of operation. If not the record, it certainly was close to it. Naturally prejudiced, I believe that Misty deserved to be one of the most highly-decorated groups of the war.

Heading back from our Thailand refueling, we decided to make our next run across the Fingers Lake target from south to north. We hoped that if we could offset slightly from the place we had crossed the first time, we might be able to see the target. It was very probable that we had flown straight over it before. This time, I offset slightly to the west, again at low altitude and with a full head of steam. I was "jinking" the aircraft around pretty violently, weaving in an uncertain pattern, since we were taking a lot of fire. As we went over the target, Kip said, "Roll out, I've got it in sight!"

As I rolled out, we took a smashing blow in the aft section. It jolted the bird hard, rattling us violently in the cockpit. Nevertheless, the Hun continued to fly and seemed to be controlable. We were almost dead-center in the flak pattern.

I think we took a direct hit from a 37 mm gun, in the vitals of the tail surface controls. There was no bright orange flash that accompanies a missile detonation.

I bent the airplane around to the east in a high-G turn, heading for the water and trying to climb out of the flak. This put me some 35-40 miles north of the Dong Ha Tacan and north of Fingers Lake. As I got the aircraft rolled out on a heading of about 130° (southeast), it pitched over, nose down, in an extremely violent negative-G bunt. In effect, it tried to throw us out the top of the canopy.

Kip came up on the interphone, "We're hit!"

"Rog," I answered, "I've got it," meaning that I had control of the bird, I knew about the hit, and would work out that problem along with flying the aircraft.

All of the warning lights in the cockpit told me that the bird was getting sicker. Then the stick locked! This indicated that the normal hydraulic system which operated the controls had been shot out. The aircraft continued nosing over. At the rate we were approaching the ground, there were only seconds left. I jerked the throttle out of burner to reduce thrust, and threw on the ram air turbine to see if it would power the hydraulic system. The guages read little or nothing.

I pressed the trim for takeoff button to my left, hoping that the slab would respond to electrical power. No help! Our bunt became more aggravated. A couple of seconds, maximum, left for correction! I had to get the nose up or leave the bird.

I thought briefly about rolling inverted because if the stabilator remained locked in its present attitude, the aircraft would start climbing inverted instead of hurling at the ground as it was now doing. I looked at the ground, our rate of descent, and decided there wasn't enough time. If it didn't work, we'd be dead. My last thought was to blow the flaps down and increase the lift of the wings to raise the nose. It didn't work! Only one thing left — PUNCH OUT!

I had carefully briefed Kip before the flight that if we took a hit and had to eject, I would be firing my seat immediately after the canopy left the aircraft. The emergency egress system is automatic and requires only that the pilot try to position himself erect in the seat, raise a lever, and through a system of explosive squibs, blow the canopy from the aircraft, and then fire the rocket-powered seat. This took only fractions of a second and was designed for emergency situations just like this one.

It was clear that the aircraft was too sick from the flak damage to respond to any of my efforts to bring it under control. The high negative G forces were pressing me up against the lap belt. My helmet was banging against the plexiglass canopy. Every loose item in the cockpit was rattling around my head . . . an Asahi Pentax 35mm camera, two pair of field glasses, my own Canon camera, water bottles, maps and everything that was not nailed down, including the dirt off the floor of the cockpit.

I fired the canopy.

KEEP THE FAITH

Too young to know what happened,
Why Daddy couldn't be found,
Landing in some foreign woods
After jettison to the ground.

Mama sat upon her bed
As tears filled in her eyes,
Reaching hard for hopefulness,
Answered questions without lies.

So, insecure, I wondered,
And knew something wasn't right,
Why Mama sat there crying,
Such an unfamiliar sight.

Mama talked of Daddy
And his never-ending love
For his children and his wife
And for God above.

From Mama's strength we dared believe
Her feelings always true.
She never lost her faith in God.
He always pulled us through.

Then one day we heard the news.
Our Daddy was set free.
Many years had come and gone.
Would Daddy remember me?

St. Patrick's Day was a day of joy
When Daddy at last stepped down
From the silver bird that brought him home
To his beloved native ground.

Today my parents' inner strength
Is there for all to see.
It is ultimately stronger,
And they've passed that strength to me.

Love,
Sonja Day

CHAPTER FOUR

On the Ground

First things first. Once on the ground the most important thing was to get off my call to the C-130 flying command post. I snaked out the small brown case, extended the aerial with my left hand and transmitted.

"Hello, Hillsboro, this is Misty 31 Bravo. Hello, Hillsboro, this is Misty 31 Bravo. I'm on the ground OK."

As I waited for a reply, I noticed in dazed amazement what a beautiful day it was, and how peaceful it seemed. My camouflaged parachute draped through the tree limbs was wafted gently in the light afternoon breeze.

I heard shouting in the distance, and the sounds of something smashing through the light tree branches. I looked up to see a very young Vietnamese, extremely frightened, pointing a rusty old rifle at me. He was unbelievably excited. Perhaps I was the first Caucasian he had ever seen. I was in too great a state of shock to realize I was losing life's most precious possession, freedom.

He spied the watch on my arm and immediately snatched it, a treasure of unequalled value in his village. He was now the richest man there with the only semblance of the twentieth century, an automatic calendar watch. He attempted to remove my pilot school graduation ring, but I was not that dazed and fought him off. He took my hunting knife and began cutting me out of my parachute harness with such ignorant abandon that I was concerned for my safety. All the while, he was yelling like a banshee, calling for assistance from some nearby comrades in the search party.

His friends arrived and began snatching off my boots, flight suit, and other clothing. They hustled me to my feet and started to march me away. I discovered as I stood up that something was seriously wrong with my left knee. It was excruciatingly painful and almost impossible to stand on. The Vietnamese were frantic to get me moving and applied liberal blows with their rifle butts and muzzles to get me moving.

We hadn't gone more than a few yards when I heard heavy rifle and automatic weapons fire. I was surprised to hear such low-trajectory firing.

Then I picked up the "whop, whop, whop" of a helicopter and realized what was happening. A "Jolly Green" rescue helicopter had been scrambled from South Vietnam. He was roaring in after me, homing on the electronic beeper in my chute to give the rescue people a direct bearing on my position.

He came in very low, and that was the reason the guns were depressed. The Viet gunners were having a hard time bringing the muzzles to bear on him, particularly since they were sunk into a doughnut-shaped enclosure for protection. They were firing above the chopper, letting the rounds air burst, hoping they would explode close to him. It was interesting to speculate how many Vietnamese they might have "done in" on this day with such low-angle fire. Probably part of the fire came from the same site that shot me down.

In spite of the barrage, the helo pilot pressed on with total disregard of the flak, acting as if there were no way he could be shot down. Words fail to describe his incredible courage. I could see a man standing in the open door of the chopper with a rifle in his hand. I couldn't identify him. I didn't know for a long time that it was Corwin Kippenham.

It would have been an encouraging memory to know that Kip was alive and that he had tried to assist in my rescue. By the same token, my friend Kip did not know for years whether I lived or died, and he worried constantly about my fate. The chopper had flown up from its base in the South, picked up Kip and loaded him safely aboard. Giving him a rifle, they posted him in the door and said, "We're going in after your buddy. Shoot anyone that shoots at us."

Kip had not been injured in the ejection and was glad to assist. The chopper homed in on my chute and stopped, all men aboard looking for me. They could see that I wasn't there! Heartsick, I watched them tip and turn the chopper in order to see more clearly. Finally, unable to find me, they were forced to leave.

It was heartbreaking to see the pilot elect to make a left turn. Had he made a right turn and withdrawn or even turned east, my primitive young captors would have dropped to the ground in frightened paralysis. It was not to be.

My captors were elated, almost dancing, realizing how close it had been, how near to success my rescue attempt had been. My own spirits sagged! It was shattering, and the sickening feeling lingered for hours.

One can choose to believe in predestination to the point of being a fatalist. He can also believe that he has charge of everything and that he makes things happen as he chooses. On this dreadful day, I certainly could not claim that I was in charge.

My captors forced me to a shabby hut and gave me some ragged clothing, reversing the American dream. I went instantly from riches to rags. It was almost six years before I saw decent clothing again.

They tried to force me to march barefoot to their camp, but I could scarcely hobble due to the severe pain in my left knee. Bone-jarring whacks from their rifle butts landed on my spine as they tried to get me moving. I moved at my own pace, believing there was hope of being picked up by a chopper. As I limped into my first village, I received a baptism in abuse that was to become a routine for many months to come.

A wizened prune of a man called the Cadre seemed to be the leader of the people. His sing-song harangue was obviously enumerating my sins against their country. Women and children pummeled me with their fists. The men aimed half-hearted kicks at me with their rubber sandals. Some spit at me, and when I fell to the ground, I was raised quickly to my knees or feet with tugs at my hair or ears.

While the beating was bruising and painful, it seemed to me that the onslaught was lacking in fury. No hate shown through the eyes of my persecutors. The veins did not stick out on the necks of my tormentors. They seemed insensitive to the fact that I was a human. They could just as well have been pounding on a tree. It may have been that such acts were so commonplace that there was no fun in it.

I was led from village to village, finally arriving at a built-up camp at dusk. I was in a state of shock and had developed a dusty-dry, unquenchable thirst. The guard ushered me into a hole carved out of the side of a bunker. It was about the height and length of a coffin. I lay on the dirt floor which had been carved out of the side of a large mound of earth. It was slightly elliptical in shape, with two small entrances. The roof was a layer of logs, covered with several feet of dirt. The walls were carved hard clay, the floor slightly damp and cool from the subsurface moisture. My left hand was raised upward and wired to the ceiling logs, my legs wrapped and tied with ropes.

I was taken with the thought that my fate was parallel to the Bishop's in Dante's *Inferno*. But this time, it was not a man of the cloth. It was me, plugged into a ring of the Malebolge. The comparisons to Dante's fantasy would plague me all through my capture.

After crawling into the hole, I could barely sit erect. A number of Vietnamese came by to stare at me curiously and to look at my arm. A small piece of bone was protruding from the skin of my wrist, and my arm hung in a strange fashion. They made some hand signs and kept pointing at my face. Their pointing and chattering baffled me since I was not able to see what injuries I had taken to the eye. Later I discovered that the right side of my face had been mangled and my eye blinded.

The guard brought me a small bowl of rice, a metal tin can full of thin, lukewarm tea, and a very small bowl of what looked like plain weed soup. I learned that this was the food pattern common to North Vietnam. Food was incredibly plain. Luxuries, such as meat, fish and spices were generally unknown. When your food is boiled weeds and rice, it is barest level of existence.

It became clear to me in this camp that it was going to be *all* uphill from now on. I was in enemy hands, and a chopper rescue was out of the picture. All of my equipment for signaling was gone. I had no compass or radio. Any escape attempt had to be made with no resources or outside help, through cunning and deceit.

A medic came by after several days. He wanted to put some drops in my eye from a horse needle large enough to go through my arm. He was quite unbelievable, looking and acting more like a sewer cleaner than a man of medicine. I didn't speak Vietnamese and he didn't speak English, so it was a standoff. I kept rolling and dodging around on the floor, determined that he wasn't going to put anything into my eye, or do anything else to me.

This area of Vietnam adjoined the demilitarized zone separating the North and South. If there was a front to the war, it was just south of here. My little hole in the mound of earth was roughly 20 or 30 miles, as the crow flies, directly north of the DMZ.

From the first day, I thought of nothing but escape and began to set the scene. I resisted all attempts to force me to move. I began feigning maximum injury and inability to escape. I had already determined that since I was able to walk, I could and would escape.

The Vietnamese pressured me to move around, but I would move only a few inches to pick up my food and for nothing else. Apparently, the combination of the damaged arm and leg, and the mangled face convinced them I was helpless. I took a couple of heavy beatings for refusing to move, and I began to wonder if I would be able to retain that ability.

The guards had to bend down uncomfortably low to look at me. I could tell they were coming when I saw their shadows and made sure I dispelled any notion that I could fend for myself. By Monday, August 28, my guards concluded that I could not move, and carelessly stopped wiring my hand to the ceiling, only wrapping and tying my legs with ropes at night. This was essential to my plan for making good an escape.

The next day the first English-speaking Vietnamese showed up. He was extremely simple, very poorly educated. His English was barely intelligible. We hardly passed the stage of "Who are you?" and "What organization are you from?" I gave him my name, rank and serial number as was provided for in the Geneva Convention and refused to answer any other questions.

I understood generally that he wanted military information: the

ON THE GROUND

organization I was from, my takeoff base, which aircraft I was flying, who was commanding officer of the base, and some military questions of this nature. I did not answer because I was required not to do so and he did not torture me to answer. He told me that on the following day a doctor would come by to look at my leg.

On Wednesday morning, a tiny Vietnamese wearing a ball cap appeared. He was about five feet tall, very slight, and perhaps 100 to 110 pounds, an average product of their poor diet. He looked at my ring and said in French, *"Ah, vous etes pilot Americain,"* and I answered, *"Oui."*

He was reasonably friendly and was able to converse in understandable French, although my visits to Casablanca had only partially prepared me for this exchange. He told me he was a doctor, had attended the University in Paris, and had interned in Hanoi. He said he had a Vietnamese nurse with him, and he would attempt to set my arm. He told me he had plaster of paris and that my arm was badly broken.

I could see a piece of bone sticking through one part of my arm, and there was a very bad break in the upper part. Even I could verify his diagnosis. The nurse washed my arm with warm water, but without soap, which surprised me. The fact is, they probably didn't have any soap.

The procedure for setting my arm was pretty wild. The doctor sat me on a wooden bench. He had a Vietnamese sit on the bench beside me and take hold of my neck. With that, he grasped my thumb and while the Vietnamese on the bench pulled me in one direction, the doctor pulled me in the other direction.

"Sweet Jesus," said my brain cynically, "isn't this fun?" The pain was excruciating. The guards smiled derisively. Finally, the doctor decided that it was impossible to set my arm without giving me anesthetic and he dropped my arm in disgust.

Out came another long needle! Horse doctors with horse needles, I thought. It left a gaping, bleeding hole in my arm. However, it was filled with novocaine and he pumped a large shot in the upper arm and two or three shots in the lower arm. Soon the guard returned, sat by my side, put one leg up over my legs in front of me and one behind my back and began to pull my neck. The doctor again grabbed my thumb and started extending my arm. The novocaine worked great. No pain!

It was staggering to see how far an arm could be stretched without the bone to restrain it. When he was satisfied that everything had been pulled out straight, the doctor began talking to the nurse. They folded my arm back into the 90° position very carefully, as you would do if you extended your arm in front of you and then brought it back parallel to your chest.

The nurse prepared the cast and applied it. After an hour, I had a massive, clumsy cast which ran from the shoulder bone to my fingertips. It was crude by American standards, and it was clear that this "doctor" was not up to American standards. Most were called assistant doctors, even by the Vietnamese.

All in all, Vietnamese medicine was at about the same technical level as the United States practiced in about 1850, or earlier. Despite this fact, I was convinced that my arm had received the best repair work possible under these primitive conditions, and I was a happy man to have it fixed at all.

I limped back to my hole in the ground, taking a great deal of abuse, examined my cast and thought that it hadn't been too bad a day. When one sits around with the bone protruding through the skin, harrassed continually by persistent flies, the probability of infection is not remote. Neglect of wounds or primitive care was to be the lot of many American airmen who did not have their wounds treated for days, weeks, months, and sometimes never. I soon learned that a great deal of healing takes place purely through the grace of god and nature. The human body repairs itself very well in many cases.

Back at the Malebolge, a delightful surprise awaited me. The guards, lazy as they were, did not like to carry water or tea to the hole for me, so they had devised a system to bring me water once a day. To my delight, they had brought a canteen, which was a key utensil in my escape, but I had been certain it was too much to expect.

Time passed slowly and, as I took closer notice of my environment, I gained some practical lessons in biology. I learned that ants preferred live worms for dinner to grains of rice dropped from my bowl. They crawled into holes where the earthworms lived and an army of them would rip out a fat protesting earthworm, dragging him off to be eaten. I was very surprised to find that they were cannibals who preferred eating other flesh to eating dried food. I dropped a few pieces of greens from the soup to see if they had any interest in those, and they showed zero interest. Smart ants!

I watched a spider who made his web in my little home. It was fascinating to watch him fly into action from his dormant state. He folded himself into an innocuous lump but came roaring to life when a mosquito would bumble into his web. I intended to emulate the spider. I intended to spring out of my hole and be gone like a shot.

That Wednesday evening, two armed Vietnamese came for me. They motioned with their weapons for me to get out of the hole. I refused. One of them furiously took hold of my leg and seized me by the trouser, ripping off the leg. He dragged me out of the hole, got me onto my feet and marched me about five or six yards away where a young Vietnamese sat stiffly on a rickety chair. The interpreter told me this man was the camp commander and a Vietnamese colonel. He also said that since I was a major I was ordered to answer all questions this colonel directed to me.

ON THE GROUND

I was 42 years old and would guess that this man was about 25. The chances of his being a Vietnamese colonel were the same as floating an ice cube through hell. It was hard to believe they expected that story to sell. The "colonel" sat on his chair and stared at me while the interpreter insisted that I must answer the questions.

The man said that if I did not answer the questions, they had the authority to shoot me, and the officer would simply execute me on the spot. I stood mute. He then asked me my name, rank, serial number and from which base I had departed.

I gave him my name, rank, and serial number and told him that I refused to answer any other questions. The interpreter spoke to the guards who immediately struck me with their fists, rifle butts, and slapped me violently. With their rifles, they banged on my back and chest, but did not convince me that they were going to kill me.

The officer snapped the flap on his holster two or three times, toyed around with his pistol. He pointed it at the ground, then at me, and then put it back in the holster. The interpreter was telling me in the meantime that I was definitely going to be shot if I didn't shape up and speak. It was an unproductive session.

I feigned dizziness and fell to the ground. They banged me around with their rifles, kicked me, and finally sat me up. It was just about dark and I now had a fix on due west, the setting sun. Not good, but a fair idea.

My respite was only temporary. The following day, Thursday, August 30, at about 7:30 A.M., I was forced to an A-frame type shelter constructed of logs, and covered with a heavy layer of dirt and mud. The interrogator began his questioning again as I sat in stoic silence.

"I order you to answer!" he shouted.

I remained mute. My tormentor sprang into action.

A hemp rope was coiled tightly around my ankles and cinched up to the point where I no longer had any feeling in my feet. The other end of the line was thrown over a beam and I became the dead weight at the end of a tug of war. My captives pulled with abandon until I swung freely off the floor. The agony was indescribable. The bones in my useless arm were mashed together and pulled apart alternately, making grating noises. Blood rushed to my head, blurring my vision and piercing my skull with an excruciating throb.

This was the beginning of hours of purgatory, hanging inverted like a side of butchered beef. Things that would normally have been minor nuisances, such as the attack of a fly or mosquito, or an itch, became an avalanche of discomfort on my crawling skin.

Beads of sweat broke out all over my body, and rivulets coursed their way into my dusty nostrils and mouth. It took several hours for the rope to mercifully stretch to the point where my head touched the ground and progressively lowered further until the weight transferred to my shoulders.

This insane and inhuman procedure brought me moments of despair. Midway between the time my head first touched the floor and my shoulders assumed some of the burden, I was convinced that my neck would break. At times I nearly strangled as the full weight of my body forced down my twisted head. As incongruous as it may seem, I took courage in the realization that I had experienced as acute and intense pain as the body can withstand and I had endured it.

My mind was a kaleidoscope of vivid and fleeting memories. Dorie . . . hunting in Iowa . . . the unfinished scotch glass back at my bedside . . . God . . . a swimming pool . . . all ran together, interrupted at times by a squadron of insects, intent on chiseling holes in my crusty skin.

I couldn't help but think that this was going to be a long war. I wondered if they did the same thing to a man with a broken back or internal injuries. Could a man live under those conditions?

My twisted leg hurt like sin! I wondered if there was another human in the world being hung like this, at this same instant. How much of this could a man tolerate?

I refused to answer questions. If they were going to exploit me, they would have to work hard and long at it. "I will return with honor, or I will not return," I told myself.

It appeared that I was going to hang until I answered questions. Day dragged slowly into late afternoon. Still I hung, and still I hurt. It was a welcome relief to become free of the rope at dusk, and to go back to the hole. This day's torture drove the message home to me that things could only get worse. I must escape.

CHAPTER FIVE

Behind the Bamboo Curtain

"Well," I thought dejectedly "Some escape it was! Now look at you! You're shot up, emaciated and on your way back to real captivity. Looks like you have driven yourself into the world's deepest hole!"

My porters continued a steady trotting pace uphill and down, on and on. At the end of each hour, two fresh bearers would take the pole, never dropping me, although they ran over very wet, slick terrain.

At what I estimated to be 10:30 P.M., we arrived once more at the Ben Hai River. My only contact with reality was the sound of the paddles, the splash of the water, and the feel of the rough, wet floor of the boat against my legs. Totally disoriented, I knew only that we were north of Ben Hai River and the DMZ again.

After a long, hard day, they stopped and I could hear the babble of many excited voices. Someone ripped the blindfold off my face, and I found that I was in front of an underground bunker. They crammed me down into the earthen carved entrance and dragged me in. Shadows flickered from the kerosene lanterns. It was smoky and foul-smelling. Like Dante's *Interno*, it seemed that Vietnam had a never-ending series of smelly, smoky, filthy holes. Which ring of hell was this? And which lay in the future?

There was great curiosity about who I was, and much ugly animosity. A couple of the porters, who had been carrying me, looked at me and raised their fists in a sort of victory salute. Then in a clear gesture of triumph, they cheered a hearty hurrah. This clearly convinced me that I was now back in North Vietnam.

"Balls!" I thought.

These were NVA regulars. No question about it. They all possessed a new AK-47 rifle, wore good-quality Chinese tennis shoes, and top-quality Chinese uniforms. Their equipment was so superior to the militia that the difference was immediately obvious.

In the morning, my bearers trotted north at a brisk pace. They brought me to within an eighth of a mile south of the town of Vinh Linh and took the blindfold off. They pointed ahead. I could see the ruins. It had been a town of about forty to sixty thousand population before it had been levelled. Gaunt and weathered skeletons of building walls or chimneys stood in quiet desolation. Nothing above ground was fit for habitation.

My bearers pointed and smiled. They were oh so very smug, and I realized how satisfying it must be for them to return me to this camp. Apprehension and fear coursed through me. I was in for some very hard times. Since I had escaped by walking out of the camp, I was also going to walk back into the camp! This may not make sense to a human, but it's very logical to a Communist!

I limped along at a snail's pace, taking a shower of kicks, jabs and curses. It was torture, but an improvement over the spine-rattling rifle butts. I re-entered the camp under my own power. The cook, a couple of guards and the so-called colonel were standing there staring at me. The camp commander sneered nastily, and pointed to my former domicile, the "hole." Back into the Malebolge!

One of the guards produced a piece of double-strand telephone wire wrapped with plastic insulation. He bound my feet together, then wired my left hand to one of the overhead beams. While so doing, he hit me, punched me with his fist, and said some things I had to conclude were hateful.

A few minutes later the "Colonel" showed up wearing his holster. He entered the hole, a black angry look on his face. He jabbered at me in Vietnamese, shook his finger and gestured, sputtered and spit. Finally, he took the nearly new pistol out of the holster, put it hard against my forehead and said several things. I could feel the muzzle of the pistol, cold on my forehead, right between my eyes.

I told myself half-heartedly, "This jerk is not going to shoot. They would never go to all the trouble of carrying me here to permit him to shoot me." I tried desperately and unsuccessfully to convince myself that he wouldn't shoot.

I wondered, "If he does shoot me, will I hear the bullet before it goes through the back of my head?"

After what seemed in eternity, he struck me a sharp blow on each side of the forehead, and on the side of the head, dazing me and addling my senses. With more cursing, he backed out of the hole. I was vastly, but prematurely, relieved.

Soon the real ordeal began. The guard who had been on duty during my escape appeared. He looked in, obviously delighted to see me, wearing a malicious, evil smile on his face. He was shaking his fist and there wasn't any doubt in my mind what was going to happen next. He began to pound and beat me.

He smashed his fist into my face, neck, ears, jaw and stomach. When he was totally spent, gasping for breath, and wet with sweat, he stopped. He backed out of the hole, gestured, spit on me, and glared viperously.

"What a rotten bastard," I thought. I wondered if this was the lot of Jesus after being captured by the Romans.

Within a few minutes, other guards and members of the camp came by to pay their respects. They seemed thrilled to have me back. They beat me with their fists and feet. I couldn't defend myself, hanging as I was from the roof. I lacked the mobility to dodge the blows. I tried to avoid any additional direct blows to my head, knowing that I couldn't stand many more.

The worst beating was from an old woman, the cook. She appeared in her late sixties. She carried a short stick about 20 inches long with which she began striking me. I couldn't evade her, and she laid one hard blow after another on me, many on the head. She really hurt me. I lunged around frantically trying to present a moving target, but it was nearly impossible to avoid her.

Finally composing myself, I drew my feet into a ball and waited until she was in a position where I could kick her. I lashed out with both feet and smashed her violently in the face, nearly tearing her head off. This blow propelled her backward out of the hole. I hoped I had broken her nose. She shook herself off, dazed and befuddled, for I had hurt her. I drew my feet back again to signal that I was going to smash her as soon as she came back. Sputtering and scolding, she decided that she had had enough. I was relieved and her absence truly made my heart grow fonder!

The old woman's beating took the last of my strength. My mouth and jaws were so swollen I could scarcely move my eyes. In addition to everything else, I had to urinate. I told the guard that I had to relieve myself.

"No! No!" he shouted violently, pointing his gun at me.

I insisted that I had to. I had not urinated since that morning. He could not have cared less! I thought I would burst. The armed guard sat on a chair, bent over, staring into the hole and I continued to ask to get outside to urinate. The only answer was threatening gestures and impending violence.

This kind of low-forehead reasoning was a familiar pattern for many years. Any action which could make a prisoner more comfortable had to be denied, for that very reason. Eventually the demands of nature overcame my distaste and I finally emptied my bladder on my leg. It had to happen sooner or later, and the scene would repeat itself over and over again in my POW years.

As darkness fell, the ranking enlisted man came to move me out of camp.

RETURN WITH HONOR

Several "V" suited up with traveling equipment, packs, and rifles stood outside the hole. I waited to see how they were going to move me, hoping they would carry me. After the sun set, I found they intended for me to walk.

The senior NCO entered my hole, untied my arm from the ceiling, and unwired my feet. He jerked his head to indicate that I should come out. I attempted that, but my wounds were so painful that it took a long time to move. My right leg was enormous, twice its normal size, and stone-hard from the swelling. The bandage was intact on my left leg where the Viet Cong medic had bandaged it.

As I made it out of the hole, the sergeant indicated I should stand up, and I noticed that he had three other Vietnamese with him. I would come to know two of them very well, since they were to be the guards escorting me all the way to Vinh. The third person was an oversized, heavyset Vietnamese who was the guide.

I was paired up with two Vietnamese. One was a runt who reminded me of a pint-sized reproduction of Stoneage man. His forehead was no more than half an inch high. His eyebrows almost met his hairline. He was about four-feet-nine, with a well-founded inferiority complex. He was totally inferior. I nicknamed him "Stoneage" because it approximated his appearance and mentality.

The second guard was taller, about five-feet-two, a little taller than average. He was slender and his most prominent feature was the two eye teeth that protruded, long and narrow, like the fangs of a snake. He had a long skinny face, and I decided his name had to be "Fang." He was considerably more intelligent than Stoneage, which prompted more imaginative cruelties. I believe their cruelties were a result of my escape from the camp.

Both of the guards displayed maximum hatred every moment they were around me. Not once did they exhibit the slightest hint of kindness. They made up their minds that I would be allowed to urinate once a day. They ignored every request to clean or treat my wounds. Every interaction with them was characterized by cruelty, neglect, and brutality.

CHAPTER SIX

The Bloody Shoe March

CODE OF CONDUCT

For members of the armed forces of the United States:

(1)   I am an American fighting man. I serve in the forces which guard my country and our way of life. I am prepared to give my life in their defense.

(2)   I will never surrender of my own free will. If in command, I will never surrender my men while they still have the means to resist.

(3)   If I am captured, I will continue to resist by all means available. I will make every effort to escape and aid others to escape. I will accept neither parole nor special favors from the enemy.

(4)   If I become a prisoner of war, I will keep faith with my fellow prisoners. I will give no information or take part in any action which might be harmful to my comrades. If I am senior, I will take command. If not, I will obey the lawful orders of those appointed over me and will back them up in every way.

(5)   When questioned, should I become a prisoner of war, I am bound to give only name, rank, service number, and date of birth. I will evade answering further questions to the utmost of my ability. I will make no oral or written statements disloyal to my country and its allies, or harmful to their cause.

(6)   I will never forget that I am an American fighting man, responsible for my actions, and dedicated to the principles which made my country free. I will trust in my God and in the United States of America.

Executive order by President Dwight Eisenhower
Commander in Chief of the Armed Forces of the United States.

ARTICLE 104, UNIFORM CODE OF MILITARY JUSTICE

Aiding the enemy:

Any person who —

(1)   aids or attempts to aid, the enemy with arms, ammunition, supplies,

money, or other things; or

(2) without proper authority, knowingly harbors or protects or gives intelligence to or communicates or corresponds with or holds any intercourse with the enemy, either directly or indirectly; shall suffer death or such other punishment as a court-martial or military commission may direct.

ARTICLE 105, MISCONDUST AS A PRISONER

Any person subject to this chapter who, while in the hands of the enemy in time of war -

(1) for the purpose of securing favorable treatment by his captors acts without proper authority in a manner contrary to law, custom, or regulation, to the detriment of others of whatever nationality held by the enemy as ... military prisoners ... shall be punished as a court-martial may direct.

* * *

The "bloody shoe" march began after dark. My captors put my boots back on my feet, minus the laces. They wrapped a piece of wire around the boots at the ankle, leaving the top flapping. As I limped and staggered, pebbles and rocks began accumulating in the boot tops. Each was trapped by the wire, and they chewed the ankle meat to ribbons.

The heavyset "V" was acting as guide. It was a black, black night. As I stumbled and limped, I stopped every few minutes, bringing a rain of rifle butts down on my back and shoulders.

Although the VC who had captured me at the end of my escape were competent, these men were second-rate. We walked from village to village on oral instructions, totally lost most of the time. There is no real road network in the paddies of North Vietnam, only a series of paths.

Our group would walk into a village and one of the men would bang against the side of a hooch with his rifle. The peasant inside would respond, "Who is it?" In an authoritative voice the reply would be, "Viet Cong."

There was no doubt that this meant, "The Viet Cong is here. You better get out here and find out what we want." The villager would appear in the doorway, and Meathead would demand assistance. If I had not been in such pain, I would have thought myself in the midst of a Three Stooges movie.

A fine escape opportunity presented itself as we forded a shallow river that night. I simply lacked the courage and the energy to try it. When we arrived at our destination, a middle-aged man came out and ordered me

THE BLOODY SHOE MARCH

into another hole, similar to a bomb shelter.

The "bloody shoe march" was an obvious title. My canvas boots, capped with leather toe and heel, had once been green down to the sole. When they were unwired and removed, my ankle was a solid red stripe of raw, bleeding meat, and my boots were full of blood. The green canvas, from the wire to the instep, was blood red.

My new home was a primitive dugout with a tiny entrance followed by a right angle turn to the room. It was excavated several feet underground. In the center of the room was a single wooden slab about two and one-half feet wide and six feet long.

"Hot damn, another nice hole! I'm beginning to feel like a mole," I thought. The villager took a huge piece of wire, which accompanied me all the way to Hanoi, and wired me in the prone position. The wire ran under the bed and across my body.

At that time, I used profanity liberally. I began cursing him, calling him a son of a bitch for strapping me down on the board. He ran the wire across my wounded leg uncaringly. The idea was to try to make things as painful as possible. I believe this maximum prone position would hurt even if you were in perfect condition.

I continued cursing him, and even though he didn't know the words, there was no doubt in his mind about the meaning. He slapped me across the mouth several times to let me know that he understood what I was saying and I had better stop.

As uncomfortable as I was, I fell exhausted into sleep. It was about mid-morning when I awakened. A huge group of children crowded into the entrance of the hole, staring, giggling, pointing, and talking. A few minutes later, the villager who had wired me in returned to untie me. A woman, perhaps his wife, came with him, and they brought an attractive helping of food in enamel bowls.

The food looked wholesome, pieces of rice mixed with sweet potatoes, a plate of small Spanish-style peanuts. They had been handcooked in a bed of coals, judging by the burned and undercooked nuts. Nevertheless, they were delicious!

This was my first real food in nearly three weeks. Shortly, the woman came back with a second serving of food, a bowl of rice and gravy, similar to chop suey. I had to force-feed my stomach since it was satisfied with only a few spoonfuls. I was determined to eat everything I could, and my appetite seemed to please the woman slightly. I tried to let her know that I was appreciative. She showed no emotion, straining to remain passive.

Approximately an hour later, the man returned with an article of clothing that was similar to basketball trunks. They were very short-legged, and tied with a string. He told me to take off the old green breech clout that was all that remained of my trousers. The shirt had been ripped off in the beating at Vinh Linh. He gave me the shorts and made motions that I interpreted to mean he was going to get me a shirt.

I was concerned about the hardness of the wound on my right leg and the bloody bandage. When a medic showed up, I could have cheered! He had some containers that looked like spice bottles. One contained cotton balls soaked in mercurochrome. The other held a yellow-looking solution with an oil base which would be useful on my scabby feet.

I pointed to the wound on my leg and made washing signs. He nodded and went away, returning in minutes with lukewarm water. He allowed me to wash my wounds and injured feet. I slipped the bandage off the wounded leg. It looked bloody but uninfected, so I left it alone. I cleaned the wounds on my feet and ankles and painted them with the yellow solution and mercurochrome.

The medic treated me decently, displaying neither hatred nor friendliness. He did his job and went away. I was grateful for the food and medical care.

I discovered that evening that the man who had wired me to the bench was the Communist cadre for the village. He had treated me somewhat decently because he'd been told to. I was marched out of the hole and Fang and Stone-age showed up. They began pushing me and banging me on the head with their rifle butts.

The cadre led me through the village in the familiar routine. He began his "hate the aggressor act," in all of its Communist dialectic. The war monger ... American Imperialist ... dead women and children. He got the people so worked up that he had to fire his rifle in the air to calm them down.

The crowd charged me, striking me and spitting on me. I was pounded from villager to villager and kicked, but no serious damage occurred. This was the pattern in most villages that I passed through.

Because of denial of medicine en route to this village, my wounded finger swelled to sausage size. I examined my arm frequently, concerned about blood poisoning. I had decided that at the first sign of a red streak, I would chew the finger off. I urinated frequently on the wound to sterilize it. This disgusted Fang and Stoneage, who beat me each time.

It took a long time to get to Vinh, located half-way up the coast of North Vietnam. When we finally arrived, I was taken to a long bamboo hut, partitioned down the center. Each side had been cut into cubicles by bamboo screens.

Unknown to me at first was the presence of another American prisoner, Major Norris Overly, a B-57 pilot shot down on September 10 near Dong Hoi. He was quite sick, with a huge pilonidal cyst on his tailbone. At this

THE BLOODY SHOE MARCH

time, all I was aware of was strange noises coming from his cell.

The guard took a large log chain and wrapped it around my ankles, pulling it tight enough to cut the flesh as painfully as possible. I was locked in with two padlocks. I was so tired I didn't bother to complain.

Early in the morning, I was unlocked, blindfolded and taken at rifle point to a "quiz." The quiz building was a pagoda, ornate and elaborately carved in the old Chinese style. It had a high peaked roof and fancy flying buttresses curling upward over a concrete or stone floor. The entire front of the building was open like a carport and there was a stone wall around the whole thing.

Sitting at a battered table was a thin-faced Vietnamese with protruding ears. He had closely-spaced, sharp, bright, dark eyes. He reminded me immediately of a rodent, so that is what I named him. In poor English, he directed me to sit down.

"Have you ever heard of Riner Robson?"

I thought about that for a minute and then asked, "Who?"

He repeated, "Riner Robson." It occurred to me then that he was talking about Robinson Risner. The mispronunciation and diction made them all difficult to understand.

I thought I'd play dumb, so I answered, "No, I don't know anybody by that name."

"Do you know Hayden Lockhart?" He mispronounced this one so badly that I didn't know until months later when I heard Hayden's name in a POW camp who the Rodent was asking about.

I told him, "No. I cannot understand you."

"What is your name and military unit?"

"I will give you my name, rank and serial number."

He acted amused and became sarcastic. "You aren't going to get away with many answers like that. You might as well understand right now that you are a criminal. You are in the hands of the people, and we aren't putting up with any bad acts from criminals!

"What do you know about Vietnam?"

I replied, "It doesn't matter what I know about Vietnam."

He said, "Well, I know, I've found from talking with other Americans, that you know nothing. You're very ignorant about Vietnam, but I will tell you a little bit about it."

Showing no interest, I told him, "That's up to you."

He launched into a remanufactured version of history, which is typical of all Communist countries. He told me that over their 4,000 years of history, the Vietnamese had overthrown all aggressors and driven everyone out of their country. They had won great victories over everyone, and defeated this or that country.

RETURN WITH HONOR

More and bigger victories! Few non-communists would ever recognize this version. He attempted to explain to me that we were violating the Geneva agreement.

"Do you have any questions?" he asked.

"Yes. I want some medical attention for my leg."

"Your medical attention will depend on your attitude. The Vietnamese people are very short of medicine, supplies and equipment. They don't have to use any of it on you. The basic policy of the Vietnamese people is to be lenient and humane. However, we are not required to be that way with enemies of the state and enemies of the people.

"Your future treatment will depend on your attitude. You could help yourself by showing a cooperative good attitude toward the people. Then the people would probably be lenient and humane."

"Sure!" I thought. "The Vichy French and the Quislings also showed 'good attitude'."

Again he questioned me on military matters. "I don't remember anything. I don't know what you're talking about. I don't understand."

I continued to be unable to remember. He kept bringing up things I refused to understand, like the type of plane I had flown.

He seemed amused by my answers, and said, "I'll be talking with you again. I'll give you a chance to see more clearly!"

I went back to my cubicle and into the chains. I was given a little weed soup and rice, and at this point I heard a noise down the hall. I was convinced that another American was there. I don't know how I knew it was an American, but I did.

The next time the guard was around, I shouted, "This is Air Force Major George Day. I need to go to the toilet, guard." I got a tacit acknowledgement from the other room.

As I went by the door of his cell, I said to the guard, "This is Major George Day. I need to go outside and urinate." On my return, when it appeared that the guard was not around, I shouted down to the other room, "I'm Major George Day. Do you hear me?"

The guard raced down and gave me a hard beating on the head with his fists. He let me know that I was not to shout or make any noise. I still had not received a significant response from the other party. Nevertheless, I was more and more positive it was another American.

I heard moaning sounds, the agony of someone in deep pain. I could hear them take someone outside and that was followed by a noise that sounded like two pieces of 4×4 pine studs being banged together. This was almost correct.

They had Overly in a set of bamboo stocks that folded across his legs. They drove a wodden wedge into place to hold the stocks in position. He could not pull the wedge out. He was lying on his face, with the pus and blood from his wounds running down over his anus and genitals as he lay on the plank.

I went to quiz again the following morning. Once more I was put through a series of political lectures followed by questions.

Later, "V" radio was to tell us every day that the "aggressors" only bombed churches and pagodas and only killed old men, women and children. According to the "V," our bombs were never directed at fuel dumps or missile sites. Thus, it was an unusual historical event just to see this pagoda. It had to be the only one left in the country!

Rodent got increasingly angry that I would not answer. I told him that I couldn't remember. He produced a Vietnamese, whom he told me was a nerve doctor. He was obviously a low-caliber corpsman who could not have diagnosed daylight. The "doctor" had little basic medical equipment, not even an otoscope for examining the eyes, ears, and throat. He gave me a very cursory examination.

When he was finished, Rodent said, "Well, I've had the nerve doctor examine you. He says there's nothing wrong with you and nothing wrong with your memory."

Had it not been for the surroundings, I would have burst out laughing. I responded, "I'd have to assume the doctor doesn't know too much . . . I can't remember!"

Rodent said, "I'll teach you to remember."

CHAPTER SEVEN

Crippled For My Faith

I found out immediately what Rodent meant. He had two of his hooligans wrap a set of ropes behind my back and underneath my armpits. They pulled the ropes up hard and tried to make my shoulder blades and elbows meet. It was excruciating.

"Now, I'm going to force you to tell me," he said.

I protested, "I'm compelled by my code of conduct to give you only name, rank, and serial number. That's all I can give you. Besides that, I was injured by bailout and I can't give you answers to things I can't remember."

He repeated, "I will make you remember."

One of the henchmen put a stick into the ropes and began to turn it like a captain's wheel. My arm joints tried to pop out of the shoulder socket. Circulation stopped and my hands puffed into huge swollen sausages. The pain could be compared to passing a kidney stone or permanent appendicitis.

Muscles in my chest ripped and I felt that my chest would tear apart down the center. The surprising thing was that my right arm, still in its cast, was the least painful of the two arms. Pressure was applied for short periods of time and the pain would vary, depending on how hard he leaned on the stick. I was able to get through it.

I knew that if this kind of dreadful torture continued, it would be difficult, probably impossible, to adhere to the rules of the Code of Conduct and the Geneva Convention. I was expected to withhold assistance to the enemy.

What did "assistance" mean? To me, it was simple. I was not to do anything for the enemy, or say anything to or for the enemy that would hurt my country or my fellow men.

While these tortures were going on, many thoughts passed through my mind. I recalled that some 19th century city had solved 90% of its unsolved serious crimes with a rubber hose. Holding a moral and physical contempt for Communism previously, I now began to build a deep hatred for its agents.

CRIPPLED FOR MY FAITH

That evening, Rodent came to my cell and introduced a young man about 20 years old as the camp commander. Rodent tried to impress upon me that the commandant would not stand for any falderol. It was answer or else. I refused.

The Commander spoke to the Rodent in Vietnamese, who would then ask me a question in English. When I would not answer, a guard was sent from the room. He came back shortly with a small green willow stick which he handed to the Commander. Rodent told me that the Commander was very displeased, very angry, that I had been discourteous and would not answer his question. Then they began to ask military questions.

"What organization are you from? What base did you fly from? What kind of airplane were you flying?"

I told them, "I was injured in the ejection. I have absolutely no recall about that."

The Rodent passed my answer back to the Commander, who struck me a violent crunching blow across the head. This cruelty started about 8:00 and ended about 9:30.

I continued to say, "I don't know," to the questions. The Commander continued to hit me across the head. My head began to throb with a deep internal headache that made me feel as if the top of my skull would explode in fragments.

I was fortunate to have some mobility and was able to deflect many hard blows to my shoulders, left arm, or left hand. It was demoralizing and frightening to discover how one hard, well-placed blow rattled the thinking mechanism.

On the first question, one is sharp. After one spinerattling blow, the shock effect is paralyzing. It puts your thinking process into limbo. The body begins to shriek, "Stop this pain! Tell them something!"

The voluntary part of your will argues, "No, I can't do that! I'll take the pounding, pray for the best, and stick it out. I will retain my honor. If I can't go home with honor, I won't go home." The harder they struck me, the more determined I was to resist, and the harder I hated them.

It was during this night that I became convinced that if I had to give certain information, even under torture, I would, in fact, be a traitor to my country. I would not be able to live with myself, nor face my wife.

I could not disgrace my wife. Her entire family had been in the Norwegian Underground during World War II. Almost every member of the family fought, resisted, and were in the Underground, right down to the small children. Almost every man of army age spent years in Nazi prisons. They took great pride in their honorable conduct, and I could not do less than they.

The beating seemed endless. Smash! Question. Smash! I wondered if it would ever end, and I was overwhelmed with relief when it did. My head, ears, neck, shoulders, arms and hand were one encompassing, piercing bruise and pain. My face was so swollen, I could not move my lips.

During it all, I told them nothing. I monotonously repeated, robot fashion, my name, rank, serial number and "I don't know."

The Commander was exhausted, panting, sweating profusely, highly frustrated and emotionally disturbed. He had committed himself to breaking me and he had not succeeded.

I was amazed that he thought he could break me in such a short session of mistreatment. It was even more shocking to me to discover later that some POWs never forced the "V" to torture them for information.

The parting words of Rodent were, "Tomorrow you will pay. Tomorrow you will talk. You will tell me many things, and if you do not, tomorrow I will turn you into a 'creepull.' You will be a 42-year old pilot, unemployed, crippled, unable to take care of your family."

The following morning, early, the guard marched me to the pagoda. It was obvious that today was going to be unique. Several "V" were sitting against the wall, perhaps ten yards from the chair where Rodent sat. I thought I knew how the Christians had felt in the Coliseum. The watchers were waiting for something to happen with the anticipation of the crowd waiting for the Indianapolis 500 to begin.

The Rodent got right down to business. He had the guard put the rope behind my arms as he had before, and I figured that we were going into the rope and broomstick trick. I was wrong.

A chair was placed under the rafters. Rodent told me, "If you do not immediately agree to answer clearly and distinctly all questions, no matter what the question is about, I am going to turn you into a cripple." Then he counselled me, "Don't be a fool. There is no need for you to get up there and be injured. All you have to do is tell us what we want to know, and we will not injure you."

Calculatingly, he added, "The other man," gesturing toward the hut I had just come from, "the other American has told us all, and there is no need for you to take all this punishment."

I did not answer. What else could they say? They threw the rope up over the rafter of the pagoda, secured it, and forced me to stand on the chair. The guard tied the upper rope to the one which was under my armpits.

Having me suspended with the rope from the rafter, the Rodent looked at the crowd. Like a master of ceremonies, he smiled and looked up at me, saying in English, "And now you will pay! Diehard reactionary!"

He took the loose end of the rope and waved it under my nose. His actions were animated, and he nearly glowed. He jerked the chair from under my feet, and I crunched down, pulling the full weight of the rope on my armpits. My arms were pulled back and up, almost ripped from my body. The arm in the cast was jerked up against my chin, causing incredible pain.

It was about 8:00 in the morning. The ropes began to cut into my arms and again I found myself wondering how much pain I could take.

My body screamed, "Brain, you must stop this."

The brain kept repeating, "No way! The rotten bastards! Never give in to this animal bastard! Son of a bitch. Pig. Scum. Dung."

Overwhelming, continuous pain buffeted my courage and will. It was fantastic pain, bursting many blood vessels. My arm and shoulder seemed to part company. Trying desperately to disengage, I groaned and sweated. My own weight, about 120 pounds by now, was trying to rip my chest muscles apart and my shoulder blades pulled backward. I wondered if some of the sounds I heard were muscles ripping.

The rope cut a scar that remains clearly visible even today. American doctors told me later that this torture was exactly like the crucifixion of Christ, as well as the American Indian torture of hanging a prisoner between trees until death.

Every fiber in my body began nagging my brain to force my mouth to beg for relief. I prayed desperately for strength and courage. Within three minutes, sweat was pouring off my face.

In an effort to blot out the pain, I began counting. I hoped that if I could make a long credible show of resistance, the "V" would become discouraged and give up. At the very least, I wanted to establish enough credibility for them to know that they would never get anything from me easily.

"Help me, Father. Help me live with this pain!" I prayed. I vowed to myself they would not get answers.

So I hung. I sweated. I hurt. More sweat poured from me. Flies droned monotonously. The drops of sweat falling from my nose counted the seconds.

One drop, one second; two drops, two seconds. How many minutes? Soon an hour. How many more?

I expected that somewhere along the line, numbness would take over. The pain would begin to subside. As the hours passed, the pain never decreased. It continued to nag, tear, and punish my flesh and bones.

Every now and then, Rodent would get up and spin me around on the rope, looking over at the people hunkering against the wall. They smiled, snickered, and nudged each other in amusement. They thought this was legitimate entertainment! Meanwhile, Rodent spoke to me in English. The villagers were unable to understand what he was saying, but he pointed to me and gestured. He was obviously playing "big man."

Once, when the rope settled down, I was in a position to see the lower half of Rodent's body clearly. He was staring at me with bright eyes and massaging his legs. Suddenly I realized it was his genitals he was massaging. The sadist was having an orgasm!

I shaped a sneer on my face and looked at him with as much disgust and disdain as I could muster. The hanging continued. He got up on the chair to ask me questions.

"Now, how do you see?" he asked.

I tried to ignore him. According to my mental clock, it was about 10:00 in the morning. I had been hanging on the rope about two hours. Instead of diminishing, the pain seemed to intensify.

Another five minutes went by. Another round of questions and gestures. At about 10:15, one of the audience lost interest. Apparently, things were moving too slowly for him. He stood up, watched for another minute and then walked away.

It was almost as if he had given Rodent a cue to speed up the action. He was scarcely gone from the courtyard when the Rodent said something to the guard who had been marching back and forth and occasionally spinning me around.

The guard took the cast on my right arm and pressed it up tight against my body. He began twisting my wrist in the cast. Since it had been healing for a short time, the bone was not completely joined. This caused the most engulfing pain I had known so far. I found out quickly how the expression "seeing stars" came into being.

A nauseating blue-black sea of pain overwhelmed me. In the midst of this rich, dark color exploded some brilliant white light. I did not see stars exactly, but a beautiful white brilliance. The pain was so indescribable I was simply unaware that it existed.

"Cra-a-a-ck!" The bone snapped. It was not a sharp snap, but a splintering sound as if breaking balsa wood. I could feel each sliver separate from the bone.

I wanted to retch, urinate, or do anything unusually foul to display my total revulsion and contempt for them, for their sadistic cruelty and primitive stupidity. I simply hung.

Rodent began immediately, "Now, pig, I have broken your arm! I am prepared to break the other arm! When you come down, you are going to find you are a 'creepull.' If you do not give me the information I ask you for, I am going to make you a double 'creepull.' I am going to make you a complete 'creepull.' You will never work again, never feed your family and children!"

I looked him straight in the eye. There was no doubt in my mind that he was sincere, and that he had unlimited torture authority. I knew he would break the other arm if he felt it must be done to get an answer. I assessed my broken arm, his threat, and his sincerity.

What would it be like to spend another year, two years, in the Inferno with two broken arms? How would I feed myself? Would my arms simply rot off? Could I stay alive in prison with one broken arm?

I felt I had established some credibility, but more importantly, this was the time to adopt new tactics. I didn't seem to be winning with stony silence. The score was "V" - one, Yank - zero. I hung for a few more minutes.

Finally I said, "Put me down. I'll answer your questions."

"No!" he shouted. "I will not put you down until you answer every question."

I told him loudly and firmly, "I will not answer any questions as long as I am hanging here."

We bartered back and forth. A few minutes passed and I did not answer his questions. He told the guard to let me down and shoved the chair under my anxious feet. As soon as the ropes were untied, he began asking questions.

As I examined myself, I found I could not move either hand, or any finger on either hand. A huge blotch of blood covered my right leg. A massive gusher of pus, blood, and foul-looking body excrement had run down it, and I remembered the powerful kick they had landed as they had forced me up on to the chair that morning. Maybe it was a good thing it finally had ruptured. Maybe it would be less painful.

I looked at my fingers again and tried to move them. Rodent looked at me with delight and he seemed truly happy.

"I told you I would cripple you, pig, and you will be a permanent cripple."

I was frightened, and a sick feeling invaded me. My left hand had turned into a claw. The little finger, ring finger, and middle finger curled up against the palm of my hand, and I could move neither my thumb nor my forefinger more than a quarter of an inch. My left wrist was likewise curled and the hand was pulled down toward my forearm.

My right hand was completely dead. I couldn't get the slightest motion from it. The functions of both arms were severely restricted. I wondered if I would ever be able to shoot a shotgun again, or hold a fishing rod in either hand. More importantly, could I feed myself, or take care of my bodily functions?

As I remembered the good things these hands had done . . . squeezed the Viking, held my children, reeled in bass and crappie, stuffed down tender Iowa T-bones . . . was it all worth it? Had their loss been in vain?

It was difficult to fight off the self-pity, but Rodent interrupted my soliloquy with his questions. "What unit are you from?"

I went straight into lying mode. I gave him a false base, and began a series of lies that I used from that time on. I kept every statement as short as possible and included an insignificant amount of truth.

There had been continual and extensive news releases in the *Air Force Times* and in the *Far East Stars and Stripes*. A full photographic picture display of the base at Phu Cat, the base at Tuy Hoa, pictures of the base, pictures of the wing commander, were available to VC intelligence. I needed to stagger my lies with whatever degree of truth appeared required and which had no value. I also assumed I would have a need to tell these lies at future tortures, if they occurred.

The questions were brief. The point was not to get useful information, but to force me to answer. After the quiz, they blindfolded me and took me back to my room. As I passed Overly's room, still not knowing who he was, I told him that these rotten sons of bitches had broken my arm today. A noise indicated he must have heard me.

In later years as a POW, I made a concerted effort to stop swearing. This was both to get right with God and to prevent the profane abuse of roommates.

That evening, Rodent came to my cell in the company of three or four little girls, quite young. It was another "Big Man" versus the "Air Pirate" in which he posed a lot of questions to impress the girls with the fact that he was getting answers from me. He needed to demonstrate how tough he was.

In my view, I could have broken his spindly body in half in a fair fight, which made him not at all tough. Besides, I have always held a special contempt for wife beaters, child beaters, and people who torture prisoners.

I never saw the Rodent again, but I found later that he had tortured many other Americans in the same manner. He didn't always hang them, but he had used the ropes on many pilots. Exactly one year earlier, in August of 1966, he had put Jack Fellowes through the ropes. He totally wiped out Jack's arms for six months and partially paralyzed him for a year and a half. I discovered this three years later, when Jack was my roommate and nurse for a time.

In his case, Rodent had put Jack in a tight set of ropes and left him in for 12 hours. The ropes were pulled tourniquet tight. The "V" were trying to get him to write a confession. At the end of 12 hours, of course, he couldn't move a hand or arm. There was no confession! Score: Yank - one, "V" -zero!

Within a few days, I was introduced to Overly. He had a very heavy beard, and was a quiet and intense, goodlooking Air Force major. I was delighted to meet him. It is true that misery loves company!

CRIPPLED FOR MY FAITH

We were told by the camp commander that we were going to Hanoi together on a truck and we would not be permitted to talk to each other. We were to be shot if we violated this rule.

It took about three days by truck to get to Hanoi. I had been blindfolded to go 40 steps to the pagoda, but I was not blindfolded to go to Hanoi! I was staggered by the number of trucks that we passed on the road. I counted over 300, all heading south, during a single evening.

The trucks were small cab-type, larger than a delivery truck, but not as large, for example, as a cattle truck. The boxes were about nine feet by ten feet and seemed to be heavily loaded.

I found it mind-boggling that the United States, the strongest nation in the world, would permit this flea on the buttocks of humanity to conduct a war this way.

* * *

EDITOR'S NOTE
On March 4, 1976, President Gerald Ford presented the Medal of Honor to Colonel George E. Day, USAF, for "conspicuous gallantry and intrepidity in action at the risk of his life above and beyond the call of duty" from August 26, 1967, to October 23, 1967.

LITTLE LAS VEGAS

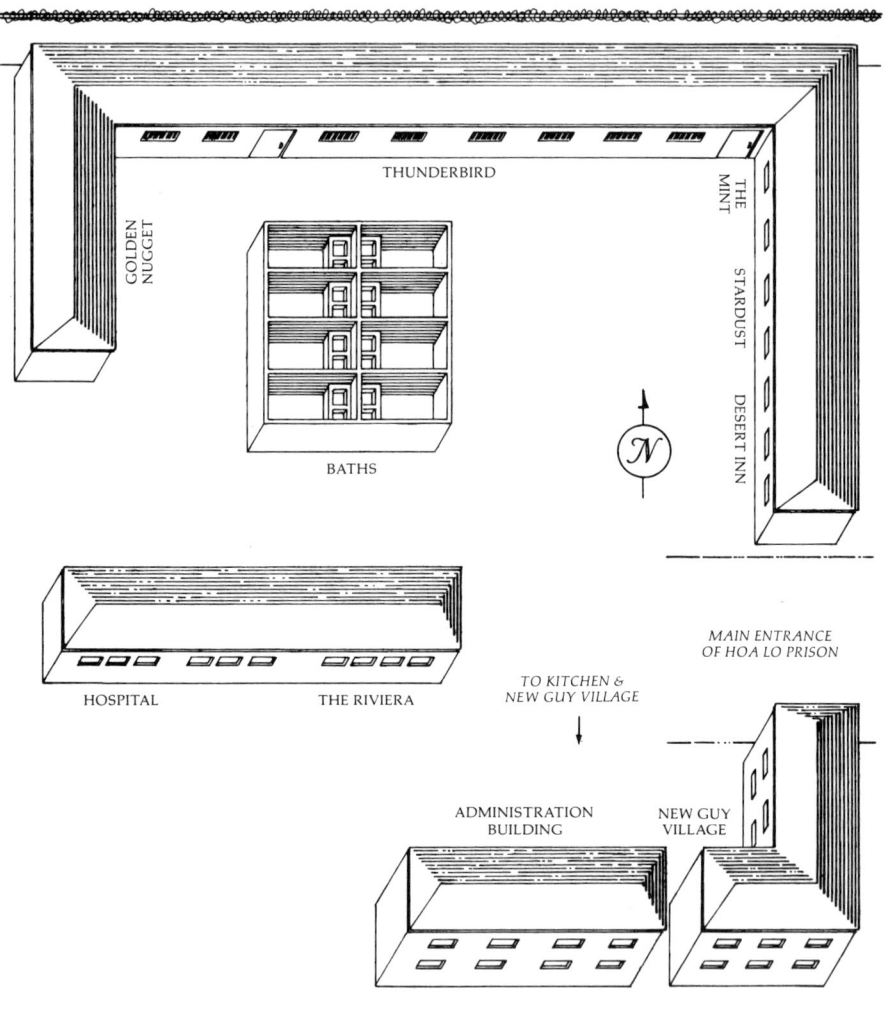

BOOK II:

CHAPTER EIGHT

The Hanoi Hilton, 1967
(The Pit of the Malebolge)

THE INFERNO
EIGHT RINGS OF THE MALEBOLGE
Prologue

THERE IS IN HELL a region all of stone,
by name Malebolges of an iron hue
like the precipitous encircling zone.

Right in the middle of the fell purlieu
there yawns a pit, exceedingly deep and wide.
Whose structure I shall tell in order due.

The belt is therefore circular, outside
the Pit to foot of the high rocky steep,
and in its bottom valleys ten divide.

—

Hither and yon along the gloomy lane,
I saw horned demons with great whips, who dealt
behindward on them furious blows a main.

* * *

The Divine Comedy of Dante Alighieri
A.D. 1336
THE INFERNO OF HELL

A blockade of Haiphong would have stopped most of those trucks I saw on my trek north. Each was a Russian, Czech, or Chinese vehicle and all came in by sea or by train.

Every truck had its own gas station on board. The driver tied a barrel of gasoline to the box of the truck right behind the cab. The discouraging thing about our trip was that I was always strapped to the barrel. It was a certainty that I would be incinerated if the truck got hit by a bomb or gunfire. We were frequently threatened by aircraft as we travelled at night. The truck would pull over to the side of the road, the "V" would run off and hide, and I would be left wired to the barrel of gasoline. Norris Overly was wired to the rack of the truck near my feet.

It was early morning when we arrived at Hanoi. Although we had not relieved ourselves in 13 hours, it was more than eighteen hours before we were allowed out.

A macabre sense of humor is required to label Hao Lo (pronounced Wah Low) Prison the "Hilton." It was a foreboding, dismal place with mouldering, faded, light stone walls, about 14 feet tall. Huge pieces of broken beer and wine bottles jammed their jagged edges upward from the top of the wall.

Even the local Vietnamese, curious as they were about Americans, lowered their eyes, or looked away as if they, too, were overtaken by a sense of fear at this dismal place. Our truck backed up to the door, where a surly, sneering young oriental stared at us hatefully. Every mannerism exuded hatred and contempt, and a chilling sense of danger crawled down my spine. I was rudely jerked and thrust out of the truck. We were led to the most frightening place in Hanoi, "New Guy Village!"

NGV was the torture center for new arrivals. It featured a knobby walled room we came to call the "Star Chamber." Every action by the guards there, every word, every motion by any Commie in the camp was designed to strike terror into the heart of a new arrival.

Despite injured arms and legs, broken backs, and combinations thereof, most POWs were taken into New Guy Village for their initial torture and indoctrination. It was a transient place with few permanent residents, the most notable being my respected friend, "Riner Robson." "Riner" was actually Air Force Colonel Robinson Risner from Oklahoma City. He was a Korean War fighter ace, one of our most decorated heroes and respected prisoners.

For the sake of maximum cruelty, Robbie was forced to live next door to the Star Chamber. He heard nearly every one of the hundreds of tortures that went on there, as well as sweating and groaning through his own.

Within minutes after entering the Chamber, I was on my knees in the kneeling torture, my left hand raised as high as possible, and my legs in irons.

A leg iron is a long rod, half an inch in diameter, holding two "U" bolts. These bolts slip over the ankles and fasten the ankles to the rod.

Torture at NGV was varied — kneeling, ropes, or beatings. For more damage, the rope trick was common, but highly versatile. A rope was passed around and under each arm, then both ends of rope were tied behind the back as tightly as possible. The guard placed his foot between the shoulders and pulled. The idea was to pull your shoulder blades backward and force them together.

The object of immediate torture was to establish a "no nonsense" rapport of calculated violence between torturer and prisoner. No regard was given to broken backs and limbs.

It was little wonder that many POWs, known to have been alive on the ground, were never heard of again. Approximately 30% of all shootdowns had broken bones.

Since I understood the effects of the rope torture already, my sensitivity to this terror was high. I began to pray for strength. It was clear it would be useless to pray for mercy.

My torturer was the "Bug." He was well known to anyone who had been through the Hilton. He was one of the most notorious and vicious torturers in Hanoi.

Bug was probably an ace on American pilots, having killed five, possibly more, on the floor of the Star Chamber. He was a loud, screaming interrogator, about five-foot-three, with extremely bushy, dark black hair which stood out from his head as if he had just taken an electrical charge. His right eye wandered slightly up and to the right. His face was unwrinkled, deceptively young and had a slight layer of fat under the roundish Buddha "Happy God" shape.

Bug was versatile in his approach to prisoners, being able to handle the friendly, greasy approach. His forte, however, was the shouting, screaming, accusing monster, striking terror into the heart as soon as possible. He always opened with an accusation of some wrong doing.

If Bug had no firm accusation, he would start by saying, "You're a criminal. I can have you shot. You killed my mother!"

There were those who learned to hate Bug so violently, they wished they had, in fact, killed his mother. He deserved it! If anyone had counted the number of people accused of this crime, the figure would have been astounding!

There was nothing at all subtle about Bug. When he used the screaming, angry act, his right eye pointed even farther off to the right. As he became more agitated — shouting, screaming and gesturing — his hair became wilder and bushier. He would work himself into a verbal rage until he was almost incoherent.

His torturing followed the same pattern. He did not participate in the physical torture, but had two assistants. One of them was a pox-marked Vietnamese whom we called "Straps and Bars," "George," or "Pig Eye," who meted out the physical mistreatment.

S & B was a real pro with the straps and the torture equipment. He was an unemotional, cold-blooded sort, very strong. He didn't enjoy his work, but he did it very quickly and efficiently.

The other assistant was a big fool, very emotional, who enjoyed the work. He was generally referred to as "Jake." Jake was more frequently a beater than a straps man. The bulk of my mistreatment in New Guy Village was by Jake.

The Bug rattled me immediately when he started asking the same questions which had been asked at Vinh and which should have been in my dossier. It was here that I confirmed the danger of putting too much fabrication in your folder, of straying too far from the truth. If the quizzer had a record to check, it became impossible for you to remember all your lies.

POWs quickly discovered it was saner policy to skirt the edge of truth as often as possible and, if asked an innocuous question, to be truthful. It didn't pay to lie about nothings. The memory cells needed to be saved for the important lies.

My thoughts churned over my current dilemma. I knew much torture and many questions were in store. My code ordered me to respond with name, rank and serial number. I had long since found it impossible to follow this code to the letter. I had to resist the enemy to the maximum, but Americans were not *kamikaze* pilots, directed to suicide rather than state whether we were married.

Whether you refused to answer the question, "What is your wife's name?" or "What is your military unit?" the torture was the same. I hoped for a chance to talk with Robbie Risner, to explain what I had done and ask for his advice. As it turned out, I knew what to do long before I met him three and a half years later.

Under the code, just what was "proper resistance?" The answer many loyal Americans found, by trial and error, was: 1) Make them torture for an answer - give nothing willingly, and after force was applied hard enough, lie! Be sure to make the lies simple and easy to remember. 2) If the question was insignificant, give an indirect, unclear, and incomplete answer. Don't lie. 3) Never be friendly or accept friendly treatment, since both lead to disaster. 4) Always use your common sense.

Those things that were wrong out of POW camp were wrong here, unless it meant lying, stealing from, or evading a Communist. When dealing with him, treat him as he treated you, with contempt, lies, and no standards of decency. Because of an inability to find this formula in conditions of isolation and pressure, a few POWs came up with the wrong answers and got "good attitudes."

A pattern began to emerge from the ropes and beatings. Most of the questions were not military, but political or personal. It was easier to answer the

THE HANOI HILTON, 1967

military questions because you could get away with some incredible answers. Political questions were harder. The "V" insisted on Communist-sounding answers and tortured more severely when unsatisfied.

An example of a military question to a carrier pilot was, "Where do they keep the pigs, chickens, and ducks on the ship?" They meant live animals. This was not hard to answer. On political questions, such as, "What is your political party?" I soon found it was better to claim I was a Democrat, for Senators Fulbright, Mansfield, McGovern, and others said many things the "V" wanted to hear.

Throughout the interrogations, Bug emphasized that we must "do good actions to repent our crimes," and to show "good attitude." That meant we must answer whatever questions they asked in the way they wanted them answered. We were always supposed to show "good attitude" and be "polite."

Being polite meant not resisting, answering all questions to their satisfaction, obeying their overbearing rules, cringing and acting deferential, saying "Sir" to privates and corporals who would be rejected by any self-respecting recruiting station. It meant bowing to runty little Communists I could break in half with one hand, writing letters to my country, President, Senator, or Representative demanding an end to the war. It meant speaking or writing against Uncle Sam.

Those who were "polite" might write war crimes confessions, propaganda describing how well the Vietnamese people ran their transportation system, and how well they stuck together. It might mean explaining certain U.S. technical aircraft equipment, how it worked and how it was used. It might mean writing statements expressing "your true feelings about the illegal, immoral U.S. war in Indo-China." Those who were "polite" long enough and often enough had "good attitude."

I was happy to have a "bad attitude." Those officers who became my friends all had bad attitudes. It should be understood there were some "good attitude" cases in Hanoi who were hated and despised by all of us.

'Bug' was the chief tormentor in three areas of Hao Lo, which means "hell hole" in Vietnamese. He supervised New Guy Village, Heartbreak Hotel, and Little Las Vegas. He ran all of them with overwhelming terror.

Among the military and personal questions, Bug would intersperse something incredible like this:

Bug: How do you think of your treatment by the Vietnamese people? (Asked after several hours of torture.)

Answer: I think my treatment is savage and barbaric!

Bug: Of course, you are "creeminal," and you must be punished for your crimes! But, we are lenient and humane; we have not killed you, although it is our right!

This would be followed by more torture. However, if the answer were a little different:

Answer: I'm happy to be alive.

Bug: Of course, although you are "creeminal," the Vietnamese people always give kind and lenient treatment to all "creeminals," even though you have killed many women and children.

Frequently, this answer would minimize the torture.

Many of the questions were so incredible they became amusing. Although I had been shot down several hundred miles south of Hanoi, I was shown a map of the city and urged to show the targets I was attacking in Hanoi. I was asked about electronics, in-flight formations, and bombing tactics of aircraft I had never flown. My torturer would twist the ropes or beat me when I denied knowledge, shouting, "You must know. You are an Air Force major!"

The terror of the situation repressed any overt smiling, but there was the sense of being a viewer of a poorly done grade "B" movie. It was one of the few times I had been given credit for knowing anything, let alone everything!

Once during my first morning's torture, the Bug had the guard move me to Room One in Heartbreak Hotel. The Star Chamber was needed for a more urgent torture. I was surprised to pass a large, faintly-attractive square courtyard, complete with dowdy blownout roses and overhead grape arbors in need of repair and trimming.

There were window shutters, left from the more civilized French days, hanging crookedly, broken, rotting, in need of paint. All the Communist buildings, roads, plumbing, walls, vehicles, fences, and sidewalks had these things in common — neglect and decay. I later attributed this axiom to the Communists, "If something cannot be fixed by neglect, to hell with it."

I did not see another American in the courtyard. It was clear from the way the guard moved me around, he was making sure I would not. Absolute isolation and insulation from all friendly or comforting contacts was the pattern.

As I entered the turn-key room, next to Heartbreak Hotel, my eyes lighted on a calendar that read October 23, 1967. I had gained three days, because according to me, it was the 26th.

The cells in Heartbreak would water your eyes. They were oppressively tiny to a fighter pilot accustomed to the vastness of the sky. My first thought was that I had seen larger closets. The cells were six feet by six and a half feet, dark and dirty. Two narrow concrete beds paralleled the walls on each side of the room. On each were rusty iron stocks, straight out of the Dark Ages, which could be operated from outside the room. The guard

THE HANOI HILTON, 1967

ordered me up on a bed and placed my feet in the stocks as I sat. Closing the stocks roughly over my ankles, he pulled my left hand forward across my right ankle and handcuffed me to the stocks.

There was no room in this position for my bulky cast. I didn't know it, but I was lucky the break was not brand new. New breaks were especially painful in this position.

Injuries were a bonus for the torturers. A man with a broken back, leg, arm, etc., is particularly vulnerable. The torture problem is minimized.

The window of the tiny room, as well as the ventilator above the door, had been pounded full of wood and covered with a bamboo mat. No light, no air.

"You must suffer because you are a 'creeminal.' Our 4,000-year history — lenient and humane."

Living in these tiny, closed-up cells was like being stuffed into a safe. The unbelievable, intentional filth was disgusting and subhuman. I could tell that having diarrhea, or having to urinate while in this position was not going to be a fun deal.

Doors banged and squeaked. "V" jabbered in their sing-song mumbles. A short time later, Straps and Bars unlocked the "Three-Circle Brand," green and chrome Chinese lock that secured every cell door in Hanoi. Quickly, he had me out of the cuffs and stocks and urged me along with points, grunts, and jerks. I told him in sign language that I had to urinate, so he snatched open the heavy door to Room Eight, across from Room One.

Huge rats leaped off the concrete beds and scurried into a slimy hole in the floor, against the outside wall. Stinking, filthy cans of garbage sat without tops on the beds. A rusted-out, broken shower head hung limply off the wall. The bamboo mats in this cell did not go all the way to the top of the window. A faint sliver of blue sky and white clouds were visible through the crack. Straps and Bars grunted and gestured.

Part of the prisoner routine was that you should have done everything five minutes ago, in order to be polite. Guards who couldn't speak another word of English, could say "queekny," meaning quickly. "Straps" continued giving me "queekny" until I finished.

Another popular word with the "V" was "bow." Whether it was because they loved this humiliating procedure, or whether it was out of revenge for the centuries they had been bowing in subjugation to the many groups who had conquered and reconquered Vietnam, was difficult to determine.

Back in the Star Chamber, Bug and an older, gray-haired "V" sat behind a rickety table covered with a deep blue cloth, overhanging it on all sides.

"Bow!" screamed the Bug. "Kneel down, hand up," he shouted.

Room 18, the Star Chamber, was sixteen feet square. The walls were concrete, plastered in patterns as though half eggshells had been filled with cement and stuck on the wall. Hooks hung down from the high ceiling, part of the "lenient and humane" apparatus.

A typewriter clicked across the hall, through the tired, weathered green-painted shutters. A piece of iron rod, about an inch long, lay bent parallel with the floor. Near the back wall, a twelve-foot piece of half-inch iron bar rested on the floor, two U-shaped devices slid over it. These were semi-portable irons. There were also built-in irons and traveling irons. You could walk in the latter with great discomfort.

An unusual thing about this quiz was a clumsy attempt to tape my answers. Bug had a tape recorder hidden underneath the blue-covered table. A combination of my mumbles and the constant power failures ruined that plan.

Ordinarily, Bug was upset if I answered above a whisper, but today he urged me to "Speak clearly! More loud!" His thrusts were transparent. He wanted me to write for the camp newspaper, to play in the band, to do some art work for my friends, and other clumsy suggestions.

It was important to conceal my true mission, my legal training, and any skills usable to the "V." I was successful to the bloody end. Had I not been, Major George Day, "International Lawyer," would have been on the Hanoi radio, and a movie and television star. Every man with a skill known to the "V" was exploited. Sometimes the torture was continuous. Since their main propaganda thrust was that the war was "illegal," I'd have been a prize. Too bad for them, they never knew.

My "Misty" operation was a top-secret, brand-new mission. If I were to divulge our secrets and tactics, it was highly likely that many of my fine, young, loyal pilots would die as a result of my admissions. I could never reveal the tactics and methods and still live with my conscience. I never revealed this information, and I take great pride in that.

My first night on a cold stone floor in late October was freezing. About 10 or 11 P.M., Jake came in and beat me clumsily for not bowing. He left a coarse, 95-cent rayon horse blanket. He threw the tan rag contemptuously on the floor, screamed "Bow," hit me again, and departed.

My ache-all-over feeling was still fresh. My stick beating at Vinh was still fresh. My current pounding left me numb, immobile, and having trouble thinking. This was exactly what the "V" wanted. They tried to keep us in that condition for years to come.

The next morning developed the same pattern of threats, accusations of lying, more beating, kneeling, questions, ropes, questions, beating and more threats. I was getting the picture. At first, I thought they couldn't be as clumsy and uninformed as they appeared. I was wrong. They were worse!

The emphasis remained on political questions. If things were said in the proper manner, a man could get away with clumsy lies about military information. Before being shot down, I had read a magazine account of Lieutenant Commander Nels Tanner's clever job. He gave his torturers a series of lies that were plausible in content and desirable politically. The "V" tortured him for the names of non-existant American pilots from his carrier who, according to the VC, were afraid to fly against the North Vietnamese gunners.

After maximum torture, Nels gave them "Clark Kent" (Superman), Jim Kildare ("Dr. Kildare"), Jimmy Doolittle, etc. The inept Vietnamese Communists then took these remarks and presented them in another Communist forum, "The Bertram Russell War Crimes Tribunal."

When these incredible fabrications were exposed to the glare of an informed international press, Bug and the "V" became the laughing stock of the civilized world. It was not a laughing matter for Nels when word of this fiasco got back to Hanoi.

Nels was again brutally tortured and thrown into the Alcatraz Gang in solitary confinement, under maximum pressure and attempted exploitation for more than two years.

I did not know Nels Tanner until late in my captivity, nor the consequences of his courageously clever acts. As a result, when I was tortured for the names of pilots from my unit, I reluctantly gave them the names of Doc Savage, Charles Lindbergh, Billy Mitchell, Wylie Post, Will Rogers, and others. Had I known of the severe consequences of Nels' deceit, no doubt I would have opted for less glamorous personalities like Jones, Brown and Smith.

On that morning I was also confronted with an amazing oversight on my part, one I at first thought to be disastrous to my cover story. As usual, Bug and the gray-haired man contronted me with the accusation that I had been lying.

In plain sight, for my benefit, a *Pacific Stars and Stripes* lay on the blue table. It was opened to a two-page center spread in which I could see the picture of a runway and pilots climbing out of their aircraft. My heart pounded, and my guts burned. The "V" might have one of these *Stars and Stripes* issues for every base in South Vietnam and Thailand!

I had flown from Tuy Hoa and Phu Cat only, and the odds were high that this photo was of Da Nang, Korat, Bien Hoa, or some other base. Nevertheless, if the picture were a display of Tuy Hoa, it would not match up with the lies I had told. My hands began to sweat.

"You lie. You are not sincere! You rotten diehard. I can have you killed for your lies!" he insisted.

"Every teng you have told me is a lie," he insisted.

"Right here it is," he complained, pointing to the paper.

"Do you deny it?" he demanded.

"Yes, I deny it," I answered, not knowing what I was denying.

My cover story was that I was a fighter-bomber pilot flying from Tuy Hoa. I claimed to be only a high school graduate, concealing my law degree and master's in international law. My master's thesis at Saint Louis University, under the world-famous international lawyer, Doctor Kurt von Schusschnigg, was entitled, "The Legality of the Flight of the U-2."

Bug ranted some more about my escape, about my being the "blackest creemenal" in Vietnam, etc. This was more of the same kind of mental abuse I was becoming used to.

Suddenly the gray-haired man popped a small white printed slip on the table. My heart sank! After I read it, and my head began to work again, I could see that it gave me some backing for part of my story. The item was a post-office money order receipt payable to my wife, who lived in Arizona. My address, as sender, was listed as the 416th Tactical Fighter Squadron, Phu Cat, S.V.N. Bug was delighted at my obvious chagrin.

"You lie, you lie, you weel be severely punished!" he cried, as Jake smashed me on the back of the head. My thinking processes were rattled, but I knew there was something good in this for me. I realized that Bug had caught me in two lies. First, I had denied having a wife. Second, I had lied about my military assignment.

I could see no way to recover point one. But, though it wasn't perfect cover, at least the address confirmed my fighter-bomber pilot story. That meant my top-secret mission was still covered. My mind raced along as Bug assailed me verbally, and Jake bashed me on the head and ears.

I collected my wits, gave Bug the crestfallen, caught-in-the-act approach, and shifted gears into a new series of lies. The receipt did clear up the gray-haired man's belief that I was a SAM hunter. They had questioned me heavily about missile detection equipment in my aircraft, and no matter how much they mistreated me, I couldn't describe something I didn't have, didn't know about, hadn't used, and hadn't seen. Now, this subject was dropped.

Bug was delighted. He raved some more about "Black Creeminal," blackest in the DRVN, escaper, and asked a flock of personal questions. It was clear that the hardest part was over.

"I have broken your stupid reactionary lies!" he gloated. I sat quietly and tried to look downcast.

Back in the cell, my thoughts were difficult to put in order. At this point, my treatment had only faintly followed the traditional pattern of brainwashing used by the Chinese against their own people, and against American POW in Korea. While there had been great emphasis on criminal guilt, repentence, confessions, and the doing of positive acts to "prove" a change in attitude, there never had been a consistent program with either enough "carrot" or enough "stick" to make the brainwashing workable. Later, I discovered the failure was because of poor timing and the amount of violence applied.

For brainwashing to be effective, a strong interrogator needs to be coupled with a subject having little sense of mission and a low degree of personal courage. Until an exceptional interrogator named Slick emerged in 1969, the "V" lacked a capable and effective brainwasher.

Slick possessed a remarkable talent and would have given sterling service in the earlier days. However, he arrived too late in the game to be of much use.

The other part of timing is the element of sheer luck. While many airmen were the only shootdown on a particular day, others had the advantage of being one of several. The "V" apparatus was poorly suited to processing more than a small number of persons. Those in larger groups could not be afforded the longer and more comprehensive tortures.

Another factor which degraded their effectiveness was the senselessness of the violence. After a victim is clubbed into submission, violence reaches a point of minimal return, which the "V" never seemed to recognize.

Still, the single most important factor which frustrated the brainwashing program was the attitude and quality of the persons being brainwashed. Because the Korean War was a surprise war, many of the first troops in were fresh from non-combat support jobs in Japan, or reservists rushed straight from civilian life. Many were post WW II enlistees who had neither been in combat, nor trained for combat.

Vietnam was not a surprise war, and the men who fought it from the air were regulars, hard-core career officers, some of whom had experienced combat in Korea. Some had both Korean and WW II experience.

These men were graduates of the U.S. Military Academy, the Naval Academy, and the Air Force Academy; the bright, clean-cut, cream of American youth. They were well educated, dedicated, and most had a working knowledge of Communism and indoctrination techniques. They also possessed that single most important ingredient for successful resistance to brainwashing - a SENSE OF MISSION.

Sense of mission channels dedication, and it is dedication that makes a man willing to take extensive physical abuse. Sense of mission generates courage to resist, courage to recover from setbacks, and it generates outrage instead of weak-kneed compliance to brutality. If there was a common denominator of the POWs in Vietnam, it was a sense of mission.

However, I didn't know all of these things at this point in my confinement and my fears were strong.

After two months of starvation, the food tasted good. An average meal at this time was a bowl of pumpkin soup and a small loaf of bread about the size of a submarine sandwich loaf. A thin layer of grease floated on the soup. Though I wanted to eat, my body ached too much to have a good appetite. My weight only ten weeks after shootdown was about 100 pounds.

I sat on the stone floor, chilled to the marrow, and thought of the incredible misery of the day. My thoughts wandered to some of my friends who had been downed before me. Men like Robbie Risner, Jim Hiteshew, Norm Gaddis, and their incredible brutal march of July 6, 1966.

Could these men possibly be alive? Living on two bowls of soup per day, no protein, and no more than 500 to 600 calories each day? Robbie had been down more than two years!

"How in God's green earth am I going to make it? Those guys came in here well, and in good condition. I'm puny, emaciated, injured. Is there any way I'll ever see the Viking and the kids again?" I wondered over and over.

Thoughts of Senator Fulbright's anti-war speeches, Robert McNamara's arrogant incompetence in military policy, and Lyndon Johnson's corrupt moral fibre coupled with his ego and ignorance in the area of foreign affairs were neither comforting nor morale-building.

"Sorrowing over this dreadful lot and the conduct of the war is not going to keep me alive, nor keep my honor intact. I must find the strength to survive!" said my mind.

Survival was going to require fantastic luck, strong will, and good health. Mere survival was not enough. I must be loyal and keep within the normal standards of decency. That would require help from God. A long heartfelt prayer for courage and faith welled up in me.

I needed faith in myself, faith in my country and faith in my God. The questions I had to ask myself were unsettling.

"Am I willing to take this mistreatment indefinitely, or am I going to start compromising my honor? What will I stand for, and for how long? Isn't George Day a cripple who can barely feed himself? Do I have the strength and guts to survive?

"This isn't really a war. It is the pit of Hell! Is there any luck left for me? Am I man enough to go home with honor? Who will George Day be? Answer God, I need help!" Answers were not forthcoming.

The next day was a mild one. A Chinese-looking man in a blue cotton uniform wanted me to explain why some majors make more money than others do, and how U.S. income tax works. The first, of course, is based on years of service, and easy to understand.

American citizens do not understand U.S. income tax, and after my explanation, the oriental did not understand, either. I gave him a lot of mathematical examples, none of which would ever add up. I kept asking him if he understood, and he kept saying, "Yes!"

THE HANOI HILTON, 1967

Immediately I knew I had him! First, *no* "V" would ever admit he didn't understand (lose much face). Secondly, I doubletalked him, not understanding what I was saying myself. That afternoon ended Yanks - one; "V" - zero!

Now that Bug felt he had broken my story, I was moved out of New Guy Village to Little Las Vegas. Vegas was located about half a block north of NGV. They blindfolded me and marched me out of the courtyard, through the kitchen, into Vegas and locked me into Riviera One. I lost my horse blanket in the move.

After two days in the Riviera, I moved into Thunderbird West. This was a bad time to arrive because a cruel camp-wide purge of the prisoners had recently been completed by Bug and his staff. Most prisoners had been badly tortured for communicating with each other. When I was put into the cell, you could hear a pin drop. Men who lived in the building at this time would tell me later that they continually talked under the doors. I must have experienced temporary deafness while they were talking, for I never heard an American voice in five weeks.

The cell in T-bird was slightly larger than Heartbreak; it was about seven and a half feet long by six wide. The walls were whitewashed a second-rate, dingy white. A stinking bucket with a poor-fitting lid was my toilet. The room had a large window facing out on a wall capped with broken green beer bottles. A sliver of sky was visible above the blocked-out portion of the window. A rough plank bed fit against each side of the room.

On the back of the cell door was a faded set of camp regulations which stated: "All U.S. aggressors, shot down in their piratical attacks against the D.R.V.N., are criminals." Almost every regulation noted that you would be "severely punished," meaning torture. These impossible and oppressive regulations gave the "V" a semi-legal basis for most of the daily torture and oppression.

The regulations ordered prisoners to answer any questions, to bow to any "V," not to communicate with or contact any American. We were ordered not to escape or help an escapee. Lastly, rewards were provided if a prisoner informed on fellow inmates. This place was one good deal after another.

An ugly green radio speaker dangled into the room from a wire. The radio broadcast the voice of Vietnam twice a day, morning and night. In between times, it played anti-war, or pro-communist, tapes attributed to Tom Hayden, David Dellinger, and other "peace" types. Tom, for example, admonished us that "I have been in plenty of fights," but he just didn't want "to fight Lyndon Johnson's war." Just as the Korean Communists tried to brainwash prisoners, the "V" had a comprehensive program.

The braying of Joan Baez, quotations by Senators Fulbright (named "Halfbright" by the prisoners), Morse and Gruening, plus the likes of Stokely Carmichael and Dr. Spock, soon identified those the Communists saw as friends and allies. The program was ordinarily narrated by female announcers who the POWs labeled "Hanoi Hannah."

The editorializing and content of the program was crude. One portion was devoted to reading letters taken from the bodies of dead American soldiers. Another favorite tactic was lifting quotations out of context and totally reversing the meaning.

The radio frequently alluded to trials of POWs for their war crimes, describing in great detail how prison sentences were to be meted out. Followers would receive five years, reactionaries would get 15, etc. Every flood, fire, riot or calamity that occurred in the U.S. was reported in painstaking detail, designed, of course, to convince the prisoner that his world was falling apart.

At first, I named this programing "Uncle Ho's Science Fiction Hour." Later I changed that to a more appropriate title, namely, "Grim Fairy Tales!"

Some programs were self-defeating. The claims were so impossible that the listener automatically tuned them out after a short time. One was so startling, so fantastic, I memorized the figures. It was a one-year summary of Communist victories in South Vietnam, 1966-67: 530,000 troops killed or put out of action; 80,000 tanks, armored cars, etc., destroyed; 7,000 aircraft destroyed, and 2,000 ships and rivercraft sunk or destroyed!

By this quick stroke of the pen, they killed and put out of action more soldiers than all of the combat units in Vietnam. They destroyed more tanks and shot down more aircraft than the U.S. Army, Navy and Air Force possessed in the entire Pacific! What a nation! What a bunch of fighters! Where did they get such men? With such fantastic losses, how could the U.S. and South Vietnam continue the war?

They claimed 2,000 U.S. aircraft shot down over North Vietnam. The figure was so unbelievable that I first thought I had not heard the radio correctly. It was almost as many combat fighters as the Air Force possessed. In truth, from June 1966 through May 1967 some 317 U.S. airplanes were lost up north — 15% of the claim.

The daily routine was oppressive. Stand up for the guards or be tortured. Hurry about or be beaten. Be absolutely silent. It began to make sense when I realized that I was in the hands of the typical "Party" hacks. All of the intelligentsia of North Vietnam, as in East Germany, and later Cuba, had run away, been murdered or imprisoned. At first it seemed impossible that everything in this country could be second or third rate!

I asked myself, "Is this total, all-encompassing, trampling cruelty the real face of Communism, or only a spastic reaction to American military action?"

The answer lies in the distorted, corrupted Communist version of the Russian revolution, the World War II take-over of East Germany, and the twentieth century Vietnamese Revolution. Neither Catherine the Great, nor Czar Nicholas Romanoff indulged in the mass murder of entire classes of society. Callous as the Czar may have been, he did not hound the wives, friends, children, or mere acquaintances of whole classes of society to prison, labor camps, or death. While the venality of Catherine and the pompousness of Romanoff were widely known, the autocracy never relied upon the lie that the soverign served the serf or citizen.

No, it was the new Party who suspended those awful "old" laws, substituting a new series of "Soviet" laws which were based upon the "new" morality. There came to be vague new crimes against the "people," crimes committed by "those rotten and corrupt intellectuals," "those lazy die-hard reactionary peasants," "that wrong-speaking, wrong-thinking clergy," "those anti-Party railroad workers," or former government officials, or writers, or doctors, or property owners, leeches of capitalism.

The new crimes were not decided by a juristic system, but tried by the Party (its revolutionary court) in the name of serving the people. That the Party had laid the charges, arrested the victim, dragged him to court, tortured him to confess, sentenced him, and then brutally turned him into a slave-labor draft animal, was not held inconsistent.

One must again ask, "Why?" The answer falls within the composition of the Party, and the morality of those men. The new morality mandated that the state did not have to prove a case against the accused, but that the defendant must prove his innocence. The new morality held that the revolutionary, who had just murdered his way to power, had the sacred, unbridled right to murder and murder until all throes of opposition and resistance on the part of those being murdered had ceased. The composition of the Party was simply the "scum" of Russian and European jails, the morality the same.

The published writings of Aleksander I. Solzhenitsyn, himself a longtime prisoner of the "Party", chronicle the never-ending waves of torture, repression, sadism, and murder of the peasant, intellectual, and citizen of the Soviet state. The cry is heard. Down with capitalism, that blood sucker of the people! Down with monarchy, that debauched self-serving institution! Down with the "old" morality and the "old" laws! Up with the new social order!

Those rotten gods of religion must go, must be replaced by a paternal and benevolent socialist state. A new god must be found, worshipped and deified by the Party and the people. The new god's name was not God, but

Lenin (not his real name), or was it "Uncle" Josef Stalin (not his real name, either)? Whether this new god smiled or frowned, millions died or were shipped to the frozen tundra or taiga as slaves.

When Uncle Joe brought his morals, his law, and his Party nipping at the heels of a devastated East Germany, some seven million Germans quickly voted with their feet, fleeing like leaves before the red wind. A heterogeneous group as large as the population of New York City left both home and family to avoid the clutch of the red bear. Whereas the mute and docile descendant of the serf marched placidly off to death and exile, his frightened German counterpart — student, doctor, intellectual, plumber, lawyer, and farmer — rushed wholesale to West Germany.

In North Vietnam, "Uncle Ho" murdered his way into control of government. Trained and reared in the violent womb of Bolshevism, an attendee at the funeral of Lenin, a representative to the 2nd Communist International in France, "Uncle" carted the total apparatus of the party from Moscow to Hanoi with all of its evil trappings.

While millions of those "rotten" intellectuals, students, lawyers, peasants, doctors, priests, functionaries, and diehards fled to South Vietnam, "Uncle" began his purge of the reactionaries, blood-suckers, and antiparties across the nation.

Like a televised replay of the Russian experience, millions of teachers, doctors, lawyers, plumbers, weavers, landowners, peasants, families, friends, and acquaintances were purged. The slogan, "God has left the North," was the byword of the evadees to the South. It was these escapees with their unfaltering distrust and hatred of Communism who formed the nucleus of government and resistance in South Vietnam.

As in Mother Russia, as in East Germany, what class of leaders and administrators was left in the North? After the frothing waves of bloodshed ebbed, and the dust of departing feet settled, only Uncle Ho and his Party remained. A Party member brayed that the peasant would no longer labor for free as a draft animal of the French, or of the capitalist, imperialist aggressor. No, instead, he would march for the Party when the Party needed a marcher, he could volunteer to work wage-free hours for the Party, or he could write songs and poems deifying Uncle, or compete to paint the finest portrait of Uncle. Likewise, he could carry the "struggle" to liberate South Vietnam, Cambodia, Laos, and Thailand from those enemies of the people.

Thus the criminals now became the witness, sheriff, prosecutor, and judge, and with the ruthlessness of a street gang, set off to cleanse the population, including his fellow criminals. Soon the executioner would also feel the cold steel of the executed.

By 1965, the Party had been pared to the bone. All of the loose fiber, fat, and corpulence, all reactionaries, diehards, and counter-revolutionaries were purged. Uncle Ho, the Party, the new law, and the new morality remained. The Party did not need laws or regulations. It could divine proper action from "social consciousness." The "decadent" Geneva Conventions on minimum standards of human decency, that shopworn bag of empty words, was discarded for divine rulings by "Uncle," omnipotent, wise, all-knowing, always showing the "people" the right line.

And what about the American aviators shot down over North Vietnam? Of 1,800 fliers downed there, only about 500 returned home. Solitary confinement, death, leg stocks, marches through the streets, tortured confessions — all of those ordinary indignities were the predictable lot of the white-skinned prisoners who, after all, deserved to be "punished" by the "people." The "creeminals" must suffer. Suffer we did.

With the abuse, the most depressing problem of the POW, was how to train oneself to waste the bulk of an entire day in a useful way. I could not spend time thinking about my wife and children. This was too painful and self-defeating. I could not afford to speculate too much on how long the war might last. That was out of the range of rational definition and demoralizing.

On initial shootdown, there was a sense of somehow failing. Some prisoners considered themselves as expended ammunition, and not worth great efforts by their nation to recover them, just as a matter of mathematics.

Positive programs of calculated waste had to be developed, and turned on and off like a radio. In order to be palatable, the subject had to be bland, such as reorganizing your account books, building a house from the ground up, etc. Few of us realized that after five, six or seven years as a POW, we would have remodeled our homes so often that they bore little resemblance to the original structure.

For me, the "creeminal," there was absolutely no amusement, books, games, or time-killing devices for many years. The only exceptions were a few "good attitude" prisoners. We improvised. I only tuned to the Viking and the children at meal time and during prayers. I mentally greeted Dorie, listening for her mildly contralto, "Hello, Daddy, I love you," and then tuning her out again. The rest of the day, I reworked the books for my apartments, remodeled apartments, or replanned flights in the F-100 from Niagara Falls, New York, to Miami, Florida, remembering headings, distances, and fuel.

On the "box" (the radio), I got some news that was of great interest to me. There was an announcement that Lieutenant Commander John Sydney McCain, III, the son of Admiral John McCain, II, Naval Forces Europe, had been shot down by the "people" in an aggressive attack on Hanoi. It also described the "great victory" of the people in shooting down Colonel John P. Flynn, vice commander of the F-105 wing at Korat, as well as Colonel Ed Burdette, the commander of the Korat wing. Two fine Irishmen, McCain and Flynn, were to become my roommates.

About the fifth day in Hanoi, I saw a Vietnamese we referred to as "Zorba," the camp doctor, talking to the guard who had brought me to Hanoi from Vinh. The guard was reading something from my dossier to him.

Zorba appeared with his assistant, opened up my cast with a dull scalpel, and removed it from my arm. My hand and wrist flopped aimlessly. The wound at the wrist, caused by the bone protruding through the skin, had healed quite well, leaving a scar the size of a half dollar.

The entire arm was thin and badly atrophied. It resembled a skeleton covered with loose skin. I could see a huge lump on the upper arm, where the bone had healed crooked. Thankfully, my elbow functioned, but unfortunately, my right hand was almost inoperative.

My left hand was still a claw, but there was consolation in being able to move my thumb and forefinger. Under certain conditions, I could hold a spoon, but I could not tie the string on my pajama pants, nor could I handle a bar of soap, take the lid off a water pot, or unfold my blankets. Zorba told me that in two or three days, they would put my arm in a cast.

The day after he took the cast off, a large amount of blood pooled in my lower arm, and my hand turned fire red. Zorba looked in my door and told me he was going to give me a bandage. He was difficult to understand, yet implied they were going to put a cast on my arm, but instead they brought a bendable wire basket.

Eventually, Zorba's office did put a new cast on my arm. I asked for a short cast because the other one had been so large that I could not manipulate it when I lay on my wooden plank bed. With the huge cast, it was impossible to get in and out of my clothing. As part of the harassment program, the "V" insisted that we be "polite" to the "people" every time we left the room. Therefore, we had to put on long pants and long shirts to leave the room, even for the most trivial things. There was no way I could wear a long shirt over a large cast, so I hoped to get one that covered only my wrist.

Zorba and his assistant shaped a bulky, arm-length cast. It had a bend in the wrist, and if my arm healed to the shape of the cast, I was going to have a very crooked arm. I pointed it out to Zorba, but he waved me off, as if this were too unimportant to discuss.

I showed him that the sling put additional pressure on the cast, causing even more bend. He looked a second time, but seemed exasperated that I complained. Obviously a "bad attitude," since everyone should want a

THE HANOI HILTON, 1967

crooked arm!

Since I couldn't vote on my medical care, or change doctors, there was nothing to do but wait and see what happened. It was a real trial to feed myself and take care of my basic needs. As it became colder, my most pressing problem was my inability to wrap up in my pair of blankets. The thin soup, when served hot, was the high point of my day.

The only reading material I saw was a propaganda book by Felix Green — an unusually warped, semitruthful, Communist-sympathizing publication, designed to impress one, through fine-quality photographs, with the nature of the unjust war. These pictures were a perfect illustration of how to convey a false impression. Next came a set of regulations that were to be memorized. These regulations were absolutely impossible for a loyal American to keep.

The rules followed the same pattern as the ones on the back of the cell door. Number one stated, "All criminals must answer fully and completely, either in writing or by voice, any question put to him by the Vietnamese authorities." This meant if they came in and asked a military question, and I refused to answer, I was liable to be tortured for violating camp regulations. The whole series followed an equally oppressive pattern.

Communications were not permitted. We could not see our fellow prisoners. All criminals had to bow to any Vietnamese civilian or any Vietnamese they met, or be severely punished.

The guards had almost unlimited authority to torture us for any actual, fabricated, or accidental violations of the "Regulations." They walked around on tip-toe listening for talking, pressed their ears to the wall listening for tapping or scratching, and over-enforced these already unbearable rules.

After a few days, the turnkeys realized it would be far easier for them to give me a roommate. They were having problems fitting me into their schedule to empty my waste bucket, to wash clothes or bathe, to carry my food, water, etc. I needed a nurse who would do my bucket, clothes, and carry my food. They assumed, apparently, that Overly and I had lived together previously. As a result, my door opened and in walked a beardless Norris Overly.

At first glance, I wasn't sure I recognized him. With a nearly-shaved head, no beard and a huge smile, it took me a moment to be sure it was he. The man who looks erect and striking in officer's uniform goes through a dreadful transformation as an abused hostage of a primitive society. In a set of purple and gray pajamas, looking tired, tacky, and seedy with sunken hollow cheeks and a barefood shuffling gait, he's a different person.

As abuse and starvation take their toll, one's shoulders seem to round, eyes grow dull, and a slight stoop appears. The "old heads" were eye-wateringly pathetic in appearance.

In spite of all this, I was delighted to see Overly, for I had been positive I would be in solitary confinement forever. Our primary concern was to get each other's complete family data. We were convinced that at least one of us would probably not return. We hoped to give the opposite family as much assistance as possible, should one person get home and not the other.

I learned about Overly's family, his relatives, and his history. I talked to him at length about my family. Norris was a boating and a skiing enthusiast. We spoke of families, homes, and experiences and I memorized a great deal of personal data about him. With the passing of the next few days, I began to understand that I would soon know this man better than I knew my wife, my parents, or my best friend. At the rate of sixteen hours per day, face to face, topics of conversation would begin to dwindle.

Delicate problems in the limit of discussion occurred. Exactly how much do you reveal? Or ask? Or limit certain personal matters? What do you talk about after you have discussed everything? Do you become a bore if you repeat the same stories over and over? Or is it proper prisoner etiquette dutifully to nod attentively at those repetitive stories designed not to provoke thought or question, but simply to pass time?

We had been together only a few days when colder weather arrived. We were moved into a room where there was not so much direct wind whistling through the bars. I was told by the "V" that this was the coldest winter in Vietnam's recorded history. The temperature plunged to almost freezing. Our clothing and blankets were inadquate.

I had no idea it could be so miserable to be barefoot at these low temperatures. My bulky cast further complicated the problem of remaining warm, since the blankets were too skimpy to fully encircle my body and cast. But we had made a step forward by being moved into another dark and dismal room in the T-bird. At least there was less wind blowing in. It was a depressing room, complete with several rats and a sour garbage smell, but it was much warmer.

Norris's mission was to be my nurse. This did not spring from motives of human kindness. There were no humane considerations in any "V" decision. It shifted the duties of emptying the buckets, shaving twice a week, etc., from the "V" to Norris. Expediency, apathetic laziness, or exploitation were always the "V" motivations.

To a man from a civilized society, our living conditions would have been inconceivable. Two men lived in a six-by-six cell. There was a five-gallon bucket for a toilet, two cheap rayon blankets, and no mattresses or pads on the rough planks. Clothing was inadequate. The cold was miserable, piercing, and numbing to both the body and the mind. Food was dreadful. We ate weed soup and rice or bread, about 500 calories per man per day.

THE HANOI HILTON, 1967

There were several sick prisoners in our wing who were not eating all of their bread. We asked the guard for the uneaten scraps which lay in empty plates on the floor to be thrown into the garbage. The request was dismissed, but occasionally the peephole would fly open and the guard would fling in a piece of partially-eaten bread.

This was a critical time. I was trying to eat the enamel off the cheap metal plates! I could almost feel my ribs begin to pop through tightly-stretched skin.

The enormous efforts to halt communications, keep us divided, and to prevent us from seeing any other prisoners were so involved that they were right out of a Three Stooges production. The "V" fear of organization and communication was more than paranoia. The Thunderbird had been constructed with many small cells in such a manner that there was no common wall that could be used for tapping or scratching messages through the wall. Try, if you will, in your mind's eye, to construct a building full of cells where there are no common walls between cells!

I emphasize again, this building was deliberately constructed in this way to cut off any contact. I didn't know the tap system at this time, and I was so busy licking my wounds and chatting with Overly all day, that I was not concerned with communicating. Later I would learn that communications were the life blood for a return with honor.

Norris was an exceedingly kind person, and treated me with genuine concern. We did not share many common interests, and would not have sought each other out as friends under ordinary circumstances. Much to my surprise, he confirmed that he had not been tortured at Vinh by the Rodent. Our views on resistance and how to respond to "V" questions were markedly different.

Norris did not intend to get hurt while resisting. He felt that the obsolete B-57 was not worth being tortured, and if the "V" asked him about it I think he answered. However, I felt that we should not confirm that the sun rose in the east — that we should give the enemy "zero" without torture. Then, if tortured, we would lie, fabricate, mislead, bullshit them . . . whatever it took not to help them.

I was plagued by a series of thoughts which eroded both my morale and confidence. I felt guilt for not having done enough for my family, not finishing this or that job well enough, or not taking the children camping after promising to do so.

Excessive self-criticism over these real or imagined sins became part of the great triumvirate - survival, release, and worry about my family.

An inordinate amount of soul baring took place between prisoners. If the POW relationship was compatible, and many were, this was satisfactory. When the initial thrill of getting a roommate wore off, it could become a special hell. With the Communist paranoic mentality for secrecy, it was obvious that prisoners would not be moved around frequently to vary roommates. They would have preferred that no one ever had one. Many POWs were solo for as long as 56 months.

A verse well stated the prisoners' philosophy:

> Whatever I do is important because I will trade
> a day of my life for it.
> When tomorrow comes, this day will be gone
> forever, and in its place will be just what
> I have exchanged for it.
> I want it to be good, not evil; gain, not loss.
> I want it to be success, not failure, in order
> that I may never regret the *price I paid for it*.

There could not have been an American in Hanoi who did not have his regrets and doubts about the price he was paying.

Norris and I talked politics at length. I held a low opinion of Lyndon Johnson, his cabinet and advisory staff. I was not surprised when I heard the news that Lyndon had fired Robert McNamara. I expressed immediate concern when I learned that McNamara was going to the World Bank. I hoped that anyone who had money in the bank would withdraw it promptly before it was managed with the great skill he had applied to the Defense Department.

After reading historian J. Evetts Haley's book, *A Texan Looks at Lyndon Johnson*, watching the Bobby Baker-Lyndon Johnson dealings, and following the accumulation of LBJ's personal fortune, my disenchantment was total. One quip about Johnson stuck with me clearly.

Question: "How can you tell when Lyndon Johnson is lying?"

Answer: "When you see his lips moving!"

Unfortunately, I was in prison before I had time or inclination to assess the war thoroughly. It was clear to me, in face-to-face contact with Communism, that Lyndon's approach could never succeed. He and his advisors had incorrectly assessed both the nature of the war and the solution.

In successful wars, the President sets policy and delegates the method to the military. With Lyndon's military expertise, he was hand-selecting all of the important targets in North Vietnam. As poor as his choices were, as bad as he was, he was better than Communists, and it was always possible to back him up on political quizzes with the "V," although it was a little like comparing Billy Sol Estes to Satan.

During the cold snap, Norris was called to quiz. When he came back, he said, "I have been told that we are going to get another roommate. We are going to move to another camp."

I asked, "What is his name?"

He replied, "John Sidney McCain, III." I remembered hearing John's name on the radio, and I had also heard it at a quiz with Bug the day after John was shot down. That day Bug had told me elatedly, "Today we shot down the Prince."

I had looked at him questioningly. I had no idea who or what he was talking about.

He emphasized, "Today we shot down the son of a big admiral. Now you, Nigh (my "V" name), you are small potatoes. Nobody cares about you, but everybody wants to know about McCain. Everybody wants to know if McCain is alive."

That evening, about 6:30 or so, Overly and I went out to the front of the Thunderbird and were loaded into a vehicle for a six-minute trip.

THE PLANTATION

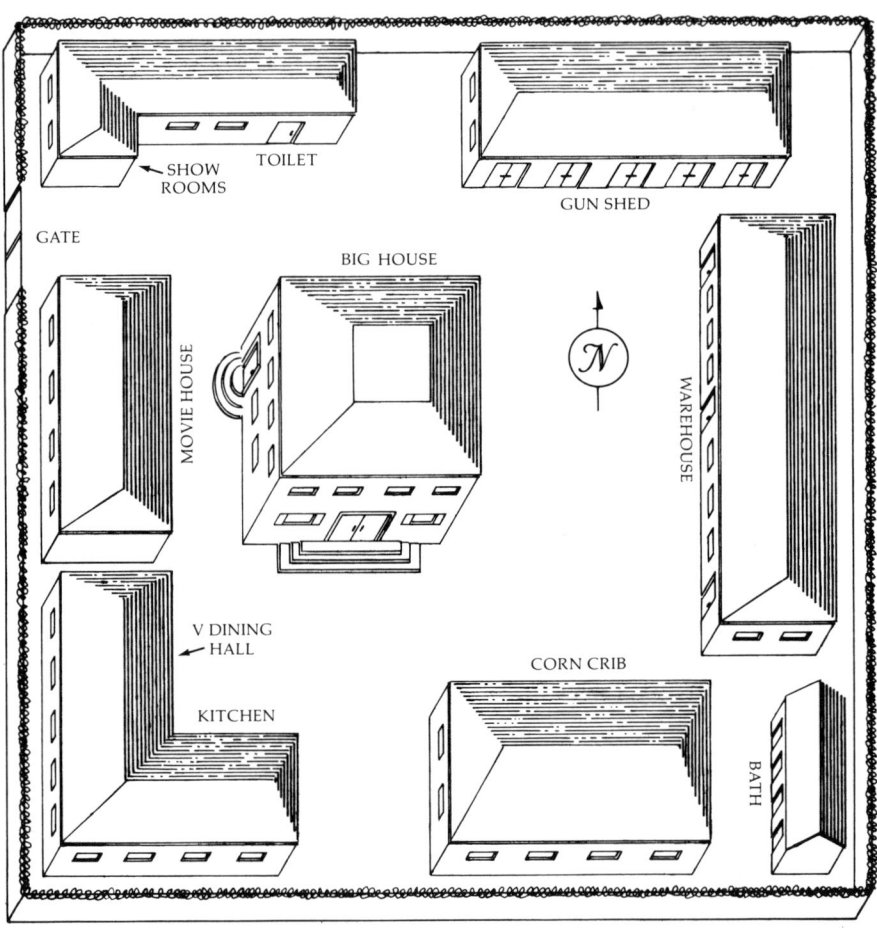

CHAPTER NINE

The Plantation, 1968
(First Ring of the Malebolge)

The new camp had been dubbed the "Plantation" by its first occupants, Arvin Chauncey, Dave Hatcher, and others, when they first occupied it in the early spring of 1967. It had been the residence of the former French mayor of Hanoi. On arrival, I viewed a pretentious old two-and-a-half story Georgian building, garnished with ornate frieze work, and sprawling, elaborate porches of old-world fashion. Although it had been an elegant building in its time, it was in the typical state of decay, needing paint and care. In the light of day it was seedy, dowdy, and unattractive.

Our new room was spacious after the wretched cell in the Thunderbird. It was approximately nine feet wide by 15 feet long, roughly twice as large as most cells in Little Vegas. Our beds were two wooden slabs about two-and-a-half feet wide, and less than six feet long.

This camp lacked the chilling, fearful look of the Hilton, and it was located only a few minutes walk from the center of town. It was rectangular and oriented north-south. The POW cells were in low, one-story buildings resembling long warehouses, each with a green painted door against the dirty yellow background. All windows were boarded or shuttered. Trees and shrubs were reasonably well cared for, and the compound was showy compared to others.

Later I learned that this was the "show place" where visiting delegations — Americans and others — were escorted to view a "typical" POW camp. It was about as representative of POW camps as the White House is of Appalachia. Much Communist movie film was made in this camp, most notably the Christmas footage, done by hidden cameras, and movies of the early releases of selected prisoners. There was a clumsy flick made by the East Germans for release in western countries, titled "Prisoners in Pajamas."

All but the last early release took place in this camp. Just as the entire Communist world ganged up on South Vietnam, so did they gang up on the few oppressed American prisoners. They came from every Communist country, as well as from many others, but the price of admission was always the same: leave speaking well of the Commies, and badly of Americans. Anyone who could not meet that criteria did not get into North Vietnam.

Under such auspices, the scum of America's lunatic fringe came and went, with one message that U.S. television happily parroted. A report by Ernest W. Lefever discusses Columbia Broadcasting System's anti-war slant during these times.

CBS reported, "The Hanoi regime is treating POWs well." The network reported this on nine occasions and gave air time to persons such as Ramsey Clark who tried to tell us POWs were happy and healthy.

Roger Mudd, the story goes, did a highly-favorable story about General Giap. Contrast this with the very biased "Selling of the Pentagon."

In *The President Steps Down*, "The late John Steinbeck complained after an extended visit to Vietnam, that news coverage of the war was unfair. Steinbeck accused the news media of sending to the war zone too many young reporters 'on the make,' who were far more interested in finding critical angles than anything else, especially if they worked for editors opposed to the war."

While many of the reporters may have been young, there was no shortage of older critics who seemed thrilled by the opportunity to work for the Communist cause, and against us prisoners. Here in the Plantation was the focal point of their operation.

A pleasant, smiling "V," later named "Soft Soap Fairy," explained that John McCain would soon arrive from the hospital. The gate rattled noisily and a dark-painted truck, the "ambulance," drove in.

"The "V" unlocked the heavy unventilated slab door, and I was permitted to walk freely outdoors. It was delightful to gaze around without threats and curses from the guards. How cheering was the simple pleasure of seeing the sky, the verdant, lush trees, and to breathe clean, fresh air. What a contrast to the putrid stench of the urine bucket that assailed our senses without respite!

Life's most basic values were becoming more and more significant with each passing day. What is the beauty of the wind, a flower, a wife, except to him who cares?

I was brought to earth by the sight of McCain. I was appalled at his condition. I knew from the radio he was a young man. I was confronted by a white-haired skeleton. There were deep, sunken pouches under his eyes, which popped bug-like from their cavities. His body was pathetically emaciated. He looked exactly like a survivor of Dachau. I guessed his weight at 100 pounds, or less. Although unbelievably puny, his eyes burned fever bright.

I said, "Welcome to the Hanoi Hilton," which, of course, was incorrect.

THE PLANTATION

I was so shaken by his appearance that I was grasping for something to say, a welcome of any kind that would distract him from the concern for his condition that had to have been mirrored on my face. My immediate thought was, "The 'V' have given him to us so he will die in American hands." Then they could blame his death on his fellow POWs.

John was in an immense body cast which started at buttock level and extended all the way over his shoulder. His right arm was propped up, sticking out of the cast like a broomstick arm protruding from a snowman. It angled out crazily. One did not have to be a doctor to recognize another butcher job.

His right knee had been torn apart. The operation on it appeared faintly professional, considering what we later saw as surgical work. His leg was nearly stiff, with only the faintest bit of movement possible at the knee.

His left arm and shoulder were broken and had neither been set nor attended to. He could not wash, relieve himself, or do any normal function of life without assistance. Without someone to feed him, he was a dead man.

John's head and body were filthy. Food particles and juices covered his chin, neck, and sideburns. He had not been cleaned after bowel movements. These things were of no concern to him. He was "on cloud nine" to have roommates.

We were the first Americans he had talked to. He had been alone for seven weeks, or more, in this terribly injured condition. As part of their attempts at breaking him, they had tried starvation. We later discovered that the Bug was his inquisitor, which made sense.

We were delighted to have him, and he was more than elated to see us. We stayed up the entire night, whispering and talking. We did not know that this was not a hard treatment camp like the Hilton and others, since we lacked an understanding of the camp system. We were not aware that we could speak in low voices, so most of our conversation was conducted in a semi-whisper.

We learned that John had a wife, Carol, two boys, Doug and Andy, and a little girl, Sydney. He shared many things from his personal and naval career, talking compulsively. I saw this repeated many times by other POWs after long or severe periods of privation. One would be so happy at the luxury of talking with another human being that he couldn't stop. This was a tender, pathetic scene for me.

John had a fantastic will to live. It was very encouraging to meet an American with his bubbly, optimistic outlook. Pessimists did not make great roommates in Hanoi! It was enough to be surrounded with gloom, without hearing more from a roommate.

McCain had a good sense of humor which surfaced quickly during a propaganda broadcast. A colored anti-war militant was ranting about the war. In his discourse, he commented unhappily that he wanted to be called "black," and that no one called him "black." He complained, "Whoever heard of a country called Negro?"

John retorted swiftly, "Right. Call him BLACK, after that *country* named BLACK!"

He had a hair-trigger mind which endeared him to me more and more, and he became one of my dearest and most trusted friends. He had a passionate love for our country and spoke straight about it. John talked of our well-written Constitution, how its guarantees set us apart in freedom from our forefathers in Britain. True personal freedom flows from this document like the bounty of our wheat fields.

He spoke of how freedom had come into being in America. He spoke of the difference in America's approach to the individual; the broad spectrum of freedom, the choices of conscience and the variety of riches. John's grasp of history was detailed, and several years later he taught history courses from memory.

McCain's discourse this night on the greatness of America would have won him a Freedom's Foundation Award, if it were reduced to writing. I desperately needed to hear these words about our country, which provided me with great mental and moral courage.

For the next several days, we were deluged by group after group of Vietnamese who came by to stare at the "Prince." These included older men, high-ranking dignitaries from the Communist Party. The enlisted men in the camp bowed to them in deference, an old Vietnamese custom and one of the highest degrees of respect that could be paid anyone. Perhaps this was one of the reasons the Commies forced us to bow.

An interesting thing surfaced in a discussion with Soft Soap Fairy, one of the most effective Vietnamese interrogators. He entered with a group of these older, obviously high-ranking Communists in their fifties and sixties. He was a slender, handsome Vietnamese officer, slightly effeminate. Although he wore no rank, it was clear that he was either of high rank, or he was the Communist cadre, because of the deference shown him by the camp "V," the camp commander, and visitors.

He spoke better-than-average English, was very low key, pleasant acting, frequently smiling, apparently a good grasp of the realities of the war. He did not parrot the ridiculous trash from the radio, i.e. Hanoi Hanna, so he had a certain amount of plausibility.

I learned that he was one of the two most dangerous "V" in North Vietnam, because he understood Americans, and was intelligent enough not to repeat the fantastic propaganda that came off the box. This would have destroyed his credibility with the POWs. He had an uncle in the

THE PLANTATION

highest of Communist Party circles, and he *was* the cadre to the camp, not a military officer. I rate him as one of the three best-appearing Communists I met, in every facet of such contacts.

The men with Soft Soap Fairy were far better dressed than most Vietnamese, although, by American standards, they looked shoddy. They entered the room and looked at John with great awe.

Soft Soap Fairy asked John, "How many corporations does your family own?" John looked back at him in surprise. Fairy continued, "I know that your father, being a big admiral in the government, is bound to have many companies under his control to deal with the government."

John replied, "You've got to be putting me on! My father is a military officer whose income is confined to his military salary."

Soft Soap Fairy translated this for the "V" standing behind us. They smiled knowing smiles, as if to say, "Oh come now, you can't put one over on us. If you are a general or an admiral, you have to be crooked. You have to be grafting!"

This was an interesting indictment of their own system, because it was clear that they expected corruption from high officials. Since they were high-ranking members in their own Party, it was probably a good measure of their honesty.

My friendship with John flourished. I was also deeply impressed with the amount of tender kindness that Norris Overly offered John and me. Norris washed, shaved, and put each spoonful of food in John's mouth.

I was surprised at some of the things the "V" did to help John improve his health. I did not realize that a unique situation was developing. There had to be some reason why the Vietnamese were being decent to John and me, when they had been so cruel in the past. Leopards do not change their spots, particularly Communist leopards. I had the gut feeling that something was awry, but I didn't know what.

As I recognized the greater press of their attention, it was increasingly clear the "V" were trying to create a special relationship with John, with the hope of getting something in return. I felt there had to be a string attached. It was a maxim of prison life that the Vietnamese gave you nothing that did not have a price tag.

Although we didn't know it, the treatment being accorded us was special. There were prisoners in other camps who were being starved, denied medical care, and tortured to death — Alcatraz, the Zoo, and Little Vegas.

We thought the Hilton had been only a temporary holding area, and failed to understand that our treatment here was better than our fellow POWs were getting elsewhere. None of us knew how many POWs there were, where they were, or who they were. Outside of the Plantation, POWs were still being put through *hell*, in the style of the pit of the Malebolge.

Christmas of 1967 arrived, and the first Christmas carol was a poignant moment, a knife in the throat. I noticed John choking up. Overly was likewise emotional.

I commented, "Someone had better tell a funny story before I burst out crying," and I nearly did.

The sound of Christmas was too deeply touching to all of us, too bittersweet. It was too reminiscent of shining childrens' faces, of church and Christmas music, of holiday greetings from friends, turkey, pumpkin pie, Santa Claus, snow crystals painting a new white world, large red stockings on the hearth. Melancholy memories of England, Iowa, Texas, Virginia, New York and Arizona washed through my brain in successive engulfing waves of nostalgia. My eyes watered. I dared not try to speak, for the sound of my voice would have caused us all to weep.

We did not have a radio speaker in our room, which ordinarily was a good deal, but tonight we treasured the music coming from outdoors. "Silent Night" was followed by "Little Town of Bethlehem." It was heart-ripping, but important to hear a Christmas carol being sung by an American. This was not a professional production, having been made by POWs. The music was not good, the fidelity and the reproduction of the song were poor. In a civilized world, it would not have drawn listeners. Here it was a perfect symphony. It was Bing Crosby and Peggy Lee to our starved souls.

We later learned that this was the famous J. Quincy Collins POW Choir. At close range, his music was beautiful, far better than we heard this night. Quincy was a great musical talent, a good POW, and a fine American.

Just after Christmas, Zorba the doctor came in with Soft Soap Fairy. Two other semi-English speaking interrogators, whom we referred to as "Kiddies," were in attendance. One of them mentioned something about lenient, humane treatment.

I said, "I have not had lenient or humane treatment. I have been very badly tortured!"

He replied, "Ah, yes, well, that was because you escaped. You must be punished for that."

I retorted, "Escapes are not prohibited by the Geneva Convention, and they are not prohibited by international law."

Apparently Soft Soap Fairy was tuned into the conversation, and relayed it to Zorba, who understood little English. Zorba then spoke in Vietnamese.

Soft Soap Fairy translated, "Jorgeday, the doctor says that you were captured about two miles from Con Thien, and you were shot being recaptured."

I answered, "Yes, I think that is the truth."

THE PLANTATION

I was delighted to have confirmation that I had made it well into South Vietnam. Though I knew it to be a fact, I was pleased to have it confirmed.

At this meeting, Zorba asked John, "Are you getting enough to eat?"

John said, "Yes."

Zorba asked, "Would you like to have something special?"

John stated, "No. I will just take what everybody gets."

He said, "Oh, no. You are very sick. We try to give you food that will help your health."

John emphasized, "I don't want anything everyone else is not getting."

The doctor persisted, "Would you like some fruit?"

John repeated, "No. I don't want anything that everyone else is not getting."

The doctor said, "Oh, we always give sick men fruit."

John said, "There isn't anything special that I would like to have, but if you want to sent some fruit, I'll eat it."

"Well," the doctor asked, "Would you eat some bananas if we send them?"

John said, "Yes."

The daily camp food was very poor because of thievery from the kitchen and the supply room. Due to incompetent camp administration, the guards were stealing a large portion of the prisoners' food. As a result, what we received was inadequate and poor quality, the leftovers. We got small loaves of bread interspersed with rice, and a thin green weed soup. Occasionally, there was a side dish of tasteless boiled turnips or hard-cooked monkey bananas. Monkey bananas taste like glue, I hasten to add.

On the following day, when Norris went out to pick up the food, there on the tray were 57 bananas! We could hardly believe our eyes. It was enough to boggle the mind. They were not the large ones found in United States supermarkets, but measure about the length of your index finger, and perhaps three-fourths of an inch in diameter. They were delicious, if not filling.

By the following morning, only six bananas remained. When the guard came by, he asked, "Do you want some more bananas?"

We responded, "Sure." Once again, they sent 57, for a grand total of 114 bananas in two days. By the time the third day had elapsed, we had eaten all of them and would have eaten another 57 had the "V" brought them. It became clear to the guards that there was no way to satiate us. That was the end of the bananas.

Soon political indoctrination began. I went to a quiz with a Chinese-looking man who started the first semi-sophisticated indoctrination that I had been exposed to. He started out with what I called building-block questions. They almost had to be answered in the affirmative. It would go like this.

If you answer A with a "yes," then you will be asked question B. If you answer A with a "yes," then you must answer B with a "yes." The next step is saying your government is wrong.

His first question was, "Do you think that it is proper for a country to have foreign troops in their country?"

Seeing the end of that one coming, I said, "Yes. There are a lot of circumstances where it is a good thing to have foreign troops in your country."

He looked at me with great surprise and said, "Oh. Give me an illustration."

I said, "O.K. The United States and some of the Allied powers occupied much of Western Europe after World War II. Through this occupation and the unlimited donation of money into Europe, we brought about its reconstruction. This was a good thing because, if it had not happened, Communism would have shot its way to power and instead of Europe being free, it would have been another Communist prison."

The answer surprised him and caught him off-balance. He became irritated and dogmatic with me, and attempted to develop another question of the same vein, which I answered in kind.

I added, "If you think having foreign troops in another country is bad, why don't you get the Russian troops out of East Germany, Hungary, Czechoslovakia, and Poland, or do you think foreign troops are okay if they are Communist troops? Why don't you get out of Laos, Cambodia and South Vietnam? South Vietnam does not like your foreign troops."

Infuriated, he responded, "Vietnam is one, the Vietnamese people are one!" That broken record sounded a little familiar.

I knew there wasn't any point in trying to be pleasant at this quiz, since it was clear where he was trying to lead me. I felt he might as well know that he was not leading me in any direction.

On the next question, I put it to him bluntly, "Look, if you think you are going to indoctrinate me with any of this cheap Communist trash, you are out of your mind. You are not going to turn me into a Communist. There is nothing about your system that I like. There is nothing about your system that I want to hear."

He lost his struggle to maintain his composure and flew into an apoplectic rage. He was an impressive sight, with his awkward-looking, round wire spectacles and prominent buck teeth. He salivated noisily, and as he tried to talk, he spit all over me.

He shouted, "I will have you transferred back to the camp you came from, you insolent dog," and continued with a long series of threats about bad treatment and punishment. It was obvious he had read my dossier, otherwise he would not have known I had come from another camp. He knew the treatment in the other camp was worse than the treatment in the Plantation.

I didn't recognize the meaning of his comment immediately. His parting words were that I would be punished, and sent back to a hard camp. That idea frightened me, as I needed a nurse, and I didn't want to go back to the old camp. The interesting thing was that I was not called back to another quiz until after Major Overly returned to the U.S. on an early release a couple of months later.

Shortly after our move to the Corn Crib, a small series of cells at the south end of camp, we were told we would be permitted outside for a few minutes of sunshine because McCain and I were injured. It sounded reasonable that sick people would get a few minutes outside. We were taken into an area which was fairly sunny. It had been a very wet, cool, miserable spring. This was the first decent weather that we had seen since the previous fall, and it was delightful to be out.

We were standing there about ten minutes when an imposing man walked up from the Big House. He was wearing a tailored Army uniform, clearly not the run-of-the-mill Army officer, or Communist weenie. He was quite dapper, with all the bearing of a professional soldier. It was obvious that he was a significant figure due to the courtesy shown him by the people in the camp. We later found out that he was the infamous Major Bai (Bye) and his claim to fame was that he was the Vietnamese officer in immediate charge of all POWs and directly responsible for all POW torture.

Hypothetically, he was the man who interpreted the elaborate Communist Party directives and passed them down to prison authorities at the lower levels. He was responsible for POW appearances on television, in posed propaganda photographs, movies, staged church services, phony banquets, and fake athletic events.

It should have been apparent to the Free World that the same persons were featured time after time in contrived propaganda programs. It was no accident that Bai was in camp this day, or that we stood outside. He was not wearing any rank, as was their custom, when he asked my name.

"Major George Day," I told him.

He responded, "Oh, we don't use that Major in here." It was their continual claim that we were criminals, not POWs.

Bai asked a number of questions of John McCain; who he was and so forth, and then asked Norris who he was. Major Bai knew full well who each of us was, and had studied our dossiers carefully. He was here on a special and surprising mission! The true purpose of this visit was to take a good look at Overly and make sure he did not have any visible scars or marks, and that he appeared to be in good physical condition.

Norris had not lost much weight. He had not been around long enough. He appeared healthy and strong. In fact, he had carried John from the room to our sunbathing area. He had no obvious torture scars, for he had never been tortured.

On February 4, Norris was called to quiz. When he came back that evening, he told us he was to meet a high-ranking Vietnamese that night to discuss his early return to the United States.

I was staggered by his suggestion that he was the candidate for release, because I was so positive that all of the friendly efforts by Soft Soap Fairy had been directed at winning over "The Prince." I was totally unprepared for any other idea. Overly was like me, a nobody! McCain, however, was the son of a famous admiral, from a respected naval family.

Who would want Overly, when the Prince would be such a trophy? The reason for the bananas, this easier camp, the casual treatment by Soft Soap Fairy, and many quizzes now fell into place. My skepticism flashed to the surface.

"What is the price?" I asked of Norris, "and, why you?"

McCain answered the question, "There is no way in the world that I would ever accept an early release! Nobody in the United States would believe that I had not done something to influence my own release, bringing me back before my fellow prisoners. Even though I am injured, and even though (speaking to me) you are injured, there are people who are sicker and more badly wounded than we.

"Because my father is an admiral, and because everyone in the world would be criticizing him, and me, whether or not I had done anything to get my own release, going home early would be absolutely unthinkable. I would absolutely refuse. I would not consider it, and they would have to drag me out of this country before I would ever accept an early release."

Shortly thereafter, Norris left our room to move to the Show Rooms in front of the camp. His new roommates were John Black, USAF, and David Mathini, USN. They were to be the first three American releasees on February 16, 1968, which turned out to be about five years earlier than those who did not have good attitudes! Soft Soap Fairy had frequently told the three of us that Norris showed good attitude, so when Norris left, we saw the positive results of "good attitude."

During our confinement in the Plantation, prior to Overly's release, the three of us were carefully kept out of the normal bathing schedule. A great deal of the communication that occurred at the Plantation took place at the bath which was split up into separate brick-walled cubicles. Communication was forbidden in there; nevertheless, a tremendous exchange of "comm" occurred each day.

THE PLANTATION

It was no accident that our room was almost never permitted to bathe and wash clothes at a time when other POWs were in the bath. The guards were also careful to keep us away from the end rooms nearest the bath. Two notoriously good resisters were located at that end of the building, Air Force Major Jack Van Loan and Navy Lieutenant Commander Charlie Plumb. There was always a word of cheer, or encouragement, or morale info popping out of their shutters, or from behind their locked door.

I agreed with John except that if the "V" simply expelled some persons, the POW would have little say over that circumstance. The Code of Conduct forbids acceptance of special favors from the enemy. Eventually, the policy of expulsion, without assistance or participation by the releasee, was established as one of the cornerstone policies of the 4th Allied P.O.W. Wing by Colonel John P. Flynn.

A special favor, of course, obviously means what it says. It means that you are getting something that nobody else is getting. In effect, the connotation also exists that you are actively assisting. You have to do something to bring about your own release. There were never any simple expulsions of POWs from North Vietnam, although a dozen POWs came home early.

Norris stated that he agreed with our views and that he had not done anything to secure his own release. Unknown to *us*, and before our arrival in that camp, an "early release" plan had been dangled in front of some POW faces. The general resistance posture here was not as strong as in other camps, such as the Zoo.

Soft Soap Fairy was in charge of this program. His extreme cunning was perfectly suited to a soft-sell program. A sizeable number of candidates for early release were competing and showing "good attitude" in a low-key way for the elusive first release.

This isolation by the "V" was good, but not perfect, because we had some small, incomplete contacts with others. Some news was relayed via Larry Carrigan, Moe Baker, then via Bob Craner, and Guy Gruters. These four Air Force officers were also housed in the Corn Crib, the six-man building John and I lived in.

Nevertheless, when Norris was released on February 16, 1968, he did not carry home any wealth of information about POWs; names, camps, living conditions, or treatment. The "V" and the anti-war groups and Communist sympathizers in the U.S. did themselves some propaganda service with this release.

The pure and simple idea of an "early release" was to dispel American apprehension that pilots were being tortured, not receiving decent treatment. There was not the slightest humane consideration involved. None of the dreadfully sick, injured, or crippled were sent to the U.S. to receive the care that would never be available in Communist Vietnam. Instead, three healthy, uninjured, recent shootdowns were returned.

The Communists solely hoped for, and achieved, a propaganda coup. They wanted to produce some truly healthy-looking specimens who would not scream torture. They had to be new prisoners; otherwise, the food, diarrhea, dysentery, worms, and beri-beri would have reduced them to the skeletons that the average prisoner resembled after losing 30 to 75 pounds. Also, the early release types could not have been tortured or aware of the horrible conditions at the other camps: the Zoo, the Hilton, Heartbreak Hotel, etc.

The release on February 16, 1968, was a real spectacle. Members of all the foreign Communist press took an active role. Flash-bulbs popped, movie cameras ground, and tape recorders spun.

On that morning, the guards came to our room and carried McCain to the Big House for the pre-release activities. I walked beside his stretcher. We were taken inside where Stone-face, the camp commander, greeted us effusively. Through an interpreter, he told us that our nurse, Major Norris Overly, was going to be released to his country by the "People."

"Norris," he said, "has shown 'good attitude' and 'repentance' for his crimes."

In a few moments, Norris entered the room from the hall, wearing a cheap, poorly-tailored cotton suit, over a cheaper blue cotton turtle-neck sweater. He was wearing a pair of tan "boondockers" with the unfinished side of the leather out.

"So long, guys!" he said, emotionally.

"What did it cost you?" I questioned.

"Not a thing," he answered. "It didn't cost a thing."

With that I gave him a squeeze and wished him, "God speed."

He handed John a pack of cigarettes with a note wishing him good luck. Overly had been permitted to take a letter written for me by John McCain to my wife, and to carry a letter from John to his wife, Carol. This letter, and subsequent actions by Overly and my wife, probably saved my life, but that is another story.

We were returned to our room, and the broadcasts went into full swing. On the speaker the next day, we heard the news of the great release. Three U.S. pilots, who had shown "good attitude" and repented their "crimes," had, in the lenient and humane 4,000-year custom of the "People," been released by the Communists.

As soon as the release was concluded, treatment toward John and me changed. We started going to bathe with other groups, the guards began to enforce rules that they ignored previously, and Soft Soap Fairy did not come to visit very often.

Colonel George E. "Bud" Day and decorations.
(Photo - Craig Chandler McDonnell)

Second lieutenant. *(1950)*

F-80 Gunnery. *(1952)* ▶

Bud and Doris —
Wethersfield RAF
Station, England
F-84s. *(1956)*

Bud and the Hun
- Sidi Slimane *(1956)*

T-bird Scott Field, Illinois. *(1959)*

Doris "Viking" Day.

Doris and kids — Phoenix. *(1967)*

The family again in Glendale. *(1969)*

Squadron Commander Vietnam. *(1967)*

Misty Group Photo: Back row left to right; Blocker, Kippenham, Dalton, Cunningham, Heiniger, Mayberry, Tompkins, Harris, Jones, Turner and Douglass. Front row; Bevivino, Meyer, Day, McHugh and Boyd. ▼

▲ Ramp — March AFB, Bud and Doris "Together again." *(1973)*

Colonel Day on POW release "How to age twenty years in five years." *(March 1973)*

Misty reunion — Bevivino, Douglass and Day. *(1973)*

Bud and F-4 friend, Eglin AFB, Florida. *(1974)*

McCain, Day and Thieu. *(1974)*

Medal of Honor presentation by President Ford to Bud with family at White House. *(1976)*

Captain Lance Sijan (deceased) and Bud Day — POW Medal of Honor recipients. *(1976)*

▲ Bud, Nancy and Ronald Reagan and Viking in California. *(1976)*

▼ Viking, President Nixon and Bud — "Richard the Lion Hearted." *(1977)*

▲ Retirement — Generals Hill, Allen, Flynn, Colonel Day, General Lane and Salisbury. *(1977)*

▼ Misty F-100 dedication - Tucson, Arizona. *(1987)*

Bud, George Jr., Sandra, Sonja, Steve and Doris. *(1988)*

Jacob — first grandson in Grandpa's jacket and gloves.▼

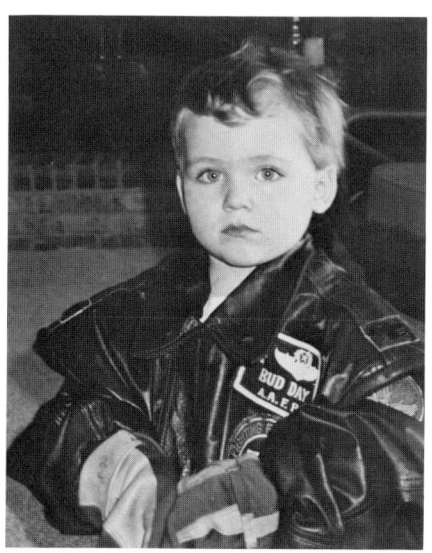

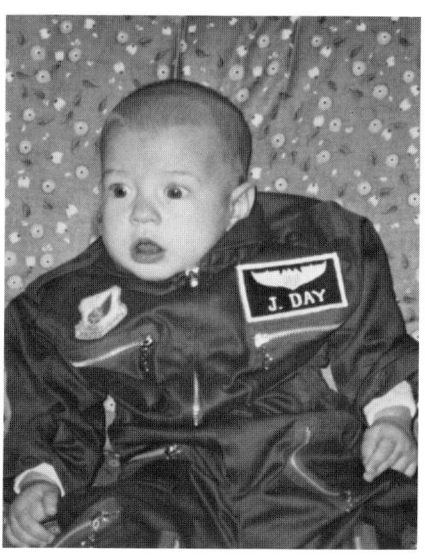

▲ Joshua Day, son of George Jr. in his first flying suit.

George Sr. and George Jr. with F-4. *(1989)*

THE PLANTATION

When my arm came out of the cast, it was heart-breaking to view. All of the arm muscle had atrophied. The upper bicep was the size of a lead pencil, all of the forearm muscle had disappeared. There were more than 70 jungle rot ulcers on my arm. The largest was the size of a silver dollar, located where the wrist bone had punctured the skin. There was a large bowing in the bone fusion between the elbow and the shoulder. However, my wrist was the disaster area.

My hand hung at an odd angle about 10 to 15 degrees out of alignment, and it was clear that only one bone was healed. The other was simply floating. I complained to Soft Soap Fairy, who sent me to the "hospital" to see the "Doctor." X-rays showed a slight fusion of one bone, with the other bone pointing into space. Soft Soap Fairy announced happily that it did not "fit."

I asked, "What is the doctor going to do about it?"

"Nothing," said Soft Soap Fairy. "It will fix itself."

My morale was rock bottom when I returned to the room. John tried to raise my spirits.

"We'll make a splint," he said, "and tomorrow I'll wrap some bamboo with rags and I'll squeeze those bones together."

Good to his word, he did just that, and within about a month, the bone was joined. After release, I explained the procedure to an orthopedic surgeon, Dr. David Martyn, of Newport Beach, California. Dave consulted with his colleagues who decided then and there that John should be awarded his degree in practical orthopedic surgery. However, they advised that I probably ought to sue him for malpractice in that his technique was not sanitary, and that if John had malpractice insurance, I could get $100,000 in damages from my injury!

At a quiz on March 14, 1968, Soft Soap Fairy asked John about his views on the Vietnam war. John responded that he fully backed the U.S., and President Johnson. Soft Soap Fairy terminated the quiz in a fit of temper, told John he had a "bad attitude," and that he would be the first POW shot after the war was over.

Next day, I had the same quiz with Soft Soap Fairy, and I stated my "true feelings" about the war. I, too, was accused of having "bad attitude," and then deposed the Prince of one of his future glories. I was told that I, "Jorgeday" (he always pronounced George Day as one word), would be the first man shot after the war, because I was the blackest criminal in the D.R.V.

A few days later, we received an advisory from the north side of the camp explaining the conditions of the first release. It said that the early releasees requested amnesty, made a statement that they had been leniently and humanely treated, promised not to come back and fight in the war, and wrote a statement expressing their "true feelings" about the war. All "true feelings" had to be anti-U.S. and anti-war to satisfy the "V."

In the bath, Charlie Plumb advised us that this was an "easy treatment" camp, and there was no torture for communicating, or other minor violations. We also received clarification of the tap code, a method of pounding messages through the thick brick walls from room to room. While it was not required much in our particular situation, it was vital at a later date in the hard treatment and torture camps, where frequently it was the only "comm" system used.

During the Tet Offensive of 1968, we were able to observe the full effect of what a completely-controlled press and radio can do. Great, all-encompassing excitement pervaded the "V" camp personnel. Soft Soap Fairy was expansive, talking of Saigon falling at any moment. He said the Communists would be riding their bicycles into Saigon, that the Commies had taken the U.S. Embassy there, and that they had captured Hue, and many other places.

A POW in another camp answered this news, saying, "The Commies won't last five minutes in Saigon. They'll be wiped out by the cars, trucks, scooters, and motorcycles." Bad attitude!

At first light each morning, one of the "V" guards posted a large chalk map in front of their mess hall with new battle lines, and indications of new victories. About this time, a rumor that Chester Bowles was in Cambodia for peace talks accelerated our speculations about the declining progress of the war, and our prospects for release.

Release is to a prisoner what water is to a man dying of thirst. We speculated and prognosticated, and the feeling began to sweep the camp that much of what the Commies were saying about their successes in the South was true. In the five years and seven months that I spent in North Vietnam, I never saw their spirits so high. They were told that all the people of South Vietnam had "risen up," the Party's expression for an invasion of troops from the North. They were positive that the war was won. Now was just a case of picking up their marbles.

Victory was not apparent at the food table. Food was still "sewer-green soup" and a bowl of rice twice a day, with an occasional plate of greasy turnips and rice. No meat, no protein.

As one wag suggested, "We don't eat, we graze!"

I had become so skeptical of enemy claims, after hearing the fantastic distortions of their fall summary of 1967, that I had trouble giving their new victories much credibility, and decided to wait and see.

As John became mobile for short periods, we spent a great deal of time peeping out the cracks and holes in the poorly constructed doors. We learned that the "V" were no longer "faceless" Orientals, but instead a

THE PLANTATION

polyglot of extremely diverse-appearing throwbacks.

Some were Mongolian, brushy haired with low foreheads. Many were Chinese peasant stock; burly, with large wide feet and strong white teeth. Others showed distinct Indian and Indonesian features. Some were uniquely Negroid, and amazingly runty. If there was common bond, it had to be their yellow-brown skin and their undernourished height.

Although young men and women existed in the camp together, the men almost shunned the women. It was strikingly apparent that some barrier existed between them.

We speculated as to how this nation of little men and seeming incompetents had defeated the French at Dien Bien Phu, and held up so steadfastly against the U.S. air strikes. While we did not like the answer, it had to be said that Ho Chi Minh had given them some pride.

Combining the victory over the French with unrelenting tales of past and future victories, a sort of national brainwashing took place as to the virtues, glories, and achievements of the Communists. With the insertion of a Party cadre into every village, the Vietnamese Communists had established control and acquired cooperation from the peasants.

Nationalism was blended into a patriotic potpourri which became their religion, morals and mores, values, sense of justice, and hope for the future. The snap judgment would say that they were ignorant and brainwashed; nothing more than robot-like automatons in the style of some of the Germans and Italians under their twentieth century dictators. That observation would be hasty and inaccurate, but partially correct.

What I did not understand about North Vietnam until I saw it firsthand, was the fact that in 1968 it was still a feudal sixteenth- or seventeenth-century state. The cadre had replaced the Mandarin and the French. The peasants still lived in filth, squalor, and ignorance on annual incomes of less than $200 per year, as their forefathers had for generation upon generation. Communism was the new exploiter, but with some promises for the future that the French never made.

I saw a parallel between the American, who in 1930 had no place to go but up, and the "V" peasant. I also saw a parallel between the totally indoctrinated Vietnamese who believed that it was fight or be killed anyway, and the Japanese soldier in 1945 who preferred death in battle to death in surrender.

Whatever the motive, cruel and ignorant as they were, they were also tougher than whang leather. They were a total enigma to the U.S. State Department and to many of the presidential advisors. What the president needed to know from his advisors was the answer to this question:

"What will happen if I take drastic, decisive action against North Vietnam? Will China enter the war? Will Russia enter the war?" Either there was no single voice that could answer these questions, or Lyndon simply did not believe the answer. I personally do not believe that anyone around the president knew.

The answer to this important question was that the Chinese would have done nothing. Relations between North Vietnam and China were lukewarm at best, for China had only recently split violently with Russia over ideological matters. Russia was both North Vietnam's sponsor and benefactor. The North Vietnamese had spent far too many years under Chinese rule to permit too much assistance from China, lest Peking assist them right into control of North Vietnam. China would not permit transshipment of certain war materials from Russia to North Vietnam.

Lacking this understanding, Lyndon could never quite summon courage to go after Hanoi in the way that President Nixon did in 1972. As a result, LBJ listened to uninformed advisors who cautioned him against the kind of military actions that would have stopped the invasion and maintenance of the war in South Vietnam.

Secondly, a significant red herring was drawn across the president's view. That herring was the tonnage of bombs dropped. In typical MacNamara fashion, bombs seemed to be raining on Vietnam. Indeed, they were.

In order to comply with instructions from Washington, commanders in the field were dropping bombs. However, they could only drop bombs on approved targets chosen by Lyndon or his close associates. When Lyndon did not choose truly significant targets for bombing, such as the port at Haiphong or Hon Gue, our aircraft would faithfully carry the bombs and drop them on the same targets that they had long since reduced to nothing. Defense would then excitedly report that another X-hundred tons of bombs had been dropped, reassuring both Lyndon and the American public that the war was moving on.

The sinister end result of this series of deceptions was that soon enough bombs had been dropped to beat a serious enemy. Despite this massive tonnage, little seemed to have happened.

In *Decade of Disillusionment*, the author comments, "The bombing raids on the North, although so intense that they made those in WW II look modest in comparison, were not producing results." The bombing in North Vietnam was exactly as if all the bombs had been dropped into the ocean or on the Sahara desert. This caused disastrous miscalculations.

A great deal of our poor treatment apparently stemmed from the barbaric ignorance of our captors. There were two groups of mongrel dogs in camp, those the "V" fed, and who barked with Oriental animosity at the POWs, and those that were fed and handled by the POWs, and who barked at the "V" with Oriental anger. The dogs all resembled Chinese Chows, with a

THE PLANTATION

fat square head and the Chow pointed nose. The pro-American dogs were ordinarily the first slain in the frequent forays for food, for the "V" enjoyed dog meat.

As we were peeping into the yard one sunny morning, we were flabbergasted to note that a young female worker, a food handler, was masturbating a male dog with enthusiasm. The dog was also enthusiastic, until the young woman lighted her cigarette lighter and put the flame directly against the animal's penis!

"Hoo boy!" exclaimed John, "I'll bet that smarts! It sure makes me feel good to know that she works in the kitchen, and is handling our food!"

Another fun diversion for the "V" was to catch the baby rats or mice that abounded in the camp. The rat was soaked in either gasoline or lighter fluid, and then torched with a cigarette lighter. This event always drew a sizable crowd, and the air would be split with shrieks and cheers as the animal raced desperately around until its tiny legs were burned off, and it fell squealing to the ground.

The most dreadful spectacle of all was the foray after the dogs, ducks, or turkeys. The dogs, at least, seemed to sense their impending doom.

Normally, the "V" would stride into the yard without the slightest notice of an animal, and should a dog venture within kicking distance, he could expect a jolting boot on one end or the other. Apparently, it was their belief that the meat would be more edible if pounded thoroughly before cooking.

On slaughtering days, the "V" would pick up a piece of brick or rock in one hand and attempt to coax the dog into lethal range with a crust of bread. The dogs were, of course, distrustful, but, like POWs, they were also hungry.

Once the dog was enticed into range, he would be dazed with a well-thrown rock, and the entire camp contingent would join in pursuing and stoning it to death. It was considered a meritorious achievement to be the lucky fellow who would disable the dog by breaking its first leg, but even better to be the one who broke the second. After all, *anyone* could cave in the skull when it was immobile.

By March 1968, both John and I had been in Hanoi five months, and together for about three months. He was getting around a little, and we were able to walk out to the table and pick up our food. We had a real problem. Although John could hardly walk, he could use his hands. I could walk well, but could not use one hand at all, and barely use the other. As we passed an end room with our food, someone shouted, "Hire the handicapped. They're fun to watch." We were amused, and glad to be noticed.

Neither John nor I understood the most important communication technique common in the Hilton and Zoo. This simple miracle was the "tap code" — a parallel of the miners' tap code in the U.S., and of the Russian prison tap code. Smitty Harris, a very early shootdown, was credited by the POWs with this splendid tool.

The code drops the letter "K" out of the alphabet, leaving 25 letters. The code is then broken into five groups of letters. A-E, F-J, L-P, Q-U, V-Z. To use the A-E group, tap once, pause . . . and tap your letter.

.	A B C D E
..	F G H I J
...	L M N O P
....	Q R S T U
.....	V W X Y Z

For B - tap once, pause, tap twice, (. ..)
For H - tap twice, pause, tap three times, (.. ...)
For P - tap three, pause, tap five times, (... .....)

This system was universally used by the Hanoi POWs and was essential to a return with honor. Communication was our life's blood.

We looked forward to the coming presidential election with immense interest and correctly speculated that Richard M. Nixon was going to be the Republican nominee, versus Vice President Hubert H. Humphrey in the Democratic corner. I strongly preferred Richard Nixon because it meant a clean sweep of many of the bureaucrats and appointees of the Democratic administration whose policies had been so incredibly unsuccessful and incompetent. I felt that the war needed a fresh point of view; we needed to win or get out. My disgust with my Democratic Party had become so complete that I had crossed over from conservative Democrat to Republican. I could scarcely recognize as Democrats many of the lint-headed liberals who had invaded the party, and abandoned the conservatives.

Speculation was rife across the camp on the effects of the impending elections on our release. It became a fixation in the minds of most prisoners that our release would be tied closely to a presidential election. Of course, it was our hope that it would be this one.

A stunning and frightening event occurred just as we learned the code. Two Misty pilots, Captains Bob Craner and Guy Gruters, were moved into the cell next to us. At first, I put the most paranoid interpretation on this move, believing that the clever "V" had set this up and "bugged" the wall. I refused to tap about "Misty," instead using the common drain pipe to whisper under the wall of the bath. I learned that Craner had been my "after shootdown officer," and had communicated with the Viking. He told me she would be in Phoenix, as that was where I left her, and that's where I'd be looking for her, and that she was doing O.K., and that the kids were fine only two months earlier! I was relieved! Bob also advised McCain through the pipe that I'd been recommended for another Distinguished Flying Cross, and four Silver Stars. On this news, McCain wisecracked, "Bud, you better pass this to Soft Soap Fairy so he can arrange for a presentation of your medals, and maybe a parade!"

"I'll settle for a couple of bananas!" I replied.

THE ZOO

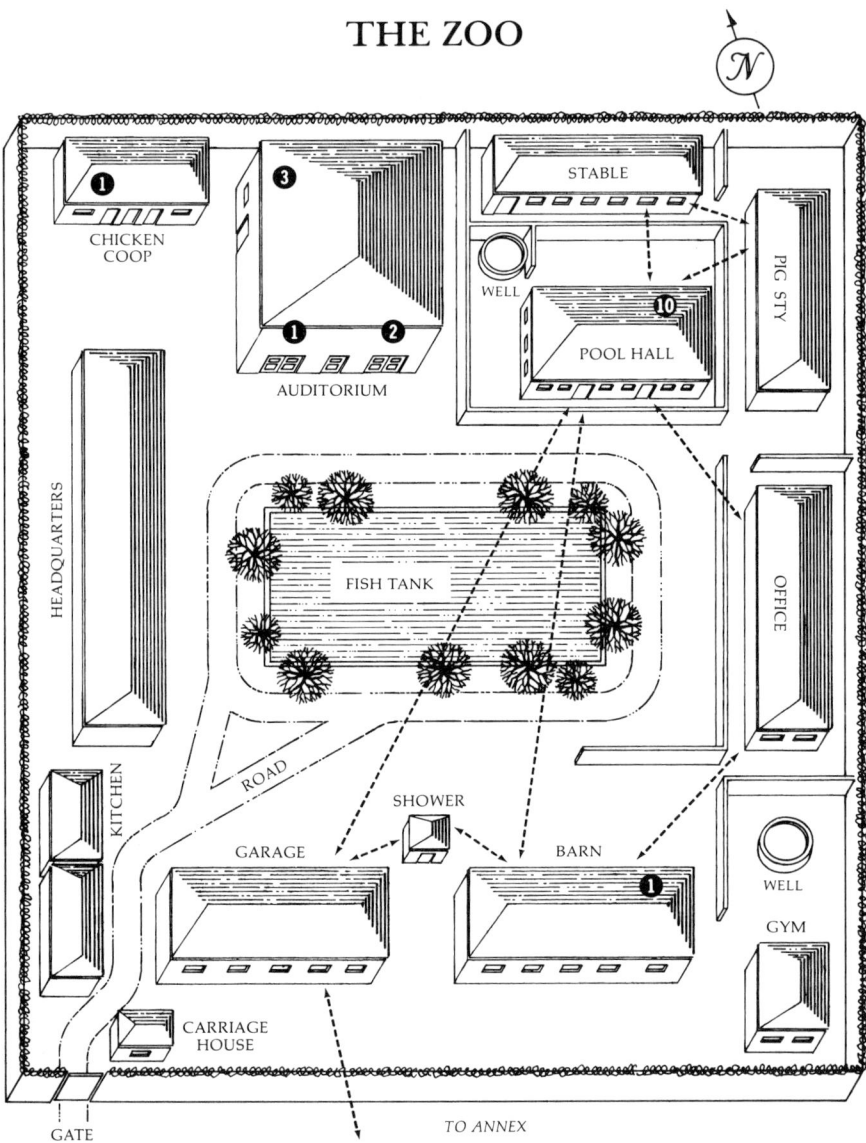

LEGEND
◂------▸ = Communication Lines
1, 2, 3, 10 = Rooms in which I lived in or torture rooms.

CHAPTER TEN

The Zoo, April 1968
(Second Ring of the Malebolge)

Shortly after Norris Overly's departure, my treatment and John's declined radically. On April 28, 1968, I was selected for transfer to the Zoo, along with several other reactionaries. Charlie Plumb, Jack Van Loan, Bob Wiedemann, Arvin Chauncey, Bob Sawhill, Dewey Smith, Kay Russell, Bill Stark and several others also would have the chance to improve their "attitudes."

The Zoo was a new world after the low-key Plantation. We realized that the Plantation was the "V" equivalent of a progressive camp, in their view, whereas the Zoo was a "punishment" camp.

This doesn't mean that there were a group of low-key resisters at the Plantation, for that is not true. Some of our toughest, most gutsy people were in that camp. It was, however, the camp the "V" selected to try to run a more "progressive" program. With several early releases generated from the Plantation, they were having limited success.

Lieutenant Commander Arvin Chauncey of Glendale, California, and Major Robert R. Sawhill of Carnegie, Pennsylvania were my new roommates. With great ears and fine hands, Arv took over as the prime communicator, while Bob and I were relegated to the menial chores of lying on the concrete and clearing, or pushing on our double doors to get a view of the outside in order to sound the alarm.

Our room was a reasonable size, with a solid door and only a faint tribute to ventilation. Some tiny four-inch holes were scattered around the walls, near the ceiling, plus a barred, round window about the size of a dinner plate near the top of the 12-foot wall. The blazing tropical sun burned on this room from first rising until last setting. When we were advised by the room to the west that this was the hottest room in the camp, one of my new roommates replied sarcastically, "No shit?"

Korean ace Jim Kasler, our neighbor in solitary, began filling us in on those things he felt we needed to know in order to survive. Despite the fact that he had no one to clear for him, and that he had already taken some of the most brutal abuse in North Vietnam, he talked through the wall using his clothing as a muffler, or he would tap to us for long periods of time. We learned that the senior POW was Major Larry Guarino, a June 1965, shootdown. Kasler told us Guarino's resistance policies, which were designed to blunt the Communist goals of reducing POWs to spineless cooperators.

These policies were:

> **First:** Follow the Code of Conduct to the best of your ability. Don't write or speak against your country or for the Gooks.
> **Second:** Do not meet or see delegations without torture to the limit of your abilities.
> **Third:** No early release, no confessions, no requests for amnesty.
> **Fourth:** You are an American. I can't tell you what to do in every case of torture. Do what you think is right. Cut off the torture before losing all self control. It's better to give a little than a lot.
> **Fifth:** I emphasize, follow the code, but if you are tortured to do something, as a hell of a lot of us have been, do it as "BAD" as you can.

We learned a great deal more about the Hanoi prison system. There was a fairly large, stable population at Little Las Vegas in the Hilton. There was an outlying camp, thought to be closed, called the "Farm." There was another small camp, variously called "Dirty Bird," "Power Plant," or the "School."

We told of seeing bread and soup hauled out of the Plantation to some other camp. We had estimated there was food for about 15 people, whom we erroneously speculated to be "the senior officers." Some full colonels — Ed Burdette, John Flynn, Dave Winn, Jim Bean, Norman Gaddis — and several other senior officers such as Lieutenant Colonel Robinson Risner, Commanders Jim Stockdale, Jerry Denton, and others seemed to be unaccounted for. We wrongly assumed that all of the senior officers were clustered together.

In reality, the food we saw go out of the Plantation went only a few doors up the street, to Alcatraz, where several escapers, doers of "bad acts," were being held in stocks and solitary. One was Nels Tanner, whose tortured false confession I have already mentioned as having embarrassed the "V" internationally. None of those whom we speculated as being at Alcatraz were actually there.

My roommates and I were deluged with questions and indignant complaints about the early release in February. We did not fully understand that these releases were designed to recoup the "loss of face" that the "V" suffered in doing a tortured interview with Lieutenant Commander

THE ZOO, APRIL, 1968

Dick "the Beak" Stratton, early in 1967, where he gave the appearance of being drugged.

Columnist Holmes Alexander expressed the POWs' viewpoint exactly when he described early release as "setting a low value on loyalty, valor, and steadfastness this country asks of its soldiers and citizens." Few U.S. newspapers picked up on the theme.

Kasler told us of a particularly savage beating received by one of the POWs a short time before. The prisoner would not bow. He had been tortured so unmercifully that he lost his mind. He was not permitted to have a roommate and, as a result, never returned. Chills went up and down our spines as we heard this bloody story in tap code through the wall.

The torture of this prisoner was directed by a Caucasion who spoke Spanish. He was named Fidel because he was believed to be Cuban. Most of us were convinced that he was the Cuban consul to Hanoi, or another member of the Cuban diplomatic group.

A tall, strong man, Fidel was idolized by the runty "V" due to his size and his fluency in English. He acted as English teacher to the guards and taught a practical, idiomatic American language course. We held him responsible for censoring the few letters that were written and teaching the "V" how to censor.

We also believed that Fidel required the biographical personal history which each POW in the camp was tortured to complete. We felt that Fidel's English was so perfect, he had either been in the U.S. Army, or had worked for them at Guantanamo Bay. Because of his insight, he was able to inform and rat on us as well as an American could have.

We could see that this was going to be a fun camp. For an insignificant, trumped-up violation, my roommate, Bob Sawhill, was hit in the face, and Chauncey had been struck. For no reason, we spent the 28th, 29th, 30th, and May Day in kneeling "hand-up" torture. Of the first four days we were in camp, we spent three on our knees! We got the message, "You are new guys! This is a tough camp. You better shape up!"

The attempted political exploitation in this camp was severe and never-ending. I was called to many quizzes, and my quiz master was a sadistic Vietnamese called "Dum-Dum" by most of us. He was also known as "Marion the Librarian" and the "Goat." The last was because his face slightly resembled a nanny goat wearing glasses.

Dum-Dum's English was atrocious, and he was angered when we didn't understand him. Like the Bug, he relied on the "icepick between the eye" technique, pure and simple terror. "You will be punished. Do this, or I will torture you. Write this, or I will torture you!" He was predictably consistent.

There were no breathing spells. We went to a joint quiz at first, and then started individual quizzes.

At the first quiz with Dum-Dum, I was told, "You *will* write!" He referred to propaganda for the "V." I was to state my "true" feelings about the legality of the war, and in what ways the United States was not adhering to the Geneva Convention. The implication, of course, was that the North Vietnamese *were* adhering to the convention.

"I don't have any intention of writing anything," I told him.

He threatened me with torture and made statements, "You will do this." But he did not follow up with torture.

I was still wearing my pilot ring. When they attempted to take it from me in the past, I had resisted with all the effort I could. At this quiz, Dum-Dum noticed that I still had it and told me I could not keep it. It was a very nice, heavy gold ring. They took it away from me by force and, I assume, Dum-Dum or some other Communist thief is wearing it today. Somehow, it could not be found when we were released. So, along with being torturers, murderers, and international outlaws, they are also thieves and have a ring with my name on it as proof.

After this encounter with Dum-Dum, I received some sound advice from next door. Since I was senior man in the building, I had said I did not want anyone to make a tape, write, or make any propaganda for the Vietnamese without being tortured significantly. One of the men tapped back, "I don't think you understand all there is to know about this camp. It is very cruel and there are *some* times when it is more intelligent, instead of absolutely refusing to do anything, to either answer indirectly, noncommitally, or just give a nonsensical answer. They almost always torture for refusal. Once they have an excuse to get you going downhill, they continue to press and escalate their demands for more and more valuable things."

Our next-door neighbors had been in the Annex and had access to a lot of names. We spent a good part of our early days accumulating the names of POWs. We operated a memory bank in which the name of every known prisoner was to be learned by every other POW. It was effective and useful. When we got together in 1971, we found our list almost 100% correct. All of this was done by tapping or scratching through the wall in code.

Our turnkey, the man who opened our door and dealt with us on all our inside-outside chores, was a spindly, vicious animal, with a permanent sneer. As time went by, his slaps, kicks, insults, and continual goading was building to a fever pitch and I was having difficulty keeping self-control. The idea of surprise punching him as hard as possible in the belly, or kicking him in the groin, made some delicious day-dreaming.

Such an act would have been pure insanity. The "V" had demonstrated their complete freedom from restraint by beating senseless a man who would not bow. An attack on a guard would not produce any less, and would probably result in death. We seethed internally and turned a bland face to all mistreatment. Our only outlet was disgust and hatred and we named him "Anus," a title he deserved.

Since I could not express my frustrations against Anus, one of my roommates would frequently bear the brunt, or vice-versa. Luckily, one roommate was absolutely non-argumentative and had amazing self-control.

At the end of nine months imprisonment, I was a changed man. I had lost my pacifier, the flights with the vastness of the sky as my front yard, a panacea for all earthly problems. I was filled with an all-consuming, malevolent hatred of Communism, and everything about it, including the ignorant camp peasants. Many of them were only a few days out of the rice paddies, although many of my contemporaries argue they were only days out of the trees.

One of our few pleasures was the camp news from the POW communications net. Some of the news was wild. "Today, Fred Cherry killed a poisonous snake in his room. It crawled under the door." "Prisoner X has a Beech Bonanza he wants to sell. Anyone interested?" "Prisoner Y had a four-inch worm crawl out of his anus (or Z had a worm crawl out of his nose) during the nap."

Communications through the camp were excellent. Leadership by our senior officer, Major Larry Guarino, was the best in the system. For example, we were able to find out in the afternoon what the mornings' quizzes had been about. Thus we were always abreast of what the "V" wanted, and were able to think ahead and avoid surprise. Because of these communications, we presented a more effective and higher resistance posture.

Our communication techniques were ingenious, and "comm" flowed every day. This prompted the comment from the Rabbit to Larry Guarino, "Americans are the best communicators in the world. Every time you leave your room for a quiz, everyone in the camp knows about it." While this was slightly exaggerated, there was more truth to it than the Vietnamese would have liked.

The only way to stave off the depression that occasionally overtook us was to use the communication net, despite the threat of torture, for morale information — even more frequently than for passing military traffic. Solitary confinement and our high-pressure living conditions took a heavy toll.

It is not by accident that the Geneva Convention prohibits solitary confinement for more than 30 days at a time. We referred to the loss of contact with the real world as "solo syndrome." Prisoners were tortured for being caught tapping the simple Friday night message dear to every fighter pilot's heart — the initials H.H., meaning Happy Hour. This was in recognition of the old days in officers' clubs across the United States.

Other information flowed freely on the comm net. Having some background in remodeling income properties, I passed on the price of construction materials, ready mix cement by the yard, the price of roofing by the square foot, the cost relationship of labor to material in remodeling, gross and net income figures, and how to offset income by depreciation. Other prisoners using this information spent hundreds of hours building apartment complexes, remodeling houses and apartments, or rebuilding or enlarging their homes.

Other exciting and precious items were the correct words to the Apostolic Creed, the Twenty-Third Psalm, or a favorite hymn. Formulas for solutions to math and physics problems brought countless hours of preoccupation and mental transfer from the hell hole of boredom and oppression.

Scarcely a day passed without some interesting, useful, humorous, incredibly trivial piece of news circulating through all six widely-spaced buildings in the camp, about 80 men in the Zoo and 100 in the Annex. The hours and effort involved in this minute transfer of information would drive an efficiency expert up the wall, but this was our life blood, and how we kept our identity.

On the morning of June 11, I was called up for a quiz with Dum-Dum. This involved some answers to questions that had been put to me by Bug concerning my family. I told him that my father made $50 a month during the depression, which was an exaggeration. I was looking for a figure they might buy, and a round figure I could remember. Dum-Dum was looking, for an excuse to torture me.

Dum-Dum knew that I was SRO in my building; they knew the SRO of every building simply by looking at the dossiers. They generally assumed that we communicated, but treated us as though we didn't. When I went to quiz, I was immediately accused of communicating.

Just like Bug, Dum-Dum's technique was to put you, and keep you, on defensive. He told me I had lied about a figure.

"What figure?" I asked.

"Your father's income. We have checked this figure with many other prisoners, and the figure you gave was a lie!" We were not getting any place, so he then raised the question he had asked me on one of the previous quizzes, "What do you think of Lyndon Johnson?"

"I support my country and I support my president, whoever he is." This matter of supporting the U.S. was a sore point with him.

He answered something like, "Oh, do you still support your president?"

"Yes," I answered.

THE ZOO, APRIL, 1968

"Get on your knees!" I did. "Hold your hands up!" I knelt for a period of time, and then he started firing questions at me. They were designed so that I would not have an answer for them.

He began to beat me in the face, across the upper part of my cheek, my ear, and eye with his open hand. He would ask a question and strike. This went on, I estimate, for two and a half hours. By the end of this time, he had bruised both of his hands so badly that he could not hit me any more.

He called a turnkey we named "Neat," who joined the fun and pounded me until *his* hands were too sore to continue. Then he brought in a third turnkey. He, too, pounded me for a substantial length of time.

They intended to break my eardrums, striking me open palmed across the ear. My left eardrum did break. It began to bleed. Some time during the beating, a blow on the temple knocked me completely unconscious. As I regained consciousness, I found they were beating me to "stop faking unconsciousness!" I was pounded unconscious a second time.

Dum-Dum continued to fire questions at me. "Do you still support your president? Do you still endorse the position of your country?"

I found myself getting so punchy, I could not answer even the simplest of questions. If he had asked me my name, I could not have answered or given him my serial number. My senses were too addled.

Sharp pains coursed through my face, neck and head. My knees ached as if nails had been driven into the joints. At the end of the beating, my left eye was closed completely. My mouth and jaw and the entire left side of my face were swollen. My right eye was a mere slit. I had to lean my head far back or lie down to see. I could not shift my eyes, look down at my feet, nor move my eyes to the side.

Before this beating, I had good vision, though I suffered from depth perception problems. After the bloody mess my eye had been following shootdown, my eye had returned to normal and looked normal before I went to the beating with Dum-Dum. After the pounding, I had new and continuous vision problems.

Finally, the day was over. I started back to the room, nearly fainting twice. It was 4:30 or 5:00, late for a quiz to terminate. My food and my roommates were waiting for me. I was so punchy that it was a full day before I could get my thoughts reconstructed enough to give them sensible answers about what had occurred, and how I had come to get this terrible beating.

Sawhill and Chauncey were kind friends, sympathetic, understanding, and terribly surprised to see me in this condition. It was pretty clear what had happened, but the question was why. I could not dredge up exactly what had triggered it. It was late the following day before I remembered the question about supporting Lyndon Johnson. They could tell from my appearance what my answer had been.

This was only part of the long-range harrassment program in a high-exploitation camp. The "V" were always after us because of good leadership in most of the buildings and in the camp in general, and because they were required to produce propaganda and indoctrination records for the "People." We held their gains to a minimum, and the "V" recognized that they were not getting the kind of propaganda they could if the conditions were more permissive. Guarino and the people who resisted were always in trouble and were punished in an effort to pound down the resistance.

Never at any time were the "V" completely successful, despite the heavy-handed torture they applied continually. To Larry Guarino's credit, they never pounded him out of his position as camp commander, no matter how much they tortured him. He had good reason many times to abdicate his position and say, "I just can't go it any more."

Even the toughest of Larry's fellow prisoners would have understood if Guarino had asked for a temporary respite from his torturers, but he never considered the idea of not doing his duty. By December 1969, Larry had completed his 390th day of heavy torture, and he looked it.

During the long hot summer of 1968, the Vietnamese military at the Zoo was headed by a Major called "Cochise," because he looked like an Indian. Most interrogators were named for their most prominent physical trait. Using this system, common names were developed for the same man by different camps with a high degree of frequency.

The Zoo acquired its name when Navy Commander Bill Franke observed the Vietnamese looking in at the Americans. He said, "This is obviously a zoo in reverse. There is no other place in the world where the animals look in at the people." The name stuck immediately.

Exploitation and mistreatment were continual during this time, and I hated to see our door open. I lived in constant fear of heavy torture for a war crimes confession, torture to see a delegation of visitors, such as Wilfred Burchett, David Dellinger, or Tom Hayden, who seemed to continually flow to Hanoi. The pressure was so high it was a relief to see your own poor beleaguered roommate go to quiz instead of you.

All three of us, and most of the others in the building, had diarrhea and bleeding dysentary. The "V" radio bleated that they had invented the double septic tank, but the story fell on deaf ears in the Barn. Only four feet from our wall in one direction, and about eight feet in another direction were *two* open toilets. Our rotten worm- and dysentary-infested urine and feces were cycled into the toilet, through the ground to the well, into our clothes, and onto our bodies, and then back into the waste bucket. Full circle. Little wonder that no one could shake the dysentary! What we

THE ZOO, APRIL, 1968

missed at the well was taken care of by the raft of rats that raced from the "septic tank" back to the room, and whose droppings littered the floor nightly.

The "V" were glad! We needed to suffer. Quizzes went hot and heavy. Dum-Dum left camp and was replaced by a deviate called Goldie, who was worse. Hate was so prevalent that we were getting rocks and broken glass regularly in the rice. Over the years, three of my teeth were broken off. Of course, dental care was nonexistent. What could one expect?

Some of the events of the summer of 1968 were the culmination of a series of downhill, and very demoralizing, steps for us. The Tet offensive of February had infused the Vietnamese with new vigor and hope. At the Plantation with John McCain during the offensive, I had the opportunity to observe camp activities in full and open view. There was no question that every enlisted man, every officer, and every Vietnamese was absolutely convinced that the end of the war was a matter of days away.

When the U.S. failed to respond to the invasion of the United States Embassy in Saigon with strong, retaliatory measures against the North, it only reinforced their belief that America was on the verge of defeat. It seemed to most of us that our country should increase pressure on the enemy, but instead, for cowardly political reasons, our president was backing off. The Vietnamese were positive of victory and that their cause was predestined for success. Their propaganda organs had them convinced that massive rioting against the war was commonplace in the United States.

During this period, we were deluged with negative news from home. Every anti-war statement made by any senator, congressman, beatnik or peacenik was played for us over and over again. We felt like we were drowning or choking in this morass of tangled half-truths, lies, distortions, and quotes.

It was disheartening at a quiz to have Senator Fulbright or some dingbat politician declaring himself on the enemy's side of the argument. Many a torture was accomplished just to force a POW to say or agree to the same things that were attributed to fellow Americans, senators and representatives.

It got to the point where the "V" did not have to write their own propaganda against the U.S. They could simply quote Senator Gruening from Alaska, Fulbright from Arkansas, Kennedy from Massachusetts, or a congressman of the same ilk.

I was sickened by these statements, for the U.S. Congress passed the Gulf of Tonkin resolution which sent me to Southeast Asia! Loyalty, I felt, was a two-way street. It's a bit disconcerting not to be able to tell the difference between the words of a U.S. Senator and those of your enemy! More devastating to our cause was the fact that the North Vietnamese thought these statements to be semi-official U.S. policy. When combined with propaganda, it stiffened the "V" backs immeasurably, adding significantly to the U.S. death list on the battlefield.

With the arrival of summer, our misery was overwhelming. The heat in our room was sweatbox temperature. We broke out in massive red rashes that covered our bodies. We were terribly sick, extremely thin, had large black rings under the eyes, and were 40 to 60 pounds underweight. The temperature stayed in the high 90s until after 9:00 p.m., our required bedtime.

Because depression was sweeping the camp, Guarino started a series of morale messages designed to raise spirits, and take our minds off our real problems. New communications links were opened. But the camp buildings were so widely spaced and visibility from building to building was so limited, that this policy was hard to support.

For example, my only link to the building next door was to have the men in Room Two push as hard as they could on their two doors to make a small crack through which they could see the "Office." For the Office to communicate to us through the crack, they had to have a man standing on someone else's shoulders. The top man would wave his fingers in a code through a four-by-four inch hole near the ceiling of their room.

To reply to them, we had to send code with a piece of paper slipped out and back from under the door. During these times of communication, almost every room in the camp had to be alert for guards who, of course, spent all the day trying to catch us doing these things.

The effect of Guarino's policy was good, as it generated some interesting news and speculation. It also killed a large part of the day by keeping us busy. Our communications effort was not unique. All of the buildings had the same general problem in going from one to the next, so Guarino achieved his desired goal. He did help morale, and he forced people to stay occupied.

The radio brought some additional demoralizing news. Hanoi Hannah told us that the second group of three pilots had been released early, amid great fanfare. Shortly after, tapes made by Americans, and attributed to these three, were played for us. The tapes, if true, were absolutely disgusting, evidencing a high degree of involvement in their own release, unacceptable to any decent man.

Sadly enough, all three releasees were Air Force officers; Majors Fred Thompson, James Lowe, and Captain Joe Carpenter. Incredibly, they came home to heroes' welcomes.

I felt I knew the voice of one of the parties involved. It was my personal conviction that the tape was made with his cooperation and assistance. In

THE ZOO, APRIL, 1968

the tape, he spoke of how he had made up his mind he was going to cooperate with the Vietnamese. He mentioned how we, other POWs, were probably wondering why he was being released after having been in camp only a few months. He happily announced that this was because he had obeyed the camp regulations.

The impact of these tapes and this release was terribly demoralizing. I was enraged and felt that if they were true, we had been sold out by fellow Americans. My immediate reaction was that when I returned to my country, I would find these men had been indicted for misconduct and would not be in positions of responsibility. I couldn't have been more wrong. Not one of them ever spent a day in jail, and none were disciplined by the U.S. Government.

About this same time, another series of disgusting tapes were played for us. These were attributed to a pair of senior POWs, Lieutenant Colonel Miller and Commander Wilber. The tapes condemned the war. We referred to one tape as the Bob and Ed show.

I quote from the *Des Moines Register* December 9, 1973 article by Nick Lamberto on ex-POW Marine Colonel Edison Miller. "Bob... became my roommate and an English-speaking political officer asked us if we would mind having our conversation taped at one of our first meetings."

Miller said, "We talked for an hour or more. It was in the fall of 1968 and we talked about the elections in America and who we thought would win and why. Both of us told about our captures, that we weren't bitter about it, but didn't like it . . . Several months later, unbeknown to us, parts of the tapes were played to other POWs. Some told me they didn't think there was anything harmful in them; some said they were harmful to their morale." Does Miller feel he got preferred treatment from his captors? "Yes, in the last year or so, yes."

When Miller said that "some" people felt it was harmful to their morale — I would comment that I did not talk to one POW about this tape who was not sickened with disgust by it. The article continues concerning another tape made by Miller. "Today, America's mothers must face the fact that their sons are killing fellow human beings and destroying foreign countries for an unjust cause, making our actions not only illegal, but immoral."

The message continued in the same vein, citing American militarism, escalation of the war, violations of international law, and abandonment of America's "basic ideals and traditions of humanitarianism and democracy," and the concept of the "rights of all men to life, liberty and the pursuit of happiness, based on freedom and equality." The message was picked up in Hong Kong and relayed to the United States by the Associated Press.

More from Miller. "Sometime in 1970, I came to believe that not only was the war wrong, but that it was my duty to speak out against it. I didn't kid myself and told others not to if they did not believe the same things sincerely. I made this decision with the distinct possibility in mind that I possibly could be courtmartialed." This was an illustration of what the "V" called "good attitude," and what they hoped to achieve more frequently.

Massive arguments raged among us over what punishment should be meted out to these cooperators. Some insisted they should be shot. Others believed in lengthy jail terms in the U.S. and others believed their knees would buckle at home and they would claim they had been tortured. Universally, their cowardly acts were despised and morale destroying.

Meanwhile, back at the Zoo, the torture and exploitation continued against the "bad attitude" cases. As the summer progressed, there were more propaganda exploitation attempts and two of my people were played against each other. Both of them were early shootdowns, from 1965. The tactics employed against them were to threaten to torture one of them if the other didn't cooperate. Then the "V" would torture the opposite person.

The "V" political department would pass the word, "Okay, interrogators, we want new propaganda. Here is the program. We want a whole barrage of tapes, letters, and statements from the POWs, expressing the determination of the Vietnamese people to continue fighting."

The next time, it would be, "We want a series of tapes and letters where the POWs condemn the illegality of the war and complain about the breach of the Geneva Convention by the United States." The propaganda thrusts would be developed by the Party and the interrogator would enforce them.

The "V" considered POWs as chattels to be exploited to help support their war effort at home, and to hurt the U.S. military war effort. They also wanted to sap the will of the people in the U.S. Additionally, POWs were tortured to meet pro-Commie and anti-U.S. people and delegations. The POW's job was to frustrate them.

In the instance of my old shootdowns, the "V" did not torture them in their room, or in front of each other. They took them individually to the theater for a quiz. They would tell the man, "If you don't give us this, we are going to torture your roommate."

He would refuse.

The "V" would then call the roommate and torture him. I was very proud of the outstanding resistance efforts of both men. They made me glad to be an American. I was so impressed with their courage, I recommended both for one of our nation's highest awards for gallantry. Their names? Bob Lilly and Dick Bolstad. Bob was a helicopter pilot shot down trying to rescue Bolstad, an F-105 pilot.

With the approach of the election in the fall of 1968, an interesting situation began to build. The Vietnamese inundated us with news about the coming election. There was no doubt in their mind that they had deposed Lyndon Johnson. They thought they had won the war on the streets of Washington, New York, and San Francisco.

This grain of sand on the beach of the world made up its mind that it could control American policy by actions with the "peace groups" in the United States. Hanoi was convinced that the kind of Communist sympathizer groups that came to visit, and those who represented the U.S. anti-administration elements were having a greater impact than they were. The "V" took encouragement from the dissention in the U.S. and visiting American delegations, and grossly misjudged the situation.

They thought they could interfere in a U.S. election at any time and influence the outcome, without the faintest problem. This was evident from what they said at quizzes.

Interrogators got into expansive moods, boasting of the indestructible strength of the Vietnamese people and claiming, "We forced Lyndon Johnson not to be a candidate." One Vietnamese tape claimed, "We chased Lyndon Johnson out of the White House."

Although we felt this was a misrepresentation, I discovered years later that there was some truth in it. At the time, they had so turned me off with their volumes of lies, I no longer believed anything they said, including the truth.

Frankly, and secretly, I hoped they *had* driven Lyndon out, for I considered him unqualified to be President of the United States of America. Because I was a resident of Austin, Texas, for three years, I knew of his FCC manipulations which kept Lyndon and Ladybird the sole television licensees of Austin. We had come from a city of 85,000 which had three television stations and I was first amazed, and then outraged. Austin was a city of 250,000 with a single monopoly station!

My first Texas landlord described Lyndon cryptically. "Crookeder than a barrel of snakes." Prior to the 1964 election, a friend mailed me a copy of Haley's book, *A Texan Looks At Lyndon Johnson.* It detailed how Lyndon stole his 1948 election to the U.S. Senate — and acquired the nickname "Landslide Lyndon." He was implicated in the burning of the county courthouse wherein the critical ballots lay that would have disqualified him from office.

That he proudly wore a Silver Star for riding as a passenger on an aborted bomber mission was part of the facade. Friendly association with such contemporaries as Billy Sol Estes, Bobby Baker, and Walter Jenkins was natural, as these were unusually qualified men to assist in his manipulation of a 25-35 million dollar fortune from the public largess.

Unlike Richard Nixon, who was to find the going rough with Congress on the coverup of his derelictions, Lyndon found old Senator Sam Irvin and the Democratic committees not only willing, but able, to cover up the Bobby Baker stink.

Lyndon was probably the worst wartime president in the long history of this country. LBJ liked the Vietnam War when it appeared that the U.S. and South Vietnam were going to win. It fit his Silver Star image.

Unlike Truman's "The buck stops here," Lyndon lacked the guts to either bomb the Commies into submission, which was the correct solution, or the courage to bail out. As a result, every death after his bombing halt of 1968 has to be laid squarely at his feet. If he had pursued the military solution which he never understood, he could have brought the war to a halt at that time.

The reason I belabor the point is that we failed to learn the lessons of the "20-years war" when we went into the indecisive Korean War. We failed to recognize the bankruptcy of France's long wars of attrition in Algeria and Vietnam. Then we fought the same kind of war in Vietnam. It is totally mindboggling to we who fought that many Americans still do not understand why we took Second Place in the Great Southeast Asia War Games of 1960-1973.

The *Mayuguez* incident is a perfect case in point. We were set upon by a pissant. We stomped it with our foot in a matter of hours. The identical result could have been achieved in North Vietnam in any seven-day period.

The U.S. did not militarily lose the war. We gave it away by failing to execute a winning strategy. It also must be said that the Communist-oriented U.S. press did yeoman service in helping us give it away.

It was interesting to observe the "V" that fall of 1968. They played only pro-Democratic news and the Democratic planks of the platform, describing fully their plans for ransom if Democrats were elected. There was never any mention of Republican Richard Nixon's policies. The Vietnamese had always referred to the war as Lyndon Johnson's war, never an American war. They had high hopes that American policy in Vietnam would take a 180° turn in direction with the election of Hubert Humphrey.

With Humphrey's election, the "V" were confident that the U.S. would bail out of the war. They obviously endorsed Humphrey and I am confident that every Communist in North Vietnam would have voted for him, given the opportunity to do so.

In the fall of 1968, we were curious about the political tendencies of the POWs on election matters. We suggested that the senior ranking officer (SRO) of each building offer people the chance to participate in mock elections. The results were interesting. In the Barn, which had 18 people,

THE ZOO, APRIL, 1968

17 votes were cast for Richard Nixon, with one abstention. In the Garage, the vote was 16 of 18 people for President Nixon, one abstention, and one write-in vote for Barry Goldwater.

Our participation in Nixon's silent majority was the most silent of all, but it was generally indicative of the overall POW mood. We were disgusted with the "no-win" policy.

The U.S. Government and the State Department continually talked about the "political war." Not so! There was only a military problem, the aggression by and from North Vietnam. The question was, *would* we beat these Communists, not *could* we.

I was sick of continually optimistic statements by a naive people who were all theory and no practicum. I was tired of hearing about light at the end of the tunnel. One POW wag suggested that the light at the end of the tunnel "was a train coming at us."

After a couple of years waiting on the "light," another wag suggested that probably the tunnel had a cave-in!

We could not understand our country's lack of direction. The indecisiveness only encouraged the "V" to greater efforts. The timid bombing policies, the piece-meal attacks, the misuse of U.S. air power, only resulted in squandering the lives of pilots, destruction of high-priced aircraft, and the waste of young American blood on the battlefields of Vietnam.

It seems impossible to communicate to a certain section of so-called "intellectuals," the fact that you can never deal or bargain with a Communist except from a position of maximum strength. There is no other way! Berlin, Cuba, Korea, and Vietnam are all living testaments to this simple fact.

One of my troops made a prediction about the election. He stated flatly, "On the Friday before elections, Lyndon Johnson will stop the bombing, so that it will make the Friday night, Saturday and Sunday papers before the Tuesday election in November."

I was so infuriated and incensed by this comment, I could scarcely bring myself to discuss it. I was absolutely positive in my own mind that the U.S. Congress, the POW families, and the electorate would never be taken in by such a crude trick for the simple purpose of appearing to be at peace during the coming presidential election.

On the morning of Saturday, October 30, 1968, I was in the bath area pouring wormy water over myself, along with Bob Sawhill and Arvin Chauncey. It was 9:00 o'clock in the morning. This *was* the Saturday morning before election, I emphasize!

We suddenly heard a hue and cry, a roar of human voices emanating from the other end of the camp. It was exactly the same sound I heard during WW II when, at Johnson Island on May 7, 1945, we heard of the defeat of the Germans over the radio. I knew that sound positively and absolutely.

I turned to Sawhill and Chauncey and said, "The Vietnamese have just got the word that we halted the bombing. The bombing has ended!" They both looked at me with disbelief, downcast and disgusted. We shook our heads in dismay and went back to our room to await the news. A few hours later, the radio triumphantly claimed that Lyndon Johnson had unconditionally halted the bombing. We had been sold down the river for a few "Xs" at the ballot box.

The only lever left to pry us out of prison had been given away. I couldn't believe that release of POWs would not be a precondition of the bombing halt. The U.S. had stopped bombing, and the "V" still had several hundred American prisoners of war. I refused to believe that there had been no *quid pro quo*, and refused to believe the radio. For weeks I insisted in vain that some provision had been made for exchange of sick and wounded, or at the very least, a token removal of the most desperately ill.

I also knew that my former roommate, Norris Overly, had been debriefed by *my* government. I *knew* that my government *knew* from first-hand, on-the-scene reporting, how at least *one* American had been tortured. It stretched my credulity past the breaking point to believe that Lyndon Johnson did not know of our treatment as prisoners.

Nothing in my career as a prisoner affected me as profoundly as this breach of faith with us. It had been done by the same mentality that insisted the United States keep the POW matter "low key." This action had to be one of the lowest points in U.S. history, matched only by the *"Pueblo* incident" apology and the later sellout of South Vietnam in 1975.

CHAPTER ELEVEN

The Zoo, December 1968

During the period before Christmas, the Vietnamese gave us new numbers. Since they called us criminals, they painted "criminal numbers" (TU-251, etc.) on our clothing. Many small steps were taken that indicated they expected an imminent release after Johnson surrendered.

The "V" called in sick POWs preceding an "eyewash" medical examination, and made frequent notations in their records to make it appear that we had been getting medical treatment. It was pure fakery, designed to create a better image of what they had been doing for the prisoners if a release were effected.

There was a little easing of pressure on us in the late fall. It was clear that they were trying to mend their fences with the POWs, yet stay in full control in case something fell apart. They were talking about POW ransoms and no release of prisoners until America surrendered completely and unequivocably.

I quote from a news clipping, "HANOI MAY ASK RANSOM." New York, (UPI) "A Vietnamese-born correspondent for a Canadian newspaper said yesterday North Vietnamese representatives told him that Hanoi will demand six billion dollars ransom for the release of U.S. war prisoners . . . According to Ky, once hostilities cease, Hanoi would release those U.S. war prisoners who express 'repentance.' Other U.S. prisoners would not be released without Washington's payment of $15,000 to each of the 400,000 North Vietnamese war victims, Hanoi representatives told Ky."

America would ransom POWs! This was so arrogant that it was insane. Nevertheless, Hanoi believed the U.S. had surrendered.

During this period, one of my troops decided to try to make some sense out of our new numbers. He had recorded all of our numbers on a cigarette package with the handle of a spoon, using the metal as a pen. Unfortunately, in a weekly room inspection by the "V," this item was picked up and it indicated the "crime" of communication. He was dragged out and tortured.

He was forced to reveal a number of things about building policies. Being a bright, loyal man, he did the best he could, but he had been getting tortured for more than three years and was forced to say some things. He used his head, and only told them innocuous items.

Some of my policies, as he related them, were to ask for more blankets, to ask for better food, to ask for good clothing, to wash the dishes well, and to keep your health and not catch cold. These things any grown-up American would know anyway. When he came back from getting tortured, he was returned to his room fortunately, and was able to pass this info to me through the wall. Because of this, I was taken to quiz on December 5, 1968.

Later, he solved the number question. Arvin Chauncey realized they had taken the month you enlisted, or that they had on their records of your initial entrance in the service. If you were enlisted in January, your first numeral would be one. Then, if you enlisted in 1952, your number would be 152. This was a strange system, since every man who came in the service in July, 1953, for example, had 753 as his number.

Using Vietnamese logic, this was reasonable. When the "V" captured this cigarette package, the accumulation of knowledge for us or for them didn't mean anything, except that it revealed the fact that we were communicating, which they knew anyway.

The interrogator I was to see on December 5 was a young homosexual called "Goldie" because of his gold-capped teeth. He was so queer, it was a surprise that he did not show up in a dress. He had cute, mincing, flip-flopping hands. All he needed was a purse and a pair of high heels. He did an inordinate amount of hanging over his fellow Vietnamese. There could be no mistake about his tendencies.

The trait is not unexpected. The Communist doctrine in Vietnam discouraged young marriages. The orientals are trying to make big inroads into the high birth rate. So they recommend, first of all, don't go with girls! If you do go with girls, don't fall in love. If you fall in love, don't get married. If you do get married, don't have children!

When you take that as the natural foundation of social exchange between young people, it is inhibitive. In addition, every male capable of carrying a gun was in the army, leading from natural boy-girl relationships into an all-male environment.

I was taken to the quiz with Goldie at gunpoint. He had been trained by Dum-Dum in the "shout-accuse" technique. He quickly enunciated the "I-will-torture-you-immediately-if-you-resist" approach.

Goldie told me he had caught one of my people with a list of numbers and he knew that I had been communicating. He said he had a confession of this dark scheme. "What do you have to say about that? I know you are acting SRO and that is against camp policies. Nobody is in charge except the Vietnamese! You have broken camp regulations. I have the confession." He waved a paper around in his hand. This was a typical tactic. I was never permitted to see the paper and I did not believe it was a confession, just part of the props.

"You must confess your black crimes against the camp. You must tell all! You must apologize for breaking camp regulations."

"I haven't broken any camp regulations. My actions are within the Code of Conduct and in keeping with the general principles of international law and the Geneva Convention. I have no apologies to make and I have no statements to make, or any confession, or any admission of doing anything wrong."

He dispensed quickly with the small talk and sent me to Auditorium One, a torture room; one of four in the building. It was about three feet wide by seven feet long.

I was forced onto my knees right away. Goldie demanded that I confess all, since he had the whole story. His demands escalated throughout the torture, but the general thrust was "How do you communicate?"

It was no secret how we communicated. The "V" had tortured a few hundred people, thousands of times to get that information. They knew that we communicated through the walls. They knew that we tapped from cell to cell, that we talked through the wall using our cups, or rolled our clothing into horse collars to muffle our voices. They knew we passed notes, and that we coded in every manner possible. They knew the tap code at least as well as some inept prisoners, but could not translate fast enough to understand.

I knew, and they knew, that they were torturing for something that they had accumulated several hundred times before. Every camp in the system had been totally purged for "comm" many times. But, the torture was recurrent. At least 50% of the POW torture was for communication with each other.

I remained on my knees throughout the morning, afternoon, and evening. Normally there was a break for siesta. You would get off your knees to eat your meals.

Kneeling was probably the most painful and insidious long-term torture that could be applied. The sensitive human knee, when in contact with rough, bare concrete for a long period of time, generates great pain. The best comparison is that of driving a long nail under the kneecap. In addition to this pain was the pain of holding myself rigidly upright with my hands in the air. If you have any doubt about this, try kneeling on a broomstick with your hands in the air for fifteen or twenty minutes.

Goldie had not been in the torture business very long. After he put me in the auditorium on my knees, he came by every 15 minutes or so to ask if I were ready to write yet. I had already been tortured this way 20 or 30 times. While it was painful, I found it amusing to see him coming around at such short intervals. He had misjudged how easy it would be to make any mileage out of me, and I felt pleased with that.

Goldie harassed me. The guards beat me and struck me with the rifle butt if I let my arms fall. I got off my knees at every opportunity. I tried to be alert to where the guard was and return to my knees before he caught me. Since the door of the cell was louvered, I had a little visibility and was usually successful.

Goldie and I progressed through the normal series of questions on communications, and I refused to answer. I was on my knees from 7:00 in the morning until 11:30, when they let me up for lunch. Then I went back on my knees until about 6:00 or 7:00 in the evening, when I was allowed to lie down. This went on for two days.

I recalled clearly the admissions my pilot had made and the ground he had covered. I knew that if I could hold out long enough, I would probably not have to describe anything new. They would be happy to have me confirm the lies he had told them.

One of his most absurd lies was a winner. He told Goldie, "The only time we communicate is in the middle of the night."

What made this so amusing was that afterwards, I noticed the "V" posted an English-speaking night guard. It was his duty to sneak around and listen outside of buildings and catch people communicating. Since we never communicated at that time, this was sleep loss for them. Unless there was an emergency of some sort, we only communicated when the Vietnamese were away during lunch hour.

Goldie continued to press me. This was his first big chance to demonstrate what he could do to an "air pirate." He was irritated that I did not fold up immediately. After the second day, he kept me on my knees from morning until bedtime, holding frequent quizzes in the room.

He concentrated on pointless information. I was to confess that I was the SRO, and that I had put out policies. He was not looking for information. He wanted to grind me down and humiliate me into saying something I didn't want to say. One of the hard rings of the Malebolge.

Once more, I faced the problem of trying to keep my mind off what was happening to my body. One technique I used was to review my past from young boyhood, to assess the plusses and minuses, to build a better foundation to reach my children. I wanted to help them avoid those areas which had brought me to grief. I hoped that I could use my own experience more meaningfully with my children, and get them pointed in a better direction. I retraced my life from childhood through adulthood, remembering all the significant events, reconstructing them, visualizing how to

THE ZOO, DECEMBER, 1968

profit from them.

I had been born and raised on the banks of the Sioux River at Sioux City, Iowa. The Great Depression hit as I reached my fifth birthday and was ready to enter school. My father had been a laborer and his small savings were wiped out in the bank failure. As I grew up, I didn't understand why my family was so poor. I didn't understand why my father did not have a job. The social standards of my neighborhood held contempt for anyone who didn't work. There was no such thing as unemployment insurance or food stamps.

My dad was 56 when I was born, and there are some who think that is unusual. He was over 60 when the depression was in full swing in 1931, with no marketable skills, and without education. Fortunately, he was a good gardener and a hard worker. He sustained his family by smalltime farming during the summer, and cutting wood all winter. Mother canned food to carry us through winter and spring.

Since many were unemployed in those days, people traded what they had for what they needed. Slaughtered meat was traded for home canned tomatoes or peaches, coal, wood, or services. Many bills were paid this way. Doctor bills and other services were paid by exchange because no one had any money. Failing to understand all this, I was ashamed that my family did not have money and had to barter and accept occasional gifts of rice or beans that the federal government donated.

My parents' limitations were those of the poor and ignorant, but they were rich in decency, good conduct, good citizenship, and they were good parents. It was only after several of these long-term thinking sessions that I fully realized what a rock my father had been. He knew no limitations. If a building needed erection, he raised it. If a field needed cultivation, he took a fork and turned the ground. He could do anything he put his mind to. Possessing a bull-headed determination, he was the type who achieved any goal he set for himself. I was discovering this same hard headedness amplified in my own personality.

As a youngster, I had a great deal of freedom which parents would consider too dangerous today. The value of this was in the things I learned about the real world. At about the age of ten, I started caddying at a local golf course. I came into contact with a number of businessmen, some successful. I observed these people and noticed the differences between them and the laborers from my neighborhood.

The common denominator between these people and my parents was education, which my parents spoke of incessantly. I developed a strong desire to improve my social status and a burning desire to stop being poor, hungry, and cold.

Frustrated at the lack of immediate progress, I became rebellious. I could not understand why education was necessary. As I read the Horatio Alger series, the story-book characters succeeded without education, on pure grit, and did it promptly. I knew from tests I had taken in school that I was intelligent. I was an avid reader, reading at a college level by sixth grade.

I read and studied the Revolutionary War in the children's books and had a deep feeling about why America was what it was. I was convinced that the United States had the best political system in existence and that I had every reason to be optimistic about my future.

I read the daily newspaper as well as every book or magazine I could find. Every month my city policemen would pick up the magazines that lay around the station and bring them to a retired policeman who lived near me. These were both numerous and varied, every magazine known to man: *Doc Savage*; *G-8 and his Battle Aces*; *True Detective*; *Real Detective*; *Wild West*; etc. The old policeman was bedridden and did nothing but read. He passed the magazines on to me, so I always had a two-foot pile on hand. I was probably more knowledgeable on current affairs than the average citizen when I was a boy, and the effect of my reading on my future was very strong.

Because of my freedom and my discontent, I became headstrong and rebellious. In my senior year of high school, I met another youngster named James Brodie who was of almost identical bent. We became fast friends, imaginative and undisciplined. We were frequently in trouble with the school authorities for not attending class and other minor infractions.

James and I talked about the concepts of Christianity, sitting on the river bank fishing, and discussed our impressions of God. We agreed there was a Supreme Being, logically required to put the world into order. Because of our concept of government, we decided that atheistic and agnostic philosophies didn't suit us.

We saw America as being conceived in godliness and the idea of not having a God in this country was illogical. James and I had great unanimity of thought, and when we did not think alike, it seemed as if our ideas were mutually acceptable. Our continual exchange of ideas firmly set my religious views into concrete.

The Second World War began for the United States in December of 1941, and in a burst of patriotic fervor, I enlisted as soon as possible. Early in 1942 the services began drafting 18-year-olds. The notion of being drafted was repulsive, for I believed fiercely that it was every citizen's duty to don his country's armor voluntarily and without delay. I found myself a high school drop-out, proudly wearing the forest green of the United States Marine Corps.

The Leathernecks quickly made it clear why one should have an education. No officer candidate school, no pilot training, no college commissioning program, and no technical schools for high-school dropouts. A dropout was qualified to carry a rifle or drive a truck.

Slowly and imperceptibly, experience began to teach me what my parents had tried to tell me about the value of an education. This lesson, well taught, motivated me to obtain my high-school diploma while in the Marines. An immediate assignment to the South Pacific, lasting 30 months, placed officer training as far out of sight as Mars, but deprivation sometimes accelerates desire. My desire for a commission burned brightly.

My thoughts leap-frogged from subject to subject during the breaks between Goldie's visits, in spite of my concentrated attempts to maintain a chronological chain. When the hours hailed stones of pain, gloom, and despair, thoughts of Viking brought brief moments of pleasantness that transcended the pain in my knees and transported me from the miserable squalor of my trial.

Goldie came and went, demon-like, voicing garbled menacing threats of "severely punishment," decrying "bad attitude," or cursing me as a "hardhead." Promise of good treatment for cooperation was alternated with shouted threats of a "trial" by the people.

"How many pressures and tortures are there?" some silent insane voice asked rhetorically.

"Well, there are solitary, kneeling, beating, whipping, roping, hanging, starvation, lack of communication, screw-down manacles, stocks, irons, indoctrination, heat, cold, fear, concern for a family not heard from for two years, lies of a ruthless enemy, lies of the traitors who visit and speak well of the enemy, guilty thoughts from the past, both real and imagined, uncertainty of the sentence... whether two years, or five, or even ten, fear of a wasted past and the futureless present, loss of a career, life as a cripple, fear of becoming a mental vegetable, disease... but worst of all, the fear of being disgraced by cooperation with the enemy. This only highlights the most apparent fears, dumb-bell. Any more questions?"

My will was beginning to weaken before the dull scrapings of the knife of torture. Each day was more gloomy, oppressive, and difficult than the one before.

My mind clung vise-like to the belief that I could not answer questions about my fellow officers, about making propaganda, and about writing for the "V", even innocuous trash. Deep inside me, the foolish hope still smouldered that if my resolve were firm, I could win.

Persistence ebbed like the receding sunset. Dreadful illusions of the effect of bending to Goldie's will showered my numb thoughts with visions of disgrace, banishment to that never-never land of America's infamous, and raised clouds of guilt. Guilt in the future and guilt in the past.

I tuned in to a past flight to Luke AFB in Glendale, Arizona, and thought about Happy Hour. I tried to count how many Happy Hours I had missed so far. I thought about the great pizza parlors just south of Homestead Air Force Base, Florida. I wondered how many visitors from Niagara were at Homestead shooting gunnery in the balmy Florida sun instead of squatting on the freezing, wind-blown parking ramp at Niagara Falls Airport, NY.

Were Jim Cook, John Blewett, B.G., Deke, Sid, and the Thunderbird Squadron pilots from Niagara eating a pizza right now? Could the chianti be as icy cold? Could I taste it right that moment? Yes! It's souring pungency stirred my salivary glands.

Jesus, God, Lord, my knees and feet hurt! "Will there ever be another day, another year, another century when my knees do not hurt?"

Back in the real world, the 136th Tactical Fighter Squadron from Niagara Falls was not at Homestead eating pizza. They were at Tuy Hoa, South Vietnam shooting Communists and getting shot at by Communists. Three of my dear friends and former flying mates had made the supreme sacrifice, for their honor and their country.

I remembered gunnery practice at Camp Drum near Watertown, New York. A tent with the Viking and four children in the gorgeous, fresh-smelling pine forest south of the Thousand Islands of the St. Lawrence. Fresh frying bacon, cooked by my 11-year-old, towheaded Steve. The odors drilled into my brain. A cold night in the tent with the Viking. That other world. How sweet it was!

I began to understand that the torture and pressure were clouding my thinking processes. A cloud of dismay penetrated every pore and the end appeared close. My knees swelled and ached, muscles pained. The rough concrete sandpapered my knees and toes into ugly raw meat. Infection and death lurked in the wings. Medical care? "No medical care for bad attitude. Bad attitudes must suffer!"

"When will the animals terminate this charade?" My brain questioned.

I grew to hate Goldie so violently that the very sight of him would throw me into paroxysms of anger. I thought with pleasure of smashing his perverted skull through the brick wall. The deep, bitter well of hatred for him and his program of abuse began to overwhelm me.

He would ask, "How do you think now, Nigh?"

I wished that I could react as grossly as the torture warranted. The only thing appropriate would have been to vomit into his sneering mouthful of gold teeth.

As soon as Goldie left the room, I would get off my battered knees and try to get a moment of relief. It was time to retune. "Come on, mind!" My subconscious cried, "Get out of the Inferno. Even Purgatory would be an

THE ZOO, DECEMBER, 1968

improvement."

I intended to stop short of completely losing control, and the thought of stopping filled me with a bitter, all-consuming sense of shame and failure.

About the twelfth or thirteenth day, I told Goldie that I would answer some questions.

I began with admissions in the same framework that my pilot had outlined. On the thirteenth day, Goldie wanted me to write the answers, which I agreed to do, stalling and dawdling. On the fourteenth day, he wanted me to write an apology and I told him I would not. This brought on an unusually brutal session.

I was smashed with a rifle butt, kicked in the back, side, and ribs, and pounded in the face with fists and slaps. Goldie kept a guard in the room continually, and every time my arms faltered in the kneeling posture, he stepped on my feet and jerked my head back by the ears, with a knee in my back. It was impossible to keep from faltering. Muscles shook and jerked spastically. Sweat streamed from every pore. I had never feared for my life more than during that day.

Because I would not write what he wanted, Goldie brought a statement which he had written for my signature. It was a masterpiece, superbly done. It went like this:

"It is my understanding that the DRV gives lenient treatment to captured American air pirates. Therefore, I request this lenient treatment." If they *give* lenient treatment, why would one have to ask for it? "In response to your generosity, (yuk-yuk) I agree to do those things to me by the camp with the best of mine." He was trying to say, "with the best of mind," meaning willingly. I could scarcely believe my good fortune. If I had been trying to botch up a statement, I could not have equalled this beauty!

That evening he came by and insisted that I put it on a tape. I refused. He hoped to discredit me with my pilots, whom I had ordered not to make tapes. As the resulting torture began, I had to admit to myself that I could not stand any more. I then agreed to make the tape, which I botched as well as I could. When I went back to my cell, I was permitted to get off my knees at 9:00 p.m. Score: "V" - One; POWs - Zero!

It was a day full of good deals! On the morning of the fifteenth day, Goldie came by and said, "Now you will make a statement for the Voice of Vietnam. You will make a tape for the Voice of Vietnam about the determination of the Vietnamese people to fight and win."

I replied determinedly, "No, I won't. I refuse!"

Goldie promised, "I will punish you if you don't make a tape."

I said, "I refuse! I'm not making any tapes for the Voice of Vietnam!"

He sneered, "We will see!" and walked out. I could see what was coming.

It was a typical case of exploiting for more and more and more.

I had to do something drastic enough to stop this torture before it cost me my self-respect. The things I had done up to this point had not been of any significance except to me. What he wanted now was outright traitorous.

I had heard several anti-war tapes by Americans on the "V" radio whining that "Americans must face the fact that their sons are killing human beings in an unjust war." I considered statements of this kind treasonous and helpful to the enemy, and felt as my POW friends felt. I would never do it without torture to death. Most POWs speculated that these tapes were byproducts of torture; however, I learned that we had a couple of turncoats who ginned out this kind of trash with great eagerness.

I had to try to head Goldie off. I searched desperately for a solution. I had a problem with a suspected kidney stone years before, and I knew the symptoms. That had to be the answer! About 11:00 o'clock that night, I began to "Bao Cao" and shout for the guards, deciding to fake a kidney stone attack.

The guard appeared, angry as usual. I told him I needed to talk to an English speaker. Fairly soon, Goldie looked in and asked me what the problem was. I was sitting on the bucket that served as a toilet.

"Stand up and bow!"

I replied, "I have an unbelievable pain in my back and my hip. I can't stand it! I'm dying! I have to see the doctor!"

Goldie said, suspiciously, "Describe your symptoms."

I gave him all the symptoms of a kidney stone. "I can't urinate. I have a terrible pain." I gave him all the related symptoms again.

"Stand up!"

"I can't!"

Goldie ordered the guard to beat me, but I covered my head and I refused to move. I convinced him that I really was ill. After he left, I sat on the bucket all night, continuing to relieve myself as frequently as possible. Two or three times during the night, I "bao caoed" and demanded medicine. This made them furious, but it was apparent that Goldie was concerned. I insisted that I was dying! I writhed, sweated, and faked.

At about 6:45 in the morning, Novacaine, one of the camp medics, came into my cell. He waved me toward my bare plank bed. I got off the bucket and lay down. He gave me a light rap on the kidney where I complained of pain. I sprang off the bed and ham acted out some "super" pain.

Novacaine smiled knowingly at Goldie and I was sure that I had passed the first test. Perhaps 45 minutes later, old Doctor Zorba, who had done the great job of putting my wrist on at a 15 degree angle, appeared on the scene. Novacaine explained to him what my problem was.

Through an English speaker, I told him, "I can't urinate, and it hurts!"

THE ZOO, DECEMBER, 1968

Zorba had me lie down, and he tapped me on the kidney. Again, I put myself straight into orbit, frightening them as I thrashed around. I returned to the bucket, sat down, and refused to do anything else.

Apparently my act convinced Zorba that I did have a kidney problem. He sent the medic for a plastic tube which they ran into my bladder and drained off some urine. I complained bitterly and writhed about like a garter snake on hot concrete.

Zorba asked me to lie down on the bed. I watched with horror as he got out a large syringe with a long needle and poised it over my hips. He drove the shot into the kidney from the back side above the hip. This was both frightening and painful. I didn't know whether or not he knew what he was doing. If it was the technique he applied to my arm, I was a dead man!

I didn't have a choice. It was a gamble I had to take. I had never spoken or written against my country and I was positive that since they had me so ground down, if I didn't stop them now, they would get me for a war crime confession or some self-destroying propaganda. The choice to gamble with death was better than disgrace and dishonor.

Zorba picked up his bag and walked out the door. As they left, I returned to the bucket. I stayed there the entire day. The door's peep hole was stealthily opened quite often. The "V" had agreed to have the guard check regularly. Each time, I was sitting on the bucket. I assume he carried his observations to the medic. My seat on the putrid, stinking bucket would have nauseated a greenheaded garbage fly. It was delightful compared to kneeling.

They did not put me on my knees again. That evening, much to my surprise, a bowl of noodles with some chopped duck showed up for dinner. This was the first tasty food I had since arriving in Hanoi. I was on the sick list! I should have had an Oscar for the performance. Surprisingly there were no after-effects from the shot. I slept like a dead man.

The door opened early the following morning and Goldie told me to roll up what gear I had and go back to my cell. The reason for my pardon was the holiday season. It seemed that the "V" were just brimming with holiday cheer and good will. It was fantastic how a Communist could grow to love Christmas when it beat losing face.

My knees were lumps, although the holes did not show the bone, as they would in the future. I couldn't repress a slight feeling of satsifaction. It had been a loss, but it could have been much worse.

It was unusual for the doctor to interfere with torture. Ordinarily, the torturer had complete freedom to maximize the pain with a firm guarantee that it wouldn't be interrupted for any humane reasons. I have no knowledge of this happening at any other time. To the contrary, I know of numerous times that the torture was intensified against a sick prisoner.

Despite my concern over the drug pumped into my kidney, there were no after-effects. In fact, it may have arrested the almost certain infection in my knees. Apparently, it was real medicine.

We had grown accustomed to the Vietnamese Dr. Jekyll-Mr. Hyde routine, but at Christmas it was worse. When they pretended to be human, their conduct was grotesque. The beginning of the Christmas charade was taking us from our rooms and leading us by a pathetic Christmas tree decorated with toilet paper cutouts.

The "V" stood awkwardly smiling, grimaces that accentuated the stiffness of our relationship. The bulletin board was filled with propaganda letters either forced from a reluctant prisoner, or self-produced by a "V" trying to pass himself off as American. Their thrust was not comfort and cheer, but to accentuate our longing for home and family. It was rare for anyone to be tortured at Christmas or over Tet, the Vietnamese New Year. They were opposed to working at this time.

By Christmas of 1968, we were still unsure of who was sitting in the Oval Office. Oblique references on the radio later told us Spiro Agnew was vice president. We speculated about the prospects of negotiations in Paris. Johnson's bombing halt had made a more difficult bargaining position for the new chief executive.

The year ended on a more cheerful note when I was taken to an exhibit which Arv Chauncey read aloud to me, since my vision was too poor to read it. It was titled *My Nicest Christmas.*

"I was stationed at Goose Bay, Labrador in 1964, and I took a dogsled down to the airport to go home to the States for Christmas. I got on a plane, and the stewardess was so nice to me. I wanted to give her a gift to show her how much I appreciated her help. So, I gave her a big goose. When I got to Dallas my grandmother was there, so I gave her a real big goose. Grandpa didn't want a goose, but my wife sure did enjoy hers. I borrowed an old car, a 1963 Fleetwood, from my father-in-law and took the wife to a little hotel, the Dallas Hilton. The wife and I had to get something straightened out between us. Next morning I went shopping for Christmas presents, and stopped at the bar for my favorite drink, a Texas Tornado, which is one shot of bourbon, rum, gin and scotch, three ounces of grain alcohol, a shot of creme de menthe, and two ounces of Vodka. It was so good, I drank five or six of them. I went to the store looking for some balls for my boys. When I was a kid, I had a set of brass balls and I used to play with them often. However, I don't have them any more, for some reason I lost them. I also looked for a saddle because my wife likes to mount up in the morning. However, they didn't have one."

This masterpiece had undoubtedly been tortured from the author and was a beautiful case of "doing it bad," one of the best I had seen. Detection

THE ZOO, DECEMBER, 1968

would have brought on heavy torture. It took tremendous self-control to avoid breaking into laughter at this work of art, since it was read aloud by Chauncey in Goldie's presence.

It was a dull spring, punctuated by the same harrassment and oppression. On the morning of May 11, 1969, we learned of an escape attempt by Ed Atterbury and John Dramesi. They had been led back into the camp early that morning, in blindfolds, amidst great fanfare. They had been forced to run in front of the headquarters building toward the Chicken Coop. They had gone over the fence the night before and been recaptured a short distance from the camp.

Escaping was a "crime" of monstrous proportions to the "V." Much of my own abuse was because of my past escape. These two men had escaped from the most populous of camps by going out of the roof of one of their large nine-man rooms. With some assistance from their roommates, they had gone up through the roof of the building, then over the wall, and out into the rice paddies, where they had been recaptured.

The escape was bold and imaginative, and they did leave the camp. But any chance of success in departing Hanoi was low. The primary motivation of this "OTF" (Over the Fence) was our feeling that it was necessary to get the word back to our country of the full extent of our misery.

We knew that the six early releases did not have an understanding of our treatment. None of them had been tortured. Therefore, they were not qualified or knowledgeable to speak about the POW dilemma. We wanted to get our story out to the American people to generate some interest in bringing the war to a halt by bombing North Vietnam into submission. We wanted to secure the release of POWs and bring the war to an honorable end. We thought that if an escape could be successful, word of mistreatment straight from a POW's mouth would improve future treatment here and get America fully behind her abused prisoners.

We were aware of a continual flow of Communist camp followers, David Dellinger, A.J. Muste, Tom Hayden, Wilfred Burchett, etc., coming to Hanoi from America. They returned with fabricated tales of our good treatment and living conditions. The price of a foreigner's ticket into North Vietnam was to depart saying laudatory things about Communists or bad things about the U.S.

As military men, we were committed to an honorable solution to this war and felt that anything else was unacceptable. A great deal of emotion went into the deliberations concerning this escape, and it did not have the universal blessing of the room or the seniors in the Annex. I would not have approved it, either.

After the recapture, we were told by the Garage that they could hear the screams of the men being tortured. This was a distance of two blocks, and we suspected that the men being tortured were gagged. The news drove shivers of apprehension up our spines. We knew there would be a massive and bloody purge of the whole camp. We were being conservative. Several camps were purged by torture after this escape attempt.

I passed a message through the wall to the people in my building to prepare themselves. My suggestion was that if they were pulled out and tortured, as they were surely going to be, they should not take a massive beating for those things which the "V" already knew. These were such things as the methods by which we communicated, when we communicated, our knowledge of who was in the building, who was senior, etc.

We expected a great headhunting about escape committees, so I said to maintain that we had no escape committee. The Annex was filled solely with junior officers and most rooms had several men. The "V" appeared to believe that because they were young, they were brainless and leaderless. Some of the large rooms in the Annex had formed committees, because their possibilities for escape were greater than those of the Zoo.

During the torture, the Garage shut down the note drops and the most hazardous communications. We knew that our secrets had been compromised during the vicious torture. Few POW secrets were still secure and the "V" would be trying to catch us using the drops.

"Comm" flowed in trickles, but the Garage did spell out a requirement that special care be taken not to compromise Navy Lieutenant J. J. Connell, acting as the communications center for the camp. He had to be protected at all cost. To the best of my knowledge, he was never compromised, through all the beatings and torture that occurred. Everyone kept the faith with J. J., a tough guy and a hard resistor.

A tall, hawk-looking Vietnamese entered the camp. We promptly labeled him "Moses." He was to take the "V" out of disgrace and to the promised land. The Vietnamese were on the horns of a dilemma, not knowing whether to let us know there had been an escape, since this would give us great comfort, or not let us know, since this would cause them great loss of face.

It was impossible for them not to show their frustration. Goldie came to our cell and hum-hawed around. Finally, in a fit of frustration, he said to Arvin Chauncey, "Why? Why?" He was referring to why the POWs launched an escape since the DRV had just advanced their so-called "peace proposal," which they were sure America would jump at like a bass striking a frog.

The "V" were so convinced that they had defeated us a year before, they found it inconceivable that their offer would be unpalatable. They were sure that when they made their eight-point peace proposal, demanding the U.S. surrender in Paris, public opinion in America would immediately

THE ZOO, DECEMBER, 1968

force the President to snap it up.

The Vietnamese did not see how arrogant their terms were. They thought the U.S. President would be forced by the anti-war movement to bail out immediately. There is a perfect illustration of how little the "V" understood what was going on in America. It also illustrates how the anti-war movement prolonged the war by convincing Hanoi to hold out.

The ridiculous proposal was touted by the pro-Communist American delegations, and the American breast-beaters, as the greatest thing since sliced bread. With the bombing halt of October, 1968, on the heels of the Tet offensive, the Vietnamese expected that within days there would be a hue and cry in the States for acceptance of the peace proposal.

In the U.S., there was considerable demand for surrender, just as Neville Chamberlain had backers for his Munich decision. However, the "V" were not dealing with Mr. Chamberlain, and the breast-beaters and left-wingers were the "vocal minority" in both the 1968 and 1972 elections. The "V" were stunned that we would make an escape at the exact time they made their offer, since they expected the U.S. to rush into shameful defeat.

Moses was a staff officer of high rank, and it was clear that he had been sent by headquarters to oversee the purge. Cochise, the present camp commander, disappeared from sight, demoted from this 180-man camp to a 50-man camp at Hoa Lo Main Prison. He took over the Las Vegas complex.

A watery-eyed, hawk-nosed, 55 - to - 58 - year - old hatchet man, whom we titled the Buzzard, was brought in to take over after Moses established the line that the purge was going to take. Our communication links were sealed off. The air and light holes, a little larger than a dinner plate, and some smaller holes for ventilation, were plugged immediately. The cells were plunged into total darkness. Every room in this camp, and all other camps, was sealed.

May was a scorching hot month, and our room soon became an oven. On the first day it was sealed, the room temperature soared to 112°, perhaps 115°. Large screens were erected in all of the places where the "V" thought there was any line-of-sight for communications from building to building. Amazing as it must sound, they were nearly 100% *inaccurate* with their blocking efforts!

The communcation system had been completely compromised. My advice to the men not to worry about divulging comm and admitting obvious things was sound. We received fragmented information, despite the pressure, and learned that a terrible purge was under way. We did not know the exact intensity, but it was obvious that the men in the escapees' room would be brutalized first.

We knew that Room Two of the Garage, the communications link with the Annex, would be one of the next rooms picked off. It was also obvious that some of the SROs in the comm links to Major Guarino would be squashed like grapes. It was evident that the "V" would assume that Guarino had engineered this escape, so he would be tortured. Captain Konrad Trautman, a tough German who was running the Annex as SRO, would be badly tortured.

The question was simply "How many? How long? When?" "V" officers and guards sneaked around like Indian scouts looking for any infractions.

Because all the torture rooms were full, it took until July 16, 1969, for my turn to come. I was apprehensive during this time. The Vietnamese were acting poisonously hateful. The slightest mistake would bring about a good beating session, hours on the knees, or worse!

POWs were running very still, very silent, and very deep. There was no doubt that somebody was going to get hurt badly, even killed. As Guarino said, it was a "bad time to be famous." With our communications broken down, we were frightened and uneasy.

Our information was disconnected, incomplete, and seldom meaningful. We heard about the screams of the tortured. There was a story about one particular blood-spattered cell. Goldie caught Arvin Chauncey near the wall with a shirt rolled into a "horse collar" which he was using as a muffler for communicating. We denied his charges but he put us on our knees for the afternoon. He told me that he would be back after me soon.

On Wednesday morning, July 16, an ultra-cruel turnkey known as Beanpole opened our door. It was a little unusual to see him, though it happened that turnkeys were occasionally traded from building to building.

A guard stood outside my door with a rifle, as Beanpole ordered Chauncey and Sawhill out the doors, ostensibly to weed the yard. It was not unusual for me to remain inside, since I was still crippled from the hanging at Vinh, and was seldom permitted to do any work because I was unable to use my right hand at all. I could barely grasp a stick with my left hand. I made a concentrated effort for the "V" to understand that I could not write.

Beanpole took Bob and Arv around the corner and then ordered me to suit up in long clothes and go out with the guard. I did so with justified apprehension. The guard marched me to the wall at the end of the building and stopped me. As I looked around, I saw Beanpole coming out of my cell with my cup and towel. I knew that they would use the towel as a gag. I was going to be tortured!

When he saw me looking at him, Beanpole attempted to hide the cup and towel behind his back. I don't know what he thought I would do. There was nothing to do except pray.

THE ZOO, DECEMBER, 1968

Deep, powerful spasms of cold fear caused my stomach to churn and my hands to begin to sweat.

"Courage, Jesus, courage, courage, courage," I muttered to myself. "Yea, though I walk through the valley of the shadow death . . . Lord, help me not to fear."

> *"He who loses wealth loses much*
> *He who loses a friend loses more,*
> *But he who loses courage loses all."*
> — Cervantes

POWs and citizens alike have wondered if it would not have been better simply to tell the "V" what they wanted to know. This solution was unsatisfactory, because it helped the enemy to kill your own classmates and friends. It hurt your nation through the propaganda efforts of the enemy who used it against the United States.

We recalled the Korean War, where many "germ warfare" confessions had hurt the reputation of the United States with the underdeveloped and developing nations. In addition, such words as "collaborator" and "cooperator" carry disgraceful connotations to a military man. We all knew of Benedict Arnold and Judas.

Could I tough out more hours, days, months, and years of torture? The most senior POW had been in confinement more than three years. I decided I'd have to try to tough it out. Failing that, I'd resort to lying, deception, vagaries, double talk, or whatever it took to stay alive, and still give them as little as possible.

CHAPTER TWELVE

Crucifixion
(Third Ring of the Malebolge)

**THE INSCRIPTION ON THE GATE OF HELL (CORETO III)
THE INFERNO**

In the traveling order of Virgil to Dante on his route to Hell, Virgil summarizes the explanation of a Code of Conduct for his journey.

> *"HERE must be abandoned all mistrust.
> All cowardice must here be dead.
> We have come to the place where I told you
> that you would see the miserable people
> who have lost the good of the intellect."*

"All cowardice must here be dead . . . I saw horned demons with great whips, who dealt behindwards on them furious blows."

I was marched at gunpoint to Goldie's office. He accused me, "You have been communicating! I want a full confession of your crimes." He outlined a number of matters that I must disclose to him.

"I have no intention of disclosing anything," I responded. He wasted no time. I was ordered to the Chicken Coop where the massive torturing of the escapees had taken place. Icy fear gripped my heart. I remembered the screams of my fellow prisoners. Now it was my turn.

I was led to Room One, a large room with numerous brown stains, grease spots, and accumulated dirt covering the floor. I knew the brown spots must be blood. A large barred window opened onto the alley behind the headquarters building.

Goldie tore my towel in half lengthwise. When he couldn't stuff half of it in my mouth, he tore it again. He jammed about a quarter of it in and then wrapped my face tightly with the rest of it.

The guard produced a set of traveling leg irons about four feet long and roughly forced the "U" bolts over my ankles, slipping the bar through the ends, behind my ankles. He padlocked them and ordered me to drop my

CRUCIFIXION

pants.

Producing a set of figure-eight screw down manacles, he screwed them tightly on my wrists, forcing my poorly-healed arms together at an impossible angle. The manacles began to cut and gouge my wrists immediately, causing scars that remained for several years. My hands began to swell and throb.

While standing with my buttocks bared, my trousers around my ankles, the guard told me to lie on the floor, face down. Two guards were in the room standing against the opposite wall, each holding a thirty-inch length of fan belt in his hand. The belt was knotted so it would not slip from the hands of the beater. Goldie gave the order to begin the beating.

The entire scene was so bizarre, so totally out of the days of Mongol Hordes, that it boggled my mind. Springing off the opposite wall in succession, the guards charged at me, screaming like banshees, whips raised high above their heads. Carried by momentum, they would smash the whip across my buttocks, lower back, or upper legs. Cutting, searing, tearing, dehumanizing pain racked my body and assailed my mind with a series of shrieking tormented pleas for relief.

I stared at Goldie in disbelief, staggered at the kind of society and person who would inflict such unbearable pain on another human being, for no bona fide reason. After a long series of scream, run, smash, Goldie told the beaters to stand against the wall.

He began to ask questions, about communications, to which I shook my head in refusal. He generalized a group of charges against the camp, dark schemes and misconduct. Again, I shook my head.

Goldie told the beaters to go ahead. The whips cut, seared, gouged, and burned the bleeding, swelling flesh on my buttocks. A trickle of blood coursed its way down from bottocks to legs and dripped on the floor. The first sharp cracks of the whips changed into juicy-sounding *splats*.

At 11:30 a.m. the food arrived, half a bowl of tasteless pumpkin soup and half a loaf of bread. My mind was so distracted that eating was near impossible. Food and water had little significance, but I did drink all the water I could get down.

At 12:30 P.M., Goldie was back with a new team. He made statements about my escape committees. He told me the whole camp knew about them, that they knew of my role in the escape, and allied matters. This confirmed what I had suspected. This was purely a fishing expedition for information. In fact, I knew nothing of the escape, had no part in it, and had no committees, escape or otherwise.

Goldie would put a question to me; I would refuse to answer. He would order the guards to smash me. My mind raced from pillar to post searching for possible answers, refuges, dodges, and courage. Cutting, knife-like pain ripped through the swollen meat, down through the legs, up through the spine to the brain. Involuntary animal-like noises boiled out of my throat. Blood trickles and fright argued with reason and resolve. "Jesus, sweet Jesus. Courage . . . please?"

My mind screamed, "Sierra, foxtrot, hotel! Rotten filthy scum bastards. Pig - filth - animal dung!"

Sandals shuffled across the room. "Splat!" spoke the whip to the bloody, protesting meat.

"Confess your black crimes, Nigh! Answer or not?" asked the Devil.

As my head shook a silent, "No," the cells in my brain shouted in alarm, "You nutty bastard, this stupid gook is going to kill you! Tell him something. Anything . . . something."

Other cells cried "No!" Feet shuffled, Goldie smirked, and the newly-collected audience smiled and nodded in righteous satisfaction at the sight of an Air Pirate receiving his well-deserved punishment.

Ten thousand or ten million miles away in another world, Americans were taking summer vacations, eating steaks, and drinking martinis. Congressmen were contemplating how to give away American dollars, draft-dodgers were burning draft cards and fleeing to Canada to avoid service in Vietnam, an American was on his way to the moon. POW wives anxiously awaited the release of three more Americans. The President of the United States was preparing to assure the success of pacification in South Vietnam by cutting out the heart of the Communist octopus in Cambodia. H. Ross Perot was preparing plans to fly a planeload of Christmas packages to Hanoi, and the Viking was being nominated for Military Wife of the Year for her outstanding efforts on behalf of the POWs.

It was clear that the approach I was using was not winning. It was equally clear that I could not endure this ordeal forever. I began to stall. Goldie would ask me a question, and I would nod that I would answer. He would then have to untie the gag, remove the cloth from my mouth, and I would give him an obtuse answer, or stall by feigning that I did not understand the question. While these ploys sometimes made him furious, it was another two or three minutes that I was not being hit with the whip.

A pattern began to emerge from the questions. The admissions from me needed to fit a predetermined shape. Their attack seemed to be two-pronged. First, my admissions needed to fit the same pattern as some past admissions. Second, the "V" were fishing for any random additional information they might beat out of me. I knew that all the comm information had long since been compromised, as well as lineups in buildings and general policies of no significant import.

Goldie began to suggest answers to his own questions, giving me clues to

CRUCIFIXION

the direction my own answers should take. He wanted me to admit that Guarino had ordered and executed the escape. He told me that Guarino had been removed from the camp and demanded to know what messages had been sent to, and received by me, from the assistant camp senior officer.

The assistant senior officer was Wendy Rivers. He did not send any messages for the simple reason that Guarino never left the camp. It takes a warped mind to torture for nonexistent messages, but then it takes a warped mind to torture at all.

That evening several of the kiddies, the beginning English speakers, dropped by to feed me more clues about the questions the following day. By evening, I was exhausted and hoping for some relief in sleep.

A pistol-carrying guard entered the room as I half-heartedly tried to eat some cold pumpkin soup. As soon as I finished eating, I was jerked onto my knees. For the next four days, twenty-four hours per day, I remained either on my knees or on my stomach on the floor.

Immediately after eating, I was put back into the screw-down manacles, the torture cuffs, and within hours, blood was flowing from the wounds on my wrists. My feet were scratched and marked from the rough concrete, and I knew that infections would come in due course from the filth which littered that floor.

The pattern of torture, then, was this. I was to be beaten and questioned all day, then forced to kneel all night. It was the sentry's job to keep me awake at night and on my knees, to soften me up for the whip beaters during the day. It was torture in perpetual motion.

Thursday was a reprint of Wednesday . . . gag . . . cuffs . . . fanbelt . . . splat! Accusations . . . questions . . . demands . . . splat! Committees, Nigh. Confess your dark schemes . . . plots against the Camp Authorities. Denials . . . a barrage of fanbelt strokes across a ridged and bleeding mound of flesh.

Day melted into night and lost its identity through a never-ending series of agony upon agony. Twenty-four hours without sleep . . . or was that yesterday? Now it is almost 40 hours. Spike driving pains into the sockets of the knees. "Strength, Jesus. Yea, though I walk through the valley of the shadow of death, I shall fear no evil."

"Fear no evil," said my brain. "It is not a case of fearing evil, you meathead. You are being crucified. Instead of hanging you by the arms, you are being hung by the knees. Ask for relief, you bonehead. OK, relieve pain, Savior." On bended knee . . . on bended knee . . . on bended knee . . .

Bloody holes appeared in the Achilles tendons, bone began to show through the holes drilled into the knees by the relentless sandpapering of the concrete.

"Confess your crimes, Nigh!"

Some cell responded, "I hope your mother dies in a brothel, you rotten scum!"

Splat . . . splat . . . splat . . .

Sometime in the first days of this hellish nightmare, the 300th blow fell upon my abused body. My subconscious said, "You probably will not live long enough to keep counting."

By Friday evening, I was hallucinating. I was positive that I heard Americans talking next door to my building. Their voices came across the wall, from outside the camp. They were talking about shaving and showering in hot water at what I thought was about 9:00 p.m.

Some peppy ragtime banjo and guitar music played, and the announcer at Da Nang Air Base announced some of the hit parade tunes. It was the following December before I convinced myself that these were hallucinations.

While I dreamed fanciful thoughts of men in a hot shower, the population of the Zoo quaked in their sandals, prayed for my life, and prayed that they would not join me. Many simply prayed, unaware that they were praying for me, for many simply knew that some American needed prayers, and I was an unknown figure.

Later that Friday night, the "V" brought in a stool. Early in the morning, I was ordered off my knees onto the stool by an unusually cruel guard named Magoo, the curse of his building, the "Pool Hall." I suspect that I went to sleep almost immediately and fell exhausted to the floor, unconscious.

Beanpole had the night patrol and when he entered the building and discovered that I was not sitting on the stool, he flew into a maniacal rage. Jerking me off the floor by the chin and throat, he began beating me in the face with his fist. He broke a piece off my right center tooth, chipped another front tooth, then blamed me for the fact that he had cut his fist in bashing my face to a pulp. He dragged me around on the concrete, polishing the meat off my knees, and broke my left eardrum again.

The beating awakened me completely. The adrenalin pumped. I went back on my knees and remained awake with no difficulty. It was a source of amazement to me how the body could rise to the demands of heavy torture.

Before this ordeal, I would not have believed a person could remain awake for such an extended period of time. I expected to fall over unconscious into a merciful coma. But nothing merciful happens to a tortured prisoner, unless the torturer drops dead on the scene.

When Goldie began his questioning on Saturday, I was prepared. The kiddies had been on the scene again the previous evening and I knew that the questions were going to be about the nonexistent committees in my building. This was a hard day. My buttocks were now so swollen that the cheeks extended two or three inches above their normal height. From the upper part of my thigh through the middle of my back — a single stiff,

CRUCIFIXION

semi-solid mass of scabs and bruises — felt like the newly-opened wound of a mastoid operation. Being alive was almost too painful to be worthwhile.

My lower legs had swollen to the size of a cedar fence post, and were very nearly as hard. The skin and meat around the ankle and foot were rock-hard to the touch. The toes resembled massive summer sausages extending at odd angles from my unrecognizable, swollen, bloody feet. There was no room for these huge toes to extend in an orderly fashion off the foot. The excessive swelling caused the skin to stretch to the breaking point and was responsible for many of the cuts and gashes on my feet and knees. Every minor assault became a large injury.

Even without mistreatment, this Saturday would have been an uncomfortable day. With the killer instinct of a fighter who has his opponent on the ropes, Goldie came after me.

The pain of the beatings was so bad and so universal that I abandoned my usual mental escape dodges. There was no device that could tune out this misery, except death or unconsciousness. Goldie questioned me all day about my escape committee, messages from Guarino about the escape, names of members of my escape committee, and internal building functions that were part of the "escape plot."

"Jesus, if I survive this nightmare, I will have divine understanding. I am your brother, in blood and deed. I am being crucified! I know Satan. I have seen the deepest rings of Hell. I am in the pit, Lord, and I am fading. My strength is waning. Give me strength, Dear God, strength. I cannot bear the thought of my wife or children hearing I am a traitor, cooperator, "good attitude." I cannot live in disgrace with my fellow prisoners speaking these words of me.

"My pilots look to me for leadership and example. Help me not to get them tortured, God. Help! Hear my prayers, Dear God!"

My thoughts jumped from one desperate prayer to the next. Unknown to me, only a few days before, Ed Atterbury had been tortured to death on this very floor. Whether by accident or design, the overall brutality made the death cold-blooded murder in the first degree.

"Answer or not, Nigh?" asked Satan.

"Committees, Nigh, confess your black schemes against the camp . . . confess." Splat! Screams of pain tried to rip through my rag-choked mouth, and I wriggled miserably on the cruel floor as the whip ripped away at my will, sensibilities, and resourcefulness. By evening, I was beaten! My will was as strong as ever, but unable to resist the clamoring demands from my torn body to compromise.

I decide to give him his nonexistent committees and information, but to make my answers so ridiculous, that if I ever had to write them, they would be unusable.

"All right," I told him, "I'll answer." First, I reported that I had a "Transportation Committee."

"What does the Transportation Committee do?" Goldie questioned.

I replied, "They will line up trucks for our transportation out of Hanoi." I expected the roof to fall on me in the form of a barrage of smashes with the whip. The only thing that happened was that Goldie scribbled laboriously in his notebook, asking how to spell various words. Although my mental faculties were severely impaired from the fatigue and mistreatment, the fact that Goldie understood my words, but not their meaning, registered on my numb brain.

"What else?" he continued.

"Pass and Identification Committee," I responded.

"What do?"

I told him, "They are going to make up passes and papers for all men." Emboldened by his lack of understanding, I eventually gave him a committee for every function performed by every army since the conquests of the Caesars — intelligence, supply, military police, medical, morale, historical, and many others. Throughout the entire recitation, the whip could not have fallen more than five or six times. The admissions I made sounded so incredible to me, I wondered if I had taken leave of my senses.

Goldie insisted that I name members of the committees. Anyone I identified would be mauled mercilessly. To all questions on this subject, I maintained that I was the sole member. Goldie refused to accept this, and continued beating me for the names of the committee members.

Finally, I replied, "Everyone in my room is on the committee." He asked a few more times, stroked me with the whip, but I clung to this claim.

At last he seemed to be satisfied. He noted my answer in his book. I felt unclean, sick, and contemptuous of myself and my conduct. I had been awake for about 65 hours. My body was mutilated, and my mind perceived reality only drunkenly.

When the beaters departed, late in the evening, I was allowed to lean against the wall in a semi-reclining position. I tried to sit, but my buttocks were so sore, it was out of the question. I lay at a tilting angle on my hips, and immediately fell asleep. This induced another beating, got the adrenalin flowing, and I went back on my knees.

My mind churned in a groggy haze, thinking black thoughts about my failings. I felt I had betrayed a trust. For the first time, the "V" had pounded me to the point of serious compromise. I began praying for strength and more courage.

I worried through the night about the things that would happen to my roommates. How soon would they be dragged out for torture? How could they match their stories with my extensive fabrications? Disgust with my

CRUCIFIXION

weakness pervaded every consious thought.

I remembered a young Tennessee Civil War hero named Sam Davis who said, "I would rather die a thousand deaths than betray a friend, or be false to duty." I had to do better, and the only thing to do was immediately deny the entire admission, regardless of the consequences. I begged God's help in a long and anguished prayer.

In the morning, I was almost relieved to see Goldie. As soon as he entered the room, I began talking.

"I told you that if you continued to torture me I was going to lie, and I did lie. Everything I have told you, absolutely *everything* that I told you up to this point has been a lie. You started off torturing me. I told you I would lie. I *did* lie. Everything I told you last night was a lie. If you continue to torture me, I will lie again."

While I lacked the internal conviction and resolution that the words were supposed to convey, I was amazed at the strength and clarity of my voice. Goldie was surprised; amazement and disbelief showed on his face, which radiated the burning question, "How could you lie to me?"

Disbelief turned to anger, his face darkened, and he brusquely ordered, "Take down you spants!"

Turning to the beaters, he said tersely, "Wait!" Turning on his heel, he stalked toward the headquarters building at a brisk, angry pace. I moved myself into a position on my knees where I could follow his progress. He entered Room Seven, which served as office and bedroom for Buzzard, the Communist cadre.

It was early in the morning, sevenish. Eight o'clock passed. I waited apprehensively, as I sensed the oncoming fury. Nine o'clock came and brought various workers to do their routine duties. Ten o'clock, eleven. Time for a half bowl of cold pumpkin soup, and Goldie had not reappeared.

The pistol-carrying guard permitted me to get off my tortured knees to take my food and water. I dragged the meal out for the indescribable relief from the kneeling torture, and then further stalled by sitting on the rusty, rancid bucket, which drove the guard from the room instantly.

They looked on us as unclean animals, and the feeling was mutual. Sometime after lunch, Goldie returned with a new beater. He was a small, squat "V" with a huge scar on his chin and neck. He was a rifle-carrying guard normally. This was the first beater who had not been a turnkey. Because of his resemblance to a cubby-hole merchant in the New York garment center, we called him Nguyen von Firesale.

The name Nguyen is to the Vietnamese what John is to Americans. Most of the rifle-carrying guards, such as Nguyen, did not participate in POW abuse. Most of the torture and mistreatment was handled by the quizzers and the turnkeys.

Goldie stated, "You have turned your face on the people (i.e., denied the previous statements). Now you must repent, and tell the camp the truth."

I responded, "I told you the truth this morning when I said that I had lied. I will never tell those lies again about committees, or my people, and if you continue to torture me, you will only get different lies. Then I will again deny the lies."

"Drop your spants." said Goldie sternly.

As I dropped my "spants," a look of disbelief crossed the face of the guard, mirroring his thoughts. He stared incredulously at my massively-swollen testicle, and its bag which dripped fluid and blood from the lashes which had been laid down over my buttocks and between my legs. His eyes wandered to the gory meat on my torn body, battered knees, swollen legs and feet.

Our eyes locked for a brief moment, and he averted his eyes, almost shamefully. This may have been the first time that he understood the kind of savages he lived with. I lay prostrate again on the floor. Goldie gave him the nod to begin beating, and I braced for the first lash.

It was a brand new "ball game." Now I was being struck on the undamaged flesh of the upper leg with a stroke that ran parallel with the leg. Nguyen was not bearing down on the whip with the maniacal fury of past beaters. If such things exist, this was an "easy" beating.

I suspected he had been instructed to go easy. I also thought that if he had a choice, he would not be striking me at all. The tenor of Goldie's questions changed abruptly to innocuous ones about communications, comm links, and others to which they knew the most fully detailed answers.

I admitted those things freely. On items of some sensitivity, I was obtuse, but this resistance did not increase the ferocity of the beating. I took very few strokes that afternoon, none of them bloodletting. Some days were just full of good deals! Happiness is light torture.

Just as a lunch of weed soup arrived, I began to vomit violently. Bile, fresh blood, and green weeds spewed forth and the sight of the blood struck terror in my heart. I thought I was dying.

Immediately after, I was seized by a series of hiccup-like spasms, regurgitating blood and bile with every gasp. I couldn't control the urge to defecate and this, too, was a bloody liquid. I knew I had ruptured a blood vessel in my stomach. Alone in my cell with my lunch, I was afraid I would bleed to death.

I called the guard in a loud voice. Beanpole, the turnkey from the Garage, had the duty. Normally a miserable creature, he was alarmed when he saw that I was passing large quantities of blood. He disappeared to find

CRUCIFIXION

Goldie.

I could faintly hear conversation between the "V" in the distance, but nothing improved as the day and evening wore on. Another guard entered and dragged me away from the bucket, burning a hole in my shirt as he pulled me across the concrete. Within an hour or two, I had retched a circular pool of blood and bile a yard in diameter.

Despite my desperate condition, there was no softening of my treatment that night or early morning. I was still on my knees, still being kept awake.

Several times during early morning, I simply collapsed, folding up limply and sagging onto the floor. The guard would spring up and give me some temporary "incentive" to stay awake. Consciousness was only passing and I drifted between consciousness and total collapse.

Near 8:00 in the morning Goldie reappeared, bringing a chair. He unscrewed the wrist manacles and told me to go sit on the chair. He brought a pencil and a piece of the brown, rough paper that served as toilet paper.

"You will write," he announced. "You must tell how you communicate, what camp policies you have received," and a couple of insignificant questions.

Timorously, I sensed a reprieve coming, perhaps even a total escape from this pit of hell. Tentatively, I scratched stupid and incomplete answers to the questions, testing the water, expecting the furies to break loose.

"We communicate during the middle of the night with the tap code. We also sweep in code," I wrote. Had this provoked a savage onslaught, I would have known I was still in serious trouble. It brought no such response and I felt confident that I was wriggling off the hook.

In the afternoon, my irons were removed and I was driven with limping, faltering gait to the front left room of the Auditorium. My ankles were so swollen that the joints would scarcely bend. The wrist cuffs, which had been replaced after my writing, were removed again. I was put back into irons and the louvered, rickety doors were slammed closed.

The room was spartan, even for a prison cell. Other than the usual filth, there were only two items in the room. One was the common black, rusty, evil-smelling bucket; the other was a board about 30 inches wide by six feet long, lying on the floor. This was to serve as a bed.

There was no mosquito net, cup for water, blanket, towel, or anything else. The stink of fear had permeated my clothing and still exuded from my pores. I hadn't been allowed to bathe after the vomiting and bleeding of the previous night. Lord, but I needed that bath, some soap and water for my wounds, and some peace and quiet.

I was unable to stand the appearance of my feet and knees. I thought if my feet appeared so mangled, what of my backside?

An amazing psychological phenomena always follows such treatment. An uncontrollable euphoria, almost a feeling of pleasure sets in when it seems certain the ordeal has ended. Incredible as it sounds, one almost feels a sense of gratitude toward his tormentor. If the max torture has halted, even temporarily, I would be tougher and stronger when I went back. If the halt is permanent . . . could it possibly be? If I could keep from doing anything reckless or foolish, keep from getting famous, then I wouldn't have to go back into the pit.

"Great Scott!" I thought with cautious elation, "I may have made it! It is possible I got through this without being disgraced." My mind almost rejected these thoughts because I feared that just thinking such things might somehow bring on new disasters.

I was not bothered again that day and was able to lie semi-prone on my side and back and prop my huge legs into an elevated position against the wall to reduce the swelling. Several spots on my legs, ankles, and feet were showing serious signs of infection.

After the evening passed without harassment, I sighed in relief and enjoyed the blessing of my new comfort and luxury. My prayers of thanks were deep, solemn, lengthy, and tenuously hopeful that the ordeal was over.

I went through a period of semi-consciousness, jumping and jerking at the slightest noise. Hundreds of mosquitos fed on me with abandon. I simply didn't care!

The next morning, I limped to quiz with Buzzard and Rabbit. Buzzard was watery-eyed, wrinkled and balding, with thin wisps of hair combed straight back. He had deep, dark bags under his eyes and a large hook nose. His teeth were irregular and badly stained. He appeared to be about 50 years plus.

Rabbit was the interpreter, a fair English speaker, whose most obvious characteristic was his resemblance to a rabbit, even to the involuntary twitch of his nose and upper lip. He was remarkably courteous to Buzzard, I believe, in deference to his position as the ranking Communist.

Rabbit was a "comer" who had done yeoman service for the Party in torturing and exploiting prisoners. It was my view that he was struggling for Party membership, hoping to step out of the military and into the Party.

Neither of the two was wearing symbols of rank, either to confuse us, to keep in step with their Chinese brothers, or to try to pawn non-officers off to us as officers. Buzzard, speaking through Rabbit, questioned me.

"How are you?"

I replied, "Not well!"

CRUCIFIXION

His next question was even more inane, "How do you think of your treatment?"

I looked at him in disbelief. "My treatment is brutal, uncivilized, inhumane, and far below the standards of the Geneva Convention."

He made no denial or apology. "Of course," he answered, "you have committed many crimes against the camp. What do you expect?"

I replied, "I expect the same thing that I have always expected, to be treated like a man, and to be treated in accordance with the terms of the Geneva Convention."

He stared at me blankly and stated, "Ah, well, you must pay for your crimes!"

He spoke with Rabbit briefly in Vietnamese, and then launched into his prepared lecture, prefaced with what had to be the most unbelievable remark I had ever heard. "Nigh, we don't want to hurt you."

This was not hard to answer. "If you don't want to hurt me, then it's very easy to stop. All you have to do is stop what you are doing, and you will stop hurting me."

He answered, "You know how it is. You are a father. Sometimes the children do some things wrong and you must punish them." He looked at me earnestly, as if a show of sincerity would impress his logic on me.

I was nearly struck dumb. My body was a tortured, torn and battered wreck, and he doesn't want to hurt me! As I stared at him, I thought, "You have to be some kind of nut!" I wondered if I really understood what was being said.

I was disgusted with myself and ashamed. My puny, shaky body was so exhausted that my hands and legs trembled, palsy-like, as I stood before him. Trying hard to demonstrate nonchalance, strength and good possession of my faculties, I was ashamed of my frailties.

I was not quaking in fear, although I was afraid, but the trembling came from lack of control over my muscles. The quiz terminated with a warning by the Rabbit that I had turned my face on the "people," meaning that I had denied the lies they had tortured from me, and I was going to have to retell the "true" story. They wanted the facts as they really were, and an apology to the "people." As an afterthought, he added that I was going to have to "confess" my crimes.

Looking him straight in the eye, I said, "I am not confessing any crimes. I'm not going back and reconstructing anything I said before. I told the truth. You tortured lies from me. I will never tell those lies again. Never!" My words sounded loud, clear and firm. I wondered how they could be, for I knew well the fear in my heart. I had no doubt that if they applied the fan belt brutally again, I would fold.

At the same time, I knew I hated so fiercely that as soon as the pressure eased off, I would immediately deny any admissions made under torture. I will never know whether my words carried conviction, or whether the camp simply retrenched, but the policy concerning my torture was changing.

Early the next morning, Goldie reappeared with a young beater and a fan belt. He asked, "Write or not?"

"NO WRITE!" I emphasized.

"Take down spants."

I took down my trousers and lay face down on the floor. The beater lay a smashing blow across my buttocks. I bit back a scream, since I was not gagged.

"Write or not?"

"No!"

Another cutting lash, and "Write or not?"

"No, no write, never write!" I replied. Another piercing lash!

He stared at me hatefully, and said, "I will be back. Think of your crimes and when I come back, you will write."

"No," I vowed. "Never write again."

The morning passed without incident, and I was able to watch some of the camp activities through the louvers in the door and the crack caused by poor fitting. Although I hurt all over, I felt quite happy. An occasional single or a pair of POWs went to quiz. Lunch came and went, more thin pumpkin soup and bread.

At about 11:00 o'clock, Goldie reappeared. "Write or not?"

With unequivocal bravado, I replied, "No write, NEVER!" Three lashes fell, following the same question and pattern.

Goldie warned me severely, "Tonight I will return, and tonight you will write, or you will be severely punished." I didn't bother to answer.

At 6:00 o'clock, he returned. Same question, same answer, same three lashes over the pain-stricken ridged flesh, bruises, and scabs. But, each time the lashes stopped at three, and I realized he had been restricted from his orgy of unrestrained beating.

I was reluctant to think about that. If, in fact, he was now limited to this small number of strokes, I could tolerate the torture for a very long time, perhaps forever. If he did not escalate, the pattern was bearable. It was not fun, but by comparison to past days, it was moderate, even easy.

July faded into August. Goldie dropped out of sight and was replaced by one of the kiddy English speakers. He was totally ineffective in the tough guy role. My determination grew, and I was positive that, barring massive and unrestrained escalation, I would never write.

In early August, I was moved to Room 10 of the Pool Hall. Although it was miserably hot outside, I could not believe how much cooler it was in

CRUCIFIXION

the Pool Hall than in the Barn. My neighbors were Jim Bell in Room Nine, next door; Jim Kasler in front of me in Room Five.

I got on the wall as soon as I was settled into the room, passing my name and status to Jim. I was still in irons, but no longer in cuffs. I told Jim that I had been in torture since July 16th, what they were torturing me for, what answers I had given, and that I was in bad shape and did not want to know any building lineups or policies, while still in torture. I explained that I was still being beaten, and didn't want anything compromising that would get some of them tortured. I was not in condition to stand much, and if I had no info, I couldn't divulge it.

As I lolled in comfort on the boards in portable leg irons, I hoped the "V" were going to ease off on me. Otherwise, why this move to better living conditions? I wondered if I had overcome my ordeal without having disgraced myself. This was a lot to hope for.

Being a quiet, humble POW was obviously a good profile to carry. I ran silent and deep. Locked in irons and in solitary, I had no way to clear my door for the guard. All he needed to do was walk up to the door and listen, and I would be caught in a comm rap.

Although I wanted a low profile with no risk, Jim Bell forced me onto the line, demonstrating faith and confidence as he tapped me the building lineups, news, and policies. I was deeply humbled by their faith in me, and the stirring messages from the senior officer, Larry Guarino, who was not out of the camp after all.

They had far more faith in me than I had in myself. Larry advised me not to take any mistreatment on his account, tell anything I felt I needed to tell that involved him. Although I had not seen him, I knew that his torture had been as violent or more so than mine, and I had no intention of adding to his problems.

The assistant SRO, Wendy Rivers, said the same thing, telling me to manufacture some messages from him to me, if it were required. I was appreciative, but decided I would give only what they could pound out of me. I could not help but sit on the bed and weep at the POWs' kindness and concern.

Jim told me that all of the "heavies," the ranking men from camp, and all of the former building commanders were now in this building. Most of them had been tortured horribly. All told, 26 men had been beaten to the verge of death.

One of my men from the Barn, Major Leo Thorsness (an F-105 Medal of Honor recipient), was able to advise us that none of my people in the Barn had been tortured because of my actions. When I copied this message, I wept again, with relief. I felt as if a log had been lifted from my conscience, and prayed a long, heartfelt prayer of thanks to God. My deepest prayer had been answered.

I was surprised to find that I could hear the "Hooda Hooda" meetings of the "V" in the Auditorium, located a good distance away. The name "Hooda Hooda" came from the response that members gave.

Every time a massive torture took place, the "V" would hold three or four of these meetings per week. They seemed to be indoctrinations designed to pump them full of hate toward us. The families of the guards, village elders, and everyone who had a work detail that related to the camp was in attendance. Meetings had all the fervor of an old-style revival, and there was a great deal of singing of "liberate the South," Communist songs, and cheering. Everyone got emotionally involved.

The Commies told the people their version of why we were being tortured, explained our "crimes," and asked for their backing in the overall mistreatment. As a result, every person who dealt with the POW when maximum pressure was being applied knew your "V" name, used your name in speaking to you, and participated in treating you hatefully. This included the water boy, the bread boy, the guards, everyone.

There was not a kind word, gesture, or the faintest glimmer of decency from anyone. The entire camp, unified as one, applied their combined hate against *one* lonely POW. Little wonder that the victim being tortured had the sense of total, all-pervading pressure and abandonment.

I recovered slowly. As the swelling diminished in my buttocks, I began to sleep several hours per night, despite the discomfort of the irons. Healing took place, even though I still received six to nine lashes a day. My mental outlook was strong since I felt the maximum daily strokes of the fanbelt had been set low.

I was taken out of irons and marched from my room to Auditorium Two for my short beatings. The first time I entered the room, I saw that it had an unusually high number of brown spots on the floor and walls. I wondered if they were blood spots and the answer was not long in coming.

The wounds on my lower back, buttocks, and legs were now crusted into a hard overall scab, very rough and very dry. The scabs tended to break easily and pasted themselves to my shorts during the night.

My inquisitor asked, "Write or not?" He put me on the floor for my daily ritual. The beater had a stick this day instead of the fanbelt. The stick was willow, about three feet long and quite rigid, lacking the flexibility of the belt. My nose was nearly pressing the wall when the beater smashed me cruelly with the first stroke. I winced at the searing pain and noticed that the blood sprayed the wall in tiny random droplets. As the second stroke fell, the droplets were slightly larger, and blood began to trickle down between my legs. Any mystery about the origin of the brown spots was now solved.

CRUCIFIXION

My harrassment through the month of August was fairly low, confined to the maximum of nine strokes of the belt per day. Occasionally a really good day fell my way, and I received only six or even three. Happiness is three strokes with the fanbelt!

On September 2, 1969, a really nice thing happened. Ho Chi Minh died. The "V" were stunned with disbelief and temporarily paralyzed. Their god was dead, and most wondered how this could be. In the custom of Stalin and Mao, he had been so thoroughly deified that he was incapable of dying. Rabbit immediately broadcast a tape advising POWs not to indulge in provocative activities. This was sound advice. It was not a good time to get famous.

It was two days before the Voice of Vietnam and the village Communist radio informed the citizens that Ho was dead. Since there is no provision for legal succession to power in a Communist dictatorship, the Party had to reach out to every cadre in every province and village and make certain that the stranglehold on every person was complete; that there were no revolutionary plots or pockets of strength and resistance hoping to exploit this opportunity to lift the Communist yoke.

Without question, most of our mistreatment stemmed from Ho's personal policies toward us. Immediately we sensed a slight slackening of the pressure. Some thought, and it is conceivable, that it resulted from a directive from the incoming dictator to ease up on us in order to avoid a revolt of the prisoners and embarrassment for the Party. I lean toward taking the facts as they are. Ho died. Our treatment improved. Therefore, most of our pressure and mistreatment was his direct policy.

A new period of existence opened for me. I was in solitary, in irons, under high pressure, but they stopped whipping me. I was the only person in the camp still under maximum harassment, yet even I sensed things were getting better.

First, I was put on the bath schedule. I had the chance to wash the blood spots out of my clothes, and to wash away the dreadful stink of fear. My body welcomed the soothing water and cleanliness, especially my torn feet and knees. My buttocks were so painful that I could not wash them with the strong "floor grade" brown lye soap that was provided.

Walking to the bath was painful, and I wondered if the damage to my knees were permanent. A flight of three dark-colored geese flew across the bath area in a "v" formation, looking puny and bedraggled. As I stared at them and the bright open sky, I was struck with the parallel between them and me. We were puny "birds of a feather." On the same day, a "V" worker planted some red blooming moss roses inside the bath area. I wondered if I had ever seen anything so beautiful.

A new dark-blue blanket hung on the clothes line in front of Wendy

Rivers' room. It looked unreal, new and clean, out of step with the overall dirt and filth. After lockup, the guard came by and threw the same brand of new blue cotton blanket to me. It was not of good quality, but it was a third blanket. POWs who had spent cruel winters of 1965-68 with only two blankets were now going to have the warmest winter of their prison career.

The blankets were followed by a strange item dubbed a "snake basket" by Kasler. It was a round object woven from reeds, with a cover made of padded cloth. It was lined with cloth, overlaying a layer of rice straw, which was to act as insulator. After some time, I finally understood what it was for. Incredibly, this creation was designed to keep our drinking water hot! We needed to keep our water hot like we needed the worms which were crawling in our stomachs. It was sheer torture for the broken, chipped, and aching teeth that were so common among us.

The goal was decent, but the execution was typical of the "V" lack of understanding of simple human values — a smile, a friendly word, relaxation of oppressive regulations, or a retrenchment from their arrogant cruelty. They did not understand the most basic tenets of human dignity and became miffed because we were not thrilled with them.

In the future, they rejected with alarm any suggestion for improvement of our conditions, solely because an American made them. Our inane basket was aptly described by McCain as the process of making "unusable items from substandard materials." The basket was useful for hiding the forbidden nails, pieces of string, and sticks that we used for cleaning ears and fingernails. There seemed to be a silver lining even in this basket.

An unusual quiz occurred on October 2, 1969, with Rabbit and Buzzard. It was, to my relief, a "greasy" quiz — easy and friendly. I was expecting the worst, since I was still in irons and being harassed. Buzzard again mentioned that I must, like a child, be punished. I listened quietly, not wanting to disturb the status quo.

At that exact moment, I felt as if I had never had it so good. Rabbit explained that the camp authorities, in the custom of the 4,000-year history of the "people," wanted me to have "good treatment." That would be fine with me.

"Thus," said Rabbit, "the camp commander wishes you to have this package from your family."

For a moment, I thought that my brain had become disconnected from my ears. My shaking hands grasped the open package. It was a large box, but there were few items inside. Knowing the Viking, I knew the box had been full of goodies. To my amazement, they had left an envelope of pictures of the children — good quality, clear, color photos. My morale skyrocketed.

I asked Rabbit what had happened to the picture of my wife. He denied

CRUCIFIXION

any knowledge of such a picture. Also included in the package was a bottle of vitamins with the name Hansen as the issuing doctor. I knew this had to be my friend, Dr. Richard Hansen, and that he must now be assigned to Luke AFB in Phoenix, and in frequent contact with my family. This speculation was true.

My cup truly ran over. I nearly floated back to the room. I was totally and overwhelmingly happy to know that Doris and all of the children were alive and probably well. The pictures of the children were better than a letter, and in one of them I could see the shadow of the Viking in a well-fitting A-line dress. It was time for giving thanks.

For the first time since being taken for heavy torture, I realized that my prayers had been fully answered. The family was alive. I was alive. I hadn't disgraced myself. It wasn't that I had won a victory. In these circumstances, such things were not reasonably measured. It was that I had done the things that were so important to me.

No one had been tortured because of my actions. I had not put my words, name or signature to a piece of paper against my country. I had never let a word or sentence pass my lips to a "V" if it criticized my country, officials, or system in any way. I had not lost faith in my country or people. I knew fully that I needed God and His help for I could not make it alone. I knew that God's strong hand assured my survival, and my prayers had been answered.

On October 14 a new turnkey took me out of irons, and a different phase of treatment began. My lifestyle took a definite upward turn. To begin with, the turnkey threw two handkerchiefs and a pair of socks into the room. Both were treasures of inestimable value.

The radio played a tape that lifted my spirits immensely. I laughed, and laughed hard and heartily, for the first time in nearly two years.

Prisoners in other camps were forced to read propaganda tapes, and this tape was a beautiful illustration of "doing it bad." The reader began in an enthusiastic Festus accent. The first item was about a hack Australian writer who wrote a number of things glorifying the "V" communists. His name was Wilfred Bourchette, and he had also produced some color films for the "V" with himself as narrator. He had been a Communist lackey at the Panmunjon talks in Korea, and had exploited Korea POW General Red Dean.

Festus handled him in this way. "That well known author, Wellfed Bullshit, has just published . . ." Next, and with incredible courage and imagination, he took on Ho Chi Minh, in the following manner. "Our venerated leader, Horse Shit Minh, said . . ." These two items were sidesplitting at the time, but it takes a few years in jail to see them in the same light.

Two new POWs were moved into camp from Son Tay, and two of our officers were moved out, making me the camp vice commander. These changes were part of a system-wide move among all camps to spread the word that living conditions and treatment was improving in all camps concurrently.

Ned Shuman and Dale Doss arrived from Little Vegas and reported that treatment was noticably better there. We began to learn why. There had been a release of three prisoners from Hanoi during the summer of 1969, two pilots and a seaman. These releases had not been highly publicized to us as the previous two had been. We did not hear the barrage of sickening tapes that had accompanied the release in the summer of 1968.

During the late fall of 1969, Hanoi Hannah announced that they didn't care about the condemnation of Vietnamese Communists at the meeting of Red Cross International in Turkey. The radio stated that the Red Cross did not have anything to do with North Vietnam, and that the DRVN did not have to respond to any slander of their fair name by the reactionaries and lackeys of the U.S. Imperialists. This was always a clear indication that they did care.

As I put together the release of the POWs and the announcement from the Red Cross, I partially guessed what was happening. Seaman Doug Hegdahl (1969) was one of the three released. He had been the roommate of Lieutenant Commander Richard Stratton, who had been badly tortured and scarred. Doug knew this story well.

Each Christmas, a few select prisoners were trucked to the Theatre at the Plantation where a "V" preacher would explain how Christ had liberated the "people." Usually these POWs were handpicked, but some were random selectees, chosen to try to give the appearance that all POWs went to church. This propaganda worked.

Jim Barr, a Wichita, Kansas, lawyer was one of many who told me that he had the gut feeling we were being mistreated, but movies and pictures of POWs playing volleyball, going to church, etc., poured out of Hanoi with every group of Commie campfollowers.

This church service was conducted under the bright lights of many foreign movie cameras, flash cameras, etc. Several pilots from the Zoo attended in 1968, carrying with them the stories of the bloody atrocities carried out against POWs in the Zoo.

Communications during church were carried out by singing the story to the man standing nearby, or by simply blurting out some facts and taking the mistreatment after church. Naturally, POWs were forbidden to talk to each other at church services. After all, what normal man would want to talk to another American at Christmas?

One particularly blood-chilling story was related to Navy Lieutenant

CRUCIFIXION

Bob Frischman at this service. Now, Hegdahl and Frischman were back in the United States, and had certainly related these bloody outrages to our government.

I was convinced that only outside social, economic, and military pressure would influence the "V," for it was a fact that they relied totally on the Communist world for the major items that made the war go. If they were as vulnerable to world public opinion as I believed, then it was highly likely that our government had Frischman or Hegdahl and their stories on national and international television and news, and spread the facts across the world about the true nature of the "V."

This conclusion was supported by the change in treatment that was occurring. I had the highest of hopes that it was true, for I felt that this was the only way to rally national and international support for our cause. It is still my view that the most incomprehensible decisions ever taken on the POW matter was the decision to direct the families to play their role quietly and without objection to the treatment of the airmen, on the fantastic premise that delicate negotiations might be jeopardized. This was akin to being friendly with your blackmailer!

Like many other untried and unproven concepts used in this war, it did not work and was taken as a sign of weakness by the enemy. When the policy was changed by Secretary of Defense Melvin Laird, who said, "America cares about her POWs," and the story was aired like filthy linen on the clothesline of world opinion, our lot improved.

It is important to note that POW wives like Carol North, Sybil Stockdale, the Viking, and many others, were helping people get behind us, telling the story of our mistreatment, telling of the cruelties to POW families. There was no mail, no confirmation of life or death, just Limbo! Personable and patriotic H. Ross Perot likewise cared, and he focused global opinion on the cruelty of the DRV as he drove an airplane load of Christmas packages around the world in an effort to make Christmas for POWs a little more pleasant. Bob Hope and John Wayne cared, worked for us, and backed us up. My speculations as to why the "V" eased the pressure of the vise were largely correct, but it was several years before the whole picture came into focus.

When the cruel pressure began to relax, living conditions took on the cloak of ease. Men were still in solitary, rooms were small, food poor. We neither received mail nor wrote. Sunshine was a rarity, and exercise nonexistent. Still, it felt so good when the horror stopped.

About December 7, 1969, my door opened and a big handsome Navy pilot, Jack Fellowes from Tucson, Arizona, entered my room, carrying his possessions in his mat and blankets. I was thunderstruck, for I had given up on ever having a roommate again. Jack was congenial and friendly, as well as having suffered the same damage to his arms as I. He had been the front "flag man" (communicator to the Office from the Pool Hall), and all message traffic had gone through him. A veritable storehouse of POW data, Jack had been shot down a year earlier than I. He filled me in on things I did not fully understand, and gave me the historical perspective.

After his rope treatment by the Rodent, Jack was totally crippled and an Air Force pilot had been assigned as his nurse. Naturally kind and sympathetic, as well as knowing my problems fully, he began caring for me in every way possible. One of his arms was still damaged, but he was strong and capable. Happiness is an American named *Fe*, Jack's Vietnamese name.

I was stilled crippled, barely able to walk. The wounds on my knees, feet, ankles, and buttocks were still open. It was five months after these bouts of debilitating poundings and lashings before I started to become mobile and was able to function in a more routine manner. Jack stared at them in disbelief, and shook his head. His arrival was a boost to my morale, and with the pressure easing off, both of our balloons started to go up.

Such occurrences have a tendency to lead a prisoner to believe that release is imminent. When one wants to believe it so badly, the temptation is hard to resist.

Again, fortuitously, we were moved next door to Larry Guarino and Fred Cherry. Larry and Fred had been past acquaintances, and had just been moved together. Fred was a contemporary of mine from flying school, although I had not met him previously.

While Jack cleared for danger, I talked with LG through the wall with my cup. I gave him the details of my ordeal and commented that it had been a long, hard session. He agreed, wished me well, and said that he hoped my improvement would be rapid.

During the course of our conversation, Larry casually mentioned that completion of the last purge had rounded out his 390th day of hard torture, since his shootdown in June 1965. I felt humbled and awed that he was still alive and in possession of his faculties, and I was somewhat ashamed that I had belabored him with a mere 90-day story. He had the grand-daddy of horror stories!

I am not certain of this speculation, but I believe that his was a record for hard torture. I am not including solitary confinement as hard torture in this statement. Solitary is very tough going, and I do not attempt to minimize it, but it is a different type of torture than the fan belt, ropes, and other good deals.

Shortly thereafter, I had the opportunity to see Guarino through the crack in the door. He was pathetically thin, bearing huge kneeling holes on his knees and feet, massive iron burns on his Achilles tendons, and enormous black circles under his eyes, which almost seemed to pop out of his skinny, undernourished face. It was a demoralizing sight. I wondered if I would look like that at the end of four and a half years, and whether I would be in prison for four and a half years. Both Jack and I were touched by his appearance, and by the magnificent courage he had displayed. I still believe he was the greatest hero of the POW contingent.

Food unexpectedly became much better. We began to receive half a loaf of bread for breakfast. Though it sounds insignificant, it was momentous to us. The walls of the Pool Hall rattled with oohs and aahs of disbelief. Even the super pessimists began to find a certain amount of helium in their balloons, and great optimism swept the camp.

Small bits of sweet, stringy red meat began to appear occasionally in the soup. Speculation held it to be horsemeat, but whatever the source, it was most tasty and welcome.

Malnutrition, beri-beri, and various degrees of dysentary and diarrhea were common ailments. Food was a common source of concern and was responsible for many fluctuations in morale.

In due course, flour and noodles found their way into the soup, both thickening and enriching it. Odd side dishes appeared; slightly pickled cucumbers, greasy turnips, or some strange-colored and appearing vegetable.

Our meals had improved by at lease twenty-five percent. I am sure that on some days, the food value rose to over 1,000 calories, up from 500-700 per day. I learned from Jack that eating cigarettes was partially effective in killing worms, so both of us took "the worm cure." If the cigarettes smoked as badly as they tasted, they had to be truly horrid, requiring a dedicated smoker to burn them.

Another home remedy was the use of coarse salt for toothaches. I had broken three teeth on rocks in the rice, and learned that a large dab of salt or a piece of aspirin placed directly into the cavity relieved the pain.

Dale Doss passed a six-inch worm, which was demoralizing to all of us. There was no question that all of us were loaded with worms. Little wonder that we were so thin.

Jack and I decided that since the pressure was easing, it was time to stop the hated bowing and standing at attention for the guards. We had also been pressing the "V" to allow us to write. We were aware that many men had been permitted to write as far back as the previous October. Of the entire group in our building, Jack and I were the only persons who had not written a rough draft letter of six lines. We complained continuously for equity of treatment, both for letters and for outside time.

In response to our complaints about letter writing, we were taken to a joint quiz one day. Arriving at the quiz room, we were required by Boris, the quizzer, to bow. He harrangued us about not being "polite." Jack looked at me to see what I was going to do. Knowing that it was offensive, I bowed a deep bow, almost touching my nose to the floor. I was well aware that this would infuriate Boris. It did. While his reaction was momentarily satisfying, it cost us another year that we did not write. We were to find in the future that not writing might be a life and death situation.

Jack had been a prisoner for one full year longer than I, and I developed some guilty thoughts about having done him out of a letter, over a simple bow that we had been doing for years. Boris insisted that Jack apologize, although it was his roommate who did not bow correctly. Jack immediately told him, "Pound sand!" End of quiz. The parting words from Boris were, "No apologize, no write."

As we headed back for our room, we decided that was the last bow we were giving to any "V," and it was. We encountered the Fox, the new commandant, to whom we simply nodded. Our guard went into orbit at this breach of camp regulations, but the Fox only nodded in return, a first. This simple act would have brought on massive torture in the past.

During these days, one of the most humorous stories of the war was passed on to me. The date of the story was July 5, 1966. The principal character was Navy Lieutenant Commander Cole Black, an F-8 pilot shot down near Hanoi.

On capture, Black was hustled to NGV for the rope trick. After a hard day's night, he was jerked out of NGV in the morning, taken blindfolded by truck to Ba Dinh Square (the Red Square) in the center of town. There he was handcuffed to another POW, and a small, thin line of about 50 POWs was paraded through a howling mob of incensed civilians and soldiers in the long march.

The prisoners were beaten, spat upon, smashed with rocks, bricks, bottles, wooden shoes, and sticks. They were battered, bruised, and pounded to their knees time and time again. Finally, the torture ended and they found themselves in the football stadium of Hanoi, a temporary shelter and relief. For the first time, Cole got a good look at the man he was fastened to and asked, "Great Scott, do they do this often?"

Unexpectedly, a round of packages from POW families started arriving, and a blackmail program was instituted by Boris. Moon Mullen from my building was called to quiz. After getting all the items from his package and displaying them on the table, Boris told him that he wanted Moon to paint a picture for him. Moon told him he didn't care to paint.

Boris stated, "You must paint. I order you to paint."

Moon replied, "I don't want to paint, I don't know how to paint and I wouldn't paint if I could." Moon's response was good head work. The painting pitch was a crude attempt by the "V" to rebut the accusations across the world that we were mistreated and not permitted to do anything constructive with our time. They believed that actions spoke louder than words, and that a picture was worth 1,000 words.

They sought reproductions of stamps, original paintings, and copies of other paintings, hoping that this production of a POW art gallery would do much to dispel the notion of mistreatment. Simultaneously, they wanted to create the illusion that POW's simply lollygagged around in comfort, painting pictures at their leisure, and attending church on holidays.

Moon rightly refused to take part in this silly anti-POW program. Boris advised, "No paint, no write. No paint, no packages." I'm unsure whether Moon ever got his package, but I am sure he did not paint. Valueless and obvious as the bait was, nevertheless, some POWs did paint. Inevitably, a year and a half later, a prisoner received a letter saying, "We saw your painting as part of the exhibit of POW art in Moscow."

It is a long trip from Hanoi to Moscow for some crude paintings on rough toilet paper, but every little bit helps. It would surprise me if these paintings were not cited by the frequent anti-war types who visited Hanoi, as evidence of our good treatment.

It was imperative that we get our communications net back into full operation. This took some doing, as some people had gone so far underground, they could not be raised. Regardless of the reason, we were all still frightened and generally confused about the future. Even though the choice was a hard one, everyone had to choose to communicate, despite the consequence. It was a choice of communicate or lose your self-respect and the respect of others.

Jack and I enjoyed a package quiz just before Christmas, receiving a larger than normal package, perhaps two pounds each. The premium items in the packages were playing cards and a checkerboard. What a bonanza, and what a great time killer.

Everyone in the building except Fred Cherry received a package, so we chipped in and smuggled items to him from other packages. Ned Shuman and Dale Doss lived in a cell that joined ours on the front of the building, and they also received a deck of cards. We began playing bridge through the wall by tapping instructions. Jack and Shu teamed up against Dale and me. Dale had a real albatross to carry, for he had no choice but to take me for a partner. Jack and Shu were fine players, and in the last year of imprisonment, in another camp, became two of the leading bridge players.

Our packages were loaded with vitamins which we needed desperately. Diarrhea and dysentary had ravaged me badly beginning in March 1968, and I had little relief until after taking double and triple doses of the American-made vitamin pills. Diarrhea for 20 months was largely responsible for my puny 100-pound weight and my lack of strength. The food value from the improved diet and my retention of food began to charge my body with a jolt of energy. My sense of humor improved and I began to awaken rested, strong, and optimistic.

In early summer, 1970, Guarino was moved out of the camp and I became senior officer. After LG's long and horrible ordeal as commander of this camp, this was not a duty I was ambitious for. If my days were as hard as his, I probably would be dead soon.

However, there was little taking place that would indicate that more of those days were on the horizon. On the contrary, the opposite appeared to be the case! Guarino had been at the helm of a hard camp longer than any other officer in the system, a most impressive achievement. He was moved out because the resistance posture of the camp had begun to rise again. Inasmuch as I was dedicated to the same stance as he, it was obvious that I could not survive long as commander.

The "V" knew that I was adamantly opposed to the painting program, and had instructed that this foolish program be stopped. Our communication efforts began to bear fruit, and was effective again.

I was caught passing cigarettes to another room. Jack was caught with matches, a horrible crime, and then he was caught drilling a hole through the brick partition between our bath area and the Stable. This was where I had my first look at A.J. Meyers and Tom Sima, both old shootdowns.

For our crimes, Jack and I were alternately moved in and out of the newly-remodeled Ho Chi Minh room. Its dimensions were small — six feet, six inches long, thirty inches wide, and five feet, six inches tall. Ventilation was five holes about the size of nickel, surrounding the ever-burning light bulb. It looked like a bad summer coming, but our tenure in this room was very short.

HEARTBREAK HOTEL

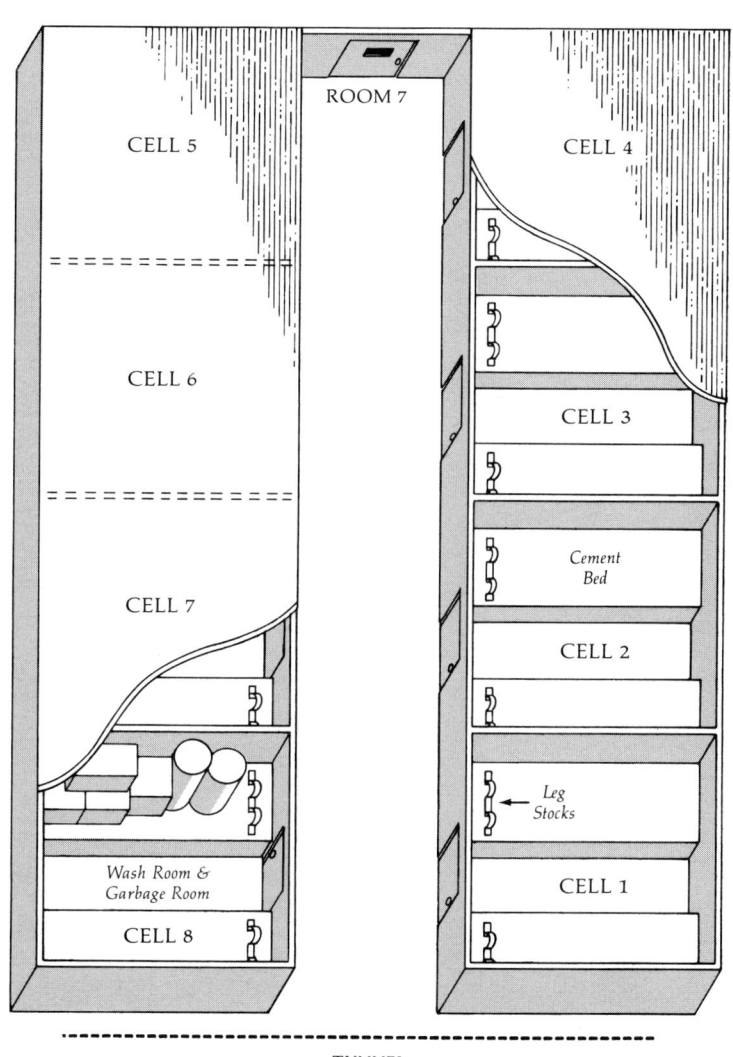

CHAPTER THIRTEEN

Heartbreak Hotel
(Fourth Ring of the Malebolge)

On the night of June 15, 1970, I found myself blindfolded, handcuffed, and on the road to someplace else. It was a typical night move. I sensed that there were other Americans on the bus. When the bus stopped. I got off, carrying my gear, and walked through familiar doors. Although I was blindfolded and could see only at foot level, I recognized the entrance to Hoa Lo Prison.

I wasn't turned to the left, so I wasn't going to the Star Chamber. I wasn't turned to the right, so I wasn't going to Vegas. My heart sank. The only place left was the Heartbreak complex. I experienced some heartbreak right on the spot.

I stepped through the doorway and into Heartbreak Hall as they ripped off my blindfold. The welcoming committee was Bug and Hack. Apprehensively, I stared at Bug and knew no good would come of this.

The Hack acquired his name from a tuberculin-sounding cough. The Bug, our old tormentor from forever, launched into his tirade. He put on the "bad attitude" record, "blackest criminal," and "going to be heavily punished." He told me this was a punishment camp and things were going to be very hard if I didn't shape up quickly.

I was locked into Room One, which was just as dismal as before. As soon as the outer door slammed, and I heard Bug walk away, I thought I heard some slight noise in the building.

I lay down on the floor and called out under the door, "This is Air Force Major George Day. My date of rank is February 6, 1962."

Right away from my right, and down the hall, came the answer, "Hi, Nigh. This is Jackie Fay." It was Jack Fellowes.

I was cheered to hear from him. Misery does love company. We talked back and forth for a few minutes, and it turned out he was in the adjoining room. We picked up the cups and began talking to each other through the wall.

Jack told me he thought there was someone else in the building. He had ears like a fox, and his four long years as a POW had given him a sixth sense. We got back down on the floor and I started calling down the hall.

I said, "This is George Day. Someone else is in this building. We are two fellow Americans. I'm an Air Force pilot. Jack Fellowes is in Room Two. He's a Navy pilot. Answer up!"

Although we called for several minutes, there was no answer. We knew someone else was there because we could hear the movements. Only a deaf man would not have been able to hear me.

As was customary, Bug made his rounds early in the morning and took head count. He started putting the press on us. He told me to stand at attention and bow. I told him I wasn't going to stand at attention and I wasn't going to bow!

Bug insisted, "You have to stand up. You have to 'stand attention' and you have to show respect. If you don't, you will be punished."

I had to stand up to get some things from him, so I did, but I did not bow. He shouted, "Bow!"

I tested the water with a nod of the head.

Unmollified, he yelled, "Either bow or you'll be punished!"

I replied, "I told you before I'm *not going to bow*!!"

He did not follow up. I was not dragged off to torture. I hoped that some of his fangs had been pulled. My responses took more courage than is apparent, but it was mandatory to face him down, or be blackmailed forever by his threats.

The next time Bug returned, I got off the bed and simply stood there. He shouted, "Bow!" in his most threatening voice. I gave him a nod of the head.

He said, "I told you to bow!"

I reminded him, "I told you yesterday that I'm *not* going to bow. If you don't knock this off, I'm not standing up, and I'm not doing anything else!"

He banged the Judas hole violently and stormed off in an angry huff. I told Jack what I had done, and we waited apprehensively. Nothing happened! We hoped camp officers had been prohibited from physical torture without good cause. This obviously was not good enough cause!

We were elated. Considering the fact that the living conditions were so poor, our morale was high. Just to feel assured that torture was over was an enormous morale builder. We had waited years for this. It was a degree of freedom, and freedom had achieved its prime perspective with us.

The cells could have been cool with a nice view of the courtyard. Unfortunately, they had been covered completely with bamboo matting. The ventilator over the door had been pounded full of pieces of wood. It was impossible to get either light or air from outside. The American POW lived in far worse conditions than the "V" who had been prisoners of the French.

As I looked around my room and experimented, I found I could displace the mat and look out, after sliding the wooden window plug out of the way. As Jack and I compared conditions, we learned that by punching holes in the mats, we had a good view of the courtyard.

For the first time in our POW life we had an opportunity, under "no torture" conditions, to watch the courtyard and develop a feel for what was going on. More importantly, we could watch the "V" and gain some understanding of them.

Again, we attempted to raise our companion in the building. We called down the hall, shouted our names, and asked for a response. We received a cough in return.

I said, "I'm Major Bud Day and my neighbor is Jack Fellowes." Then I asked, "Are you an Air Force pilot?"

He coughed a yes, in code. I inquired, "Are you being tortured?" He coughed a no.

I explained, "There is no torture in this camp. I've already confronted the Bug and he doesn't have permission to torture us. Let me have your name."

Immediately, he answered, "I'm Ben Pollard, Air Force Major Ben Pollard. I came in last night from Camp Hope (Son Tay)."

"Well, hi. Nice to know you," I answered. "Do you know anything about the guy across the hall?"

He told us, "Yes. There's more than one!"

Surprised, I questioned, "Oh, is that right?"

"Yes. I think there are two of them."

We exchanged brief biographical data by talking down the corridor under the doors, arranging a system where one of us would clear and the other person would talk. This way the "V" would not be able to listen or catch us in the act of communicating and have some excuse to torture us.

For a number of days we called and requested answers from the other men in the block. None were forthcoming. I was getting angry. We were spending a large part of the day on our knees, and mine were bloody tender, plus a lot of time in uncomfortable positions on the floor while clearing. I was furious that a fellow American would not answer me. After a long time, we got a "yes" coughed from one of them.

It turned out that there were three other people in the building. One had been beaten senseless by Fidel, the Cuban. Two people, who could communicate, had been in solo, one since 1966, the other since May 1967. They were attempting, in their own way, to do the best job of resisting they could. Due to their long time in solo, they had developed a hard, high-resistance policy which included resisting communications.

We knew it was part of the vicious and common "solo syndrome" which happens to men after long high-pressure solitary. They did not trust us and were not willing to place their confidence in us.

Coincidentally, we started to get better food at this time. Later, we discovered that two of the three men thought this food was a special favor, and would not accept it. Unfortunately, the "V" were making a strong effort to get all three of them to eat, which only confirmed their belief that we were getting special treatment.

We were still getting grunts and coughs, no real communication. The third man would not acknowledge any communication, answered nothing, and refused our repeated efforts to talk, tap or comm. The fact was, he had been tortured out of his senses and could not respond.

We passed out a huge amount of news to them, purely in the blind, by speaking loudly under the doors. Jack, Ben and I made a lot of noisy personal exchanges with the hope that these people might begin to accept us as American POWs and friends.

Part of their problem was that they had lived in the building at a time when a Vietnamese POW was also held there. The Americans thought the Vietnamese had been put there to spy on them. They also believed he was still in the building. One man had been tortured for communicating. He was sure all of our talk was a plot to get him caught communicating again.

Because of his position in the building, Pollard was occasionally able to get a look at the other three POWs from our building. His report was frightening! They were in poor physical condition, all three extremely thin.

At this time, the Vietnamese felt we would be going home soon. This brought a small flurry of tiny improvements. We had begun to get answers from one of the three unknown POWs when there was an increase in the quantity and the starchy content of the food. Soup had been primarily pumpkin. The "V" started adding large amounts of noodles, grease, some boullion, and even a little horsemeat. It was quite tasty, "for "V" prison food. It was designed to put weight on us and we began to get huge servings of soy bean cake. Six months before, our individual portions would have fed four men, but it still lacked the protein and vitamins needed to counter the widespread malnutrition and beri-beri.

The summer, fall, and winter of 1970 were the strangest time in my five and a half years of imprisonment. The greater part of the "ten most wanted men" list kept by POWs was around Heartbreak. There was Bug, torturer of hundreds, Straps and Bars, and Jake, also torturers of many. Cedric, also known as the Kid, who had assisted Fidel in torturing "Max" out of his mind at the Zoo, was there. Major Bai, or the Cat, torturer of Stratton,

Risner, and many others was also present. Moses, Chief Torturer of the Zoo purge of 1969, and many other well-known thugs were at Heartbreak.

All of them still acted and talked as tough as in the old days. But despite continuously violating camp regulations, we did not get tortured. We enjoyed their discomfort, for they had great difficulty in dealing with us without torture as their prime influence.

We refused to bow, communicated when and how we wanted, spoke to and treated the guards and officers as they treated us, usually rudely. We voiced our complaints about not getting mail, not getting to write, not getting treatment under the Geneva Convention. We griped about not getting time outside, not living with other men (although this building was well-suited for it), not getting packages from our families. We complained about poor medical care for the sick men, no intellectual material, games, or playing cards, and about the continual harassment by the guards and Bug. Our demands were merely for treatment guaranteed by the Geneva Convention.

Ben Pollard summed up our position well one morning. Bug looked into Ben's room and noticed that he had some large, painful boils on his body. Bug asked, "Why didn't you tell me?"

Ben truthfully answered, "For what? You have never cared once for our health in five years."

Buoyed by the improved food, the ability to communicate freely most of the day, to look through the cracks at the courtyard and sky, our morale grew. The simple pleasures were so dear to us. How beautiful a leaf, a cloud, or the sunset. Years of deprivation had honed our appreciation of the simple values as sharp as a pencil point.

Packages from home were delivered, highly pilfered, but good. Amazing tongue-appealing delicacies . . . toffee candy, dried apricots, chocolate pudding, and canned meat. Almost as enjoyable as the package items were the package smells. Nothing in the world smells as good as American products.

During late summer or early fall, Ben told me that two prisoners from outside our building were using the drain in our building to dump their waste buckets. All three of us began to man tiny outside peepholes, and we discovered that the men were from the Star Chamber of New Guy Village, which we could partially see.

Our hours of surveillance paid off when we discovered that one of the POWs was my friend, Colonel Robinson Risner. Robbie had been on the cover of a weekly U.S. news magazine, and had been awarded the Air Force Cross, the second-highest rated U.S. medal for heroism in combat. He had been a special subject of mistreatment by the "V". I knew he had been in solo about four years (actually 52 months), and I feared that he may have been brainwashed and tortured around the bend. Such was not the case. He was as tough as the saddle leather so dear to him.

It warmed my heart to see him, this bright sunny morning that he appeared hazily through the patchwork of grape vines that blocked our view. Jack was also eyeballing the yard and he pounded on the wall from his cell, "Who is that?"

"Robbie," I shouted to Jack delightedly. "It's Robbie, but I can't make out the other man!"

This was the start of a new program. Robbie and his partner were permitted to exercise from 11:30 to 12:00. Both men were puny, but the man with Robbie was scarecrow thin, and appeared to be in pain as he walked. He was very gray.

We all knew that some senior colonels were in the system. We guessed it might be Air Force Colonel Dave Winn, but turned out to be Lieutenant Colonel Gordon "Swede" Larson. He had become so emaciated in the three years since I had last seen him that I didn't recognize him. We could see the huge torture stripes he bore.

Jack was one of the finest communicators in Hanoi. He began flashing to Swede one day by shoving a piece of paper through an aperture. While the two were out for exercise, Swede walked, and Robbie did calisthentics in place. The "V" loved to watch Robbie's exercise routine, which was dazzling. One of the kitchen girls came out every day at 11:30 a.m. to watch. It would have been flattering, had she not been so ugly. She was one of many "V," both male and female, who considered him a prize catch.

While all the "V" were watching Robbie work up a sweat, Jack and Swede coded back and forth. This was a great morale boost for them, as they were even farther behind on news than we were. It was nice to be able to pass a little news on, for a change. Swede was a sharp, adept communicator, and our exchanges went well.

With typical concern, Robbie asked some questions about the men in Heartbreak. He shared my concern about their health and approved my program to raise cain about their treatment.

The man across the hall was code-named "Max," for maximum resistor. Max had decided that he was going to refuse to bow, and he stopped bowing altogether on May 21, 1968. He was dragged off to a torture session with Cedric (The Kid), the Cuban Fidel, who was teaching English to the "V", the Lump, and several beaters. They roped, mauled, and beat Max for more than 24 hours continuously.

"Jig" lived straight across from the Carriage House, where Max took his disastrous beating. Jig said, "Max never cried out, never screamed, and never gave them the satisfaction of hearing him acknowledge pain. When he came out of the torture session the following morning, he looked like a small child who was wondering why he had been struck." Max never regained lucidity again. Shortly after, he was put into a room with some other POWs, one of whom related this story.

"One morning the turnkey, Beanpole, came to the door harassing Max. He seized on some excuse, grabbed a fan belt and struck Max twelve times across the face with the belt. Although the belt opened a large cut under his eye, Max never flinched. The "V" were positive he was faking long after they had beaten him senseless and had long since lost all ability to feel pain. His subconscious had disconnected the feeling of pain."

It took three POWs to keep Max alive for several months, force-feeding him since he refused to eat. The team was called Choker, Stoker, and Poker. Several men held Max down while the Choker got his mouth open, the Stoker poured food into him, and the Poker rammed it down his throat.

One night, I heard Max vomiting. He sounded deathly ill, so I began to press the Bug for medical care. Bug's normal answer was, "Shut mouth, you no talk for other. All men talk for self."

I told Bug, "You have tortured him so that he cannot speak."

This only caused Bug to smash the peephole shut and storm off, threatening punishment as only he could do. Despite Bug's rebuff, Max began getting first a little, and then a lot of attention from our incompetent and arrogant medic, "Ben Casey." He was surly, foul-tempered, and frightened of Max, as were all the medics.

One day a three-star NVA officer, an army captain, came into the courtyard, took off his collar tab rank, and came over to look at Max. Because of his thick glasses, he was promptly named Sealed Beams. I was watching through a hole drilled in the board above my door. Max was in no mood for visitors. He leaped onto his feet, pressed his back against the wall, both feet spread wide apart, with his hands flat against the wall, as if he were going to spring. Sealed Beams wisely backed away and Cedric closed the door as quickly as possible. Sealed Beams and Cedric exchanged smiles of relief. They were thoroughly frightened. I had seen that Max had electric shock burns both on his arms and skull.

Sealed Beams continued to appear, and the next day Max was as docile as a lamb, only staring at the floor while Sealed Beams gave him a huge shot of what I thought was vitamins. We found some glass vials on the floor, Chinese manufacture with the word vitamins written in English.

This prompts an interesting story which may explain why he received vitamins. In the fall of 1969, as the food improved, I began taking vitamins. I threw off the dysentary that plagued me for 20 months. Everyone who received vitamins in the fall packages in 1969 reported almost identical findings. The "V" were slow to recognize our improved health related to vitamin usage, but eventually they did.

Naturally, they misinterpreted it. They considered vitamins as some new wonder drug, and began to use them indiscriminately for every ailment. If a man were to come down with appendicitis, he got vitamins. Indigestion, more vitamins. Fallen arches, vitamins. Now they were going to cure Max with vitamins.

I continued to press Bug for a quiz with Cochise, now commander of Little Vegas, New Guy Village, and Heartbreak. I was frightened about Max's health, and the other two men, Kilo and Jig. Both were emaciated to the point that they had difficulty walking.

Kilo was a tall man with a large, rawboned frame and a ruggedly handsome face. He was like many others, tough as shoe leather, and dedicated to high principles. He had not heard another American voice from May of 1967 until we moved into the building in the summer of 1970. His resistance posture was high, founded on an iron will, and a determination never to disgrace himself or his country. He lived more spartanly than we, having thrown most of his personal items away. He was determined not to take anything from the "animals," as he called the Vietnamese. Kilo's normal weight was about 200-225 pounds. At this time he weighed between 120 and 130.

Jig was an average-sized officer who had been in solitary for more than four years. He had a brilliant mind and unbelievable memory. He was also a hard-line resistor, dark-haired, dark-complected, and so frail that he would not stand on his concrete bed for fear of falling. Jig's normal weight would run about 160-170 pounds. His current weight was 105-115.

It was clear that the camp administration was growing more concerned about the health of Max, Jig, and Kilo. Sealed Beams began to show up every day, giving them vitamin shots, and urging them to eat, with no success.

In September, I was finally called to quiz with Cochise. It was a greasy, sickening quiz, starting out with what the "V" call an atmosphere of cordiality. I got straight to the point and told Cochise that unless he did something effective, very soon Max, Kilo, and Jig would die. His reaction was amused disdain.

This disregard for American life made my blood boil, but I checked my temper in an effort to save their lives. I explained carefully that they were not eating their food, that they were physically and mentally troubled, and that we needed to be moved into communal living so we could help them. Ben, Jack, and I agreed that exposure of the three to more normal living, exchange of conversation and friendship, pictures, vitamins, and tender loving care would bring both Kilo and Jig back up to speed quickly. I told Cochise that I knew them and knew all about them.

He asked with an amused air, "How?"

I told him that I communicated with them continually every day, and knew that we could help them by establishing some compound living.

He answered, "No! Kilo does not want a roommate. I have asked him and he said he didn't want one."

I told him bluntly, "That's a lie. Every American wants a roommate, and if he doesn't, it is because you have tortured him and mistreated him until he can't make the right decision. At any rate, I don't believe you. He wants a roommate!"

The quiz was so greasy that this reply did not ruffle Cochise. He gave me the typical brushoff. "The camp will study (the problem)."

Surprisingly enough, the mythical "camp" did study the problem, and I was permitted to leave my cell and visit Kilo for a few minutes each day, for a few days. Sadly, the "V" had waited too long.

On October 14, 1970, Kilo and Max were taken to the hospital. We saw a whole retinue of medics around our cell whom we were used to seeing in other camps. This caused me to believe the Bug when, in response to my question, he told me that Max and Kilo "had gone to the hospital to keep their health."

On the 16th, Jig also went to the hospital. He claimed a heart problem the day after Kilo and Max left. The three men were never seen again. On March 14, 1973, I was advised at Clark AFB, Phillipine Islands, that the "V" had reported these three men "died" in captivity. Max was USAF Captain Earl Cobeel, Jig was Navy Lieutenant J.J. Connell and Kilo was Commander Ken Cameron.

I learned from my wife later that we six — Pollard, Fellowes, Max, Kilo, Jig, and myself — were the only known POWs who were not reported by the "V" on the list of confirmed POWs which they furnished to the U.S. at Paris. I've wondered many times what fate was planned for Fellowes, Pollard and me originally. It is interesting to note that not one amputee, not one mental case, not one cosmetically displeasing prisoner was returned to the United States.

Fall was a red-letter time since both Jack and I wrote our first letters. At this time I had been a POW for more than three years and Jack for more than four years.

Bug asked with false concern if I wanted to write. Recognizing that his toadying behavior meant that the "V" wanted us to write, I told him I could not possibly write until I received a letter, a little reverse blackmail. Jack and Ben both gave him the same answer, so the following day we were called to a quiz where we all received a letter, the first for Jack and me.

I had great difficulty reading since I had not read anything for three years. In addition, my facial injuries and time's erosion of my sight made it difficult. It was ecstasy to see the Viking's signature, to see her carefully-chosen phrases of encouragement and love. The letter was only seven months old, so I knew that she and the children were alive at least a few months before. It was common practice of the "V" to hold the letters for a year before delivery.

The receipt of these long-awaited letters from home transformed us into new men, even though we were not permitted to keep them. Jack and Ben were all smiles, and we passed each other all of the details we could remember.

For some reason, the "V" took one of the speakers out of Heartbreak, and I discovered that by placing the wires together, I could short out the camp radio system. From this time on, every time the radio played something I did not want to hear, I would couple the wires and black out the radio through the entire camp.

In a cleaning session in the building, in early November, we entered the cell that Max had occupied and were entranced by a beautiful tree that he had sketched with a piece of half-burned coal. It was truly a thing of beauty, simple, stark, and lovely. It was obvious that the "V" had not pounded all of Max's senses from him. It may have been the last expression of his damaged senses.

Early November will always be remembered by me as a banner time. I received my first picture of the Viking. She was in a light-green dress, hair beautifully styled, wearing her broad comely smile, and marking a date on her perpetual succession of calendars.

What a thrill! Relief and happiness at the sight of her photo triggered waves of memories, love and joy. I suddenly felt as if another yoke had been lifted, for the picture was dated only a few months before; August, 1970.

I found out later why the "V" let us write. Our government, my wife and many families, were raising Cain about the fact that my name had not been released by the DRV. Tons of mail was flowing to Communist countries, and the animals in Hanoi were being called exactly that by civilized people all over the world. Lovers of freedom and decency across the globe were screaming in anguished voices the words a tortured prisoner could only monotonously chant to himself.

Wives and families of POWs traveled to the Paris Peace Conference and to Communist diplomatic contacts all over Europe. H. Ross Perot placed a dummy POW in a representative bamboo cage complete with rats and bugs in the U.S. capitol. The brother of John McCain lived in a cage in travels across the U.S. to illustrate our plight.

One POW wife entered the ante room of the female representative to the Paris Peace Conference with a group of reporters and photographers and hid in a closet until she burst out to confront the Communist negotiator, seizing him by the leg and shouting complaints against POW mistreatment as they attempted to drag her away.

Because of this type of action by loyal Americans, George Day, Jack Fellowes, and Ben Pollard were allowed to write, thus being tacitly acknowledged as POWs for the first time. After only three years, I had just received my first semblance of compliance with Geneva Convention treatment. It was a long time before I received more. The list of POW names was released in Paris to Senator Ted Kennedy, who was fast closing the gap on Senator "Halfbrite" as a friend of the Commies.

Following November 20, 1970, the time of the raid on Son Tay, strange things began to happen in camp. The courtyard suddenly began to fill up with a multitude of "V" interrogations. We knew many of them from the Plantation, the Zoo and some from Son Tay.

On Tuesday afternoon and evening, a total of 525 prisoners, political and criminal, consisting of many men, some women and about 150 children, were brought out of the back yard of Hoa Lo into the court yard. They were strapped together on a long piece of wood placed under their arms and behind their backs. Seven to ten people were strapped to one bar. They were led out of camp in such a panic and a frenzy, that it was obvious something had happened.

Guards ran about in the evening conducting air raid drills, running into each other, and dropping their rifles. We snickered in our cells at their clumsiness!

At about 9:30 P.M., Jack woke me by pounding on the wall violently. "They are moving hundreds of POWs into the back side," he shouted. "Ben is counting them, and I just heard Ray Vohden on his crutches."

By midnight, 225 men had been moved into the back side of the camp, into rooms that could accomodate about 40 men per room. We rejoiced, happy in the knowledge that many Americans were now living together in large rooms. It had been a long wait. We had no idea that Son Tay had been raided.

It was only one of many bold and intelligent actions taken by the new administration. Although Son Tay was not holding Americans, the raid was a great success, for it forced the "V" to move all POWs into one secure area, thus improving our conditions. Secondly, it was important for the "V" to learn that the U.S. cared that much about its POWs and it was only a harbinger of more bold and forceful things to come.

Had we known of the raid, our gratitude to our country would have welled over. We had been waiting long years for this kind of reciprocal action by our country. Loyalty was finally becoming a two-way street.

I totally disagree with the ill-conceived statement by Senator Fulbright, the *New York Times*, and the *Washington Post* that "the Nixon administration had endangered the lives of prisoners by trying to free them

HEARTBREAK HOTEL

... and ... if American prisoners had been present, as Ted Kennedy said, the North Vietnamese guards 'wouldn't have hesitated to shoot them' once the rescue party arrived. The best way to free them, Kennedy said, was to get out of Vietnam lock, stock, and barrel." Phoenix, *Arizona Republic* November 24, 1970. I heard hundreds of statements by Mr. Fulbright on the "V" radio and I cannot remember one that I agreed with. Many Arkansas voters agreed with my disdain.

The true facts of the Son Tay raid were that because of outside pressure in 1969, the "V" started a program to improve their tarnished image. They began construction of a show camp on the west side of Hanoi, which would accomodate about half of the POWs. It was finished in the spring of 1970, and the occupants of Son Tay, the most distant camp from Hanoi, were moved into the camp in June, 1970. Son Tay was run down, distant and a supply burden to the "V."

It was then turned into an NVA training camp. Perfect reconnaissance photos of Son Tay just before the raid showed the camp in its normal configuration, full of guards. Since prisoners were seldom permitted out of their cells, it was rare that a photo ever showed a POW in the yard. There is no camera in existance that will take pictures through a roof and reveal a U.S. POW sitting on a bed.

The Son Tay raid has to go down as one of the most daring, successful raids in military history. Secretary of Defense Laird, General Leroy Manor, Colonel Bull Simon, the Army Special Forces volunteers, and the Air Force helicopter crews will hold the undying admiration of the POWs for their fantastic courage!

The raid improved our treatment more than any other single act. The "V" were forced to move us into large rooms in a single camp. It was the minimum action that our nation had to take to keep the faith. It was the absolute opposite of the Lyndon Johnson kind of loyalty.

CHAPTER FOURTEEN

The Short Reunion

On Christmas Eve, Jack, Ben and I, survivors of Heartbreak, were moved into Vegas for Christmas dinner. Our gear was shaken down. Everything we had been given from our Christmas packages (toothbrushes, soap, socks, clothing, and food) was taken away from us. Most of it was never seen again. The deodorant soap and vitamins I had used so sparingly were gone! I nearly cried. With them went all of my pictures of Viking and the children.

Doors opened and we were moved en mass into Room Seven in the back courtyard of Hoa Lo Prison. Room Seven was a 25-foot by 70-foot room accomodating 45 men. One built-up concrete pedestal was located in the center of the room. We had about 18 inches per man on the pedestal for bed space, but it was as pleasurable as a boy's Sunday School picnic.

The back side area was named Camp Unity, or No OK Corral. A near-holiday mood enveloped us. Sleeping was out of the question. Everyone stayed up the entire night and talked or simply stared at all of these Americans. Happiness and joy washed through the group and built into a groundswell of relief from suffering. It seemed to be our emancipation.

People described what they speculated had prompted the moves. Some had been at Camp Faith and were able to see much of the air activity in the attack on Son Tay. There was a report that someone had contact with a South Vietnamese soldier who had described a "parachute raid." As a result, we thought a commando raid had struck near Hanoi. It was a long time before we learned the true story of Son Tay from the new "shoot-downs" in late 1972.

Delight at being in a big room was overtaken by the necessity of organizing normal activities to provide for food, cleanup and work details. We organized by seniority, sorted out our room SRO, the flight commanders, and sorted people into various flights.

It was necessary to establish comm links with Colonel John P. Flynn, the senior POW, if he were in camp, in order to get the chain of command

THE SHORT REUNION

going.

My pad lay between two friends, John McCain (later awarded the South Vietnamese Legion of Honor, that nation's highest combat award), and Jim Kasler. What a pleasure to enjoy the companionship of these dear people. Larry Guarino slept on the other side of Jim Kasler, and it was stimulating to have firsthand, face-to-face contact with this great leader and courageous Italian whom I admired so much. Billy Lawrence, a Navy Commander, now an admiral, was my flight commander; a brilliant, dynamic, fine fellow.

Our long repressed and overpowering urge of an esthetic renewal . . . a religious program, worship through hymns, participation in prayer, and thanks to God for this fantastic experience in living, began to burn in our hearts. We luxuriated in the camaraderie of each other — 45 happy, laughing, smiling men, all wanting to talk at the same time.

Astute and practical Larry Guarino psyched our situation well when he said, "Enjoy it, Pal, it will not last long. Human nature being what it is, there will be personality problems, and discord in this environment that we didn't have when the pressure was really on. We've only been in here a couple of days and people are now telling me how I should have run the Zoo. When the torture was thick and fast, I never had a person try to tell me what to do, because they knew their answers were no better than mine." How prophetic his comment!

We decided to organize a church program with Ensign George Coker as our minister. George was a fine, clean-cut young fellow, one of two early escapees from the Power Plant, and the A-6 bombardier-navigator for Jack Fellowes.

On February 7, 1971, our church program consisted of George Coker opening the church services, Commander Howie Rutledge conducting the opening prayer, and Colonel Risner giving the closing prayer. Although the Bug forbade it, we had the quiet church service. We invited Bug to attend and told him he would find that religion didn't hurt. Our welcome to him had a hollow, insincere ring. He told us that if we held a church service, it would be very bad for us. Of course, we would be punished.

As church began, Bug came to the window and ordered us to stop. He shouted, fumed, and insisted that it stop. We were in no mood to stop and continued the service. Our small four-man choir quietly sang three religious songs which touched everyone to the core: *Rock of Ages*, *The Old Rugged Cross* and *I walk in the Garden Alone*.

Early that evening, amid great commotion, the door flew open and Bug entered with many armed guards. He ordered Rutledge, Coker and Robbie to leave. They picked up quietly and as they walked out the door, I began to sing *The Star-Spangled Banner*. The notion of group resistance was not unknown to this bunch. Unlike Russian prisoners who accepted their lot with scarcely a whisper of complaint, these mice began to roar like lions.

Everyone joined in! From a low-key quiet song, it became louder and louder! The next rooms picked it up. In a few minutes, *The Star-Spangled Banner* circled the camp. It was the first time American voices had been heard united and clear in Hanoi, and was a great morale lifter for most of the POWs.

For the next two hours, we sang all of the patriotic songs: *God Bless America*, *America the Beautiful*, many hymns, *California, Here I Come*, *The Eyes of Texas are Upon You*, and many others. Three, four, five or six hard years of pent-up emotion and frustration were launched on the wings of song into the night, in a protest against our friends' having been unjustly removed from the room. A semblance of self-respect returned!

Not all POWs reacted the same, as not all supported our resistance policies. I quote the remarks of U.S. Marine Corps Colonel Edison Miller, charged by a fellow POW with misconduct, in a poem quoted from the *Des Moines Register*:

"COWARDS SING AT NIGHT"

"December 9, 1973 - WROTE POEMS. Miller wrote six poems as a POW. One of them, read over the camp radio, incensed some prisoners after several POWs were penalized after a whole camp broke into song (*The Star Spangled Banner*) one night as a showing of unity. The poem includes these lines:

> *The Valiant often stand alone*
> *And speak from heart and mind.*
> *The Coward seeks the crowd and night,*
> *His face he hides from sight and light.*
>
> *The Valiant try to understand.*
> *They often wonder why.*
> *The Coward's voice is heard in vain.*
> *He calls forth God and Flag by name.*

In answer to a question, Miller says he doesn't feel he was brainwashed, then added, 'Maybe I was a little.' " End of excerpt.

It is my guess that, according to Miller, the "cowards" were the men who sang *The Star-Spangled Banner* in protest against "V" mistreatment. Conversely, those who wrote anti-POW poems to be read on the "V" propaganda box were "The Valiant." Little wonder that the U.S. Marine Corps saw fit to dispense with the services of Mr. Miller and a pity it did not

THE SHORT REUNION

press for a court martial and dishonorable discharge, in my opinion.

The songfest frightened the Vietnamese badly. Nothing like this would dare happen in a Communist country. Such protesters would be thrown immediately into confinement, arrested, or dragged off to a labor camp. When the protesters are already in jail, it creates a real problem.

Our action indicated organization against the "camp authorities." Communists were terrorized by our unity and organization. We got their attention this time! Fearsome thoughts of riots ran through the camp administration.

"Why can't those rotten troublemakers leave well enough alone? Always wanting something. First they wanted to move together. Then they even wanted to stop bowing. When will their unreasonable demands stop? When we cracked their rotten skulls they didn't sing! When we smashed that reactionary Ngay across the ass, you didn't hear any bourgeois songs! No, he crawled like a snake on the concrete. These diehards. Give them an inch and they'll want a mile!"

Resistance fed on resistance, like a buzzard on a dead rabbit.

The SRO made it clear to Bug and the turnkeys who came to the door that the following Sunday would produce another church service; bigger, better, and louder than the last. We stated that if they did not agree (1) to allow us to have church, and (2) return Colonel Risner, Commander Rutledge, and Ensign Coker, there was going to be a lot of trouble. Our threats could not be ignored.

February 8, 1971, was an exciting day. Various of the "trouble makers" were pulled out of the room, usually singly, but sometimes in pairs. The courtyard was alive with armed guards, unlike the more normal condition of armed guards in the towers and numerous unarmed turnkeys and kitchen help milling about the yard. The atmosphere was electric with excitement. Guards held their weapons at the ready.

The area just outside of our large, rusty, double door was enclosed by a bamboo woven-mat fence about eight feet high. A partition of similar size and shape separated our courtyard from Room Six, next door. Numerous verdant trees, mostly Asian pecan and Australian pines, stirred listlessly in the light sunny morning breeze.

I was called out by Bug, who also singled out Kasler, McCain, and Fellowes. We were led out separately. After leaving the courtyard, I was steered to the right toward the Rawhide Squadron area and the run-down, tiny building that was designed as a hospital room by the "V".

The action of the guards was menacing. It was clear this was not a day in which to get "famous." I was halted at bayonet point, and waved into a room next to the sick room. A porky, puffy-faced officer, wearing the three stars of a captain, sat stiffly behind a wobbly, peeling old desk, badly in need of varnish.

He shuffled some papers nervously, mentally priming himself for the role he was going to play. The "V" English speakers acted as if there was a multi-position switch connected to their brains, and when activated, it moved them to the tough-guy, the friendly, or the sympathetic position, in robot fashion. Martinet-like, the captain stiffened his back, and looked up at me with his "toughest guy" look.

"Nigh?" he asked.

"Yes," I responded. "My name is Day."

"You, I know you nem (your name)," in butchered English. With that he went on to play the "black creemenal" record . . . killed many Vietnamese old men, women and children . . . show a "bad attitude" toward the camp authority . . . make dark schemes against the camp . . . guilty of many crimes since being captured . . . never been "sincere" . . . had even escaped from the "people" . . . never had shown "repentance" for black deeds and black crimes. Despite the fact that the camp and the people had always shown lenient and more humane treatment (meaning they had not murdered me on the spot), it seemed that I never learned my lesson, to be "polite" and to "show good attitude."

I stood mute, dulled by years of listening to this broken record. I could almost repeat it verbatim.

"Now," he said threateningly, "you have against the camp in a serious crime, and I warn you, if you show any more bad attitude, the guards have the right to kill you on the spot. There will be no more bad action against the camp, and we know, Nigh, that you are diehard reactionary and the Camp Authority will punish you heavily for your next crime. And all of your room-fellows."

I stood in silent disgust, thinking all the while that I wouldn't want it any other way. This disturbed him. He wanted me to respond, and I savored this slight discomfort on his part. Happiness is not answering a Communist who wants an answer.

"Nigh!" he shouted, half rising. "Uner stan?"

I stared at him blankly, and did not answer.

"Go home," he barked and called the guard to direct me back toward the compound.

I walked slowly back, relishing the fact that I was momentarily out from behind the bars of an over-crowded room, breathing fresh air, savoring the beauty of the blue sky and the billowy, puffy, cumulus clouds. The early spring sun was warming.

Never had the sky been so blue, the clouds so white, and the trees so green. I searched the area for any POW face, since in 1971 I could only recognize 65-70 of the 335 POWs in Hanoi. With the paranoic "V" penchant for security, that was the total I had seen, many only once, and then briefly. Even now, there are more than 200 I have not met or talked with.

Near the main gate separating Camp Unity and the Heartbreak Hotel front courtyard, a number of senior "V" officers were gathered. Lounging against the wall, hands in pockets, caps askew, in faded, wrinkled uniforms, they generated a graphic picture of what they were — secondraters, unsuited for combat commands.

In the group were Stone-Face, the former commander of the Plantation; Cochise, former and dismissed commander of the Zoo; the Fox, military commander of the Zoo; Rabbit, active torturer; Bushy, present commander of Unity, ex-commander of Son Tay; Frenchy or Hare Lip, former commander of the Briar Patch; Major Bai, liason officer responsible for all POWs; Moses, political cadre who supervised the mass Zoo torture of 1969, resulting in prisoner death; the Rat, Lump, Spot, Soft Soap Fairy, and a number of lesser luminaries well-known to the rank and file POW.

One of them said, "Nigh," nodding at me. Several of the group looked up and stared fixedly at me. Many of them were senior officers or cadres, older, slightly better groomed and a little better dressed. The punks in the group put on their sneers and disdainful faces, in a pathetic attempt to curry favor with their seniors by demonstrating "good attitude." Behind them, a few feet away, two of my future roommates, John Flynn and Dave Winn, languished in cramped, dark cells.

As I turned the corner into our yard, the sour odor of poorly-washed clothes, undergarments, and towels battered my senses. I noticed that our rectangular brick and cement horse trough was full of water. Using our cups, leaky pots or food cans, we dipped water out of this trough to bathe and wash clothes.

Thankfully, the entire courtyard was paved with a thin veneer of crumbling concrete, installed by the French, many decades past. It was filled with ruts and holes, which made walking dangerous to the unwary, but it was a blessing. With the torrential rains that fell on Hanoi, a dirt yard would have turned into a hog wallow of the worst sort.

The Hawk, our present turnkey, sour-faced and perpetually unhappy, unlocked the doors and waved me into the room. I looked over my shoulder for one last glance at the open sky, and stepped up into the room. The penetrating stink of the open urinal and the uncovered barrel that was our toilet was sickening.

Navy Commander Charlie James looked up at me questioningly. "Same thing?"

"Rog," I answered, "SOS." (Same old stuff)

"Boy," he said, "the 'V' are really excited, really panicked. I think those numbskulls think we are going to charge the walls."

"You're right, Charlie! I can't believe it. You'd think that after holding and dealing with Americans for almost seven years, they would understand us. It appears highly likely that as someone else said of East and West, never the twain shall meet."

I went straight to my flight commander, Bill Lawrence, and reported on my quiz. John McCain limped up and joined us.

"SOS, Bill!" I explained. "They are really frightened and have misinterpreted the songfest and our resistance actions. They think we are going to riot. The yard is full of all the ranking bad guys. Every high-powered "V" I have ever known from any other camp or seen around the system is out by Heartbreak Gate."

John McCain added, "This is really wild! They're terrorized! I would guess that the fact that torture has been taken away from them as a first resort, must really have them panicked. They always knew how to put out a fire when they had torture. They have no idea of how to operate when just plain ordinary human relations are demanded."

How demonstrative of my own, and many others' feelings, about this never-never land we had entered in 1970-71. How ironic that our "V" room officer in charge would be the Bug, that our bread delivery boy would be Jake, that our turnkey would be the Hawk, or that Cedric the Kid would be thrust into daily contact with us. It would be impossible to get an accurate measure of the amount of torture, starvation, deprivation, mistreatment and death that this particular group had inflicted upon the POW population. It was incredible to mix this group of torturers with the tortured, and in a semi-permissive environment, to expect the pent-up hatred and frustrations of the prisoners not to surface much more rapidly than in another environment.

Bill looked at the floor pensively as he assessed our comments, for their injection into the evening meeting of the flight commanders with the SRO. Difficult times lay ahead, for we were morally and mentally committed to an increasing pressure on the "V" until they returned Robbie and the group, as well as Navy Commanders Ned Shuman and Ed Martin, who were now being confined in hard living conditions in Heartbreak for their resistance posture. It was difficult for a prisoner to maintain a rational link with reality. The newfound freedom had a tendency to make us a little heady with emotion, as well as to push to the back of our minds the possibility of some severe punishing reaction by the camp officials.

Quite a few of our room's occupants had not taken the heavy torture of the Zoo purge of 1969, the 1967 purge at the Hilton, or carried the burdens of the Alcatraz Gang. They failed to realize how quickly and how cruelly the "V" might spring into action again.

THE SHORT REUNION

The idea behind our actions was to obtain treatment as prisoners of war under the Geneva Convention. In this situation, we had to be passive and not riotous. Otherwise, our plans to improve our lot would get us thrown back into the Dark Ages.

I had more insight into the operation of this section of the camp than most people in our room. I had spent hours looking out the back window of Heartbreak Hotel into this same yard, and I had survived the years at the Zoo.

About 525 North Vietnamese men, women, and children, including babies, had been confined in the same spaces that now held slightly more than half that number. The treatment of their own people was as primitive and oppressive as our treatment, and their living conditions were worse.

Now, in the spring of 1971, we were being treated with more restraint and less oppression that the hapless "V" civilian prisoners I had watched for hours in the previous year. I recalled how one small child, perhaps two years old, would burst into tears, scream, run and cling to her mother every time the Communist policewoman entered the yard. When a child, slightly older than a suckling babe, can recognize the obvious danger of an approaching Communist, the all-encompassing evils of Communism have to be easily perceived.

This was the first time in almost three years that I had not been a commander. During the black days from about January 1, 1966, through this spring of 1971, all of the most senior officers had been in total isolation. For years many camps were run by more junior officers. Not being in command was an awkward positon for me, for Guarino, for Render Crayton, Bill Lawrence, and other ex-commanders. We had some good experience to draw on, but in this group, we were very junior.

As this day drew to a close, a strange new phenomenon appeared. Ladders were placed against the outside of our building, and on the roof of the small lean-to attached to our room. Various "V" turnkeys and guards sat on the roof, or stood on the ladder, looking into the room, and making notes on a piece of paper about the movements occurring in the room.

This interesting drill went on for several days, and amounted to the guard spying on our activities and reporting what "black schemes" the "creemenals" were up to. The notes provided the basis for selecting certain officers from the room to go back into hard living conditions in the future.

Frequently, the guard did not have the faintest idea what was going on in the room. This was demonstrated when they removed two men from the room because they had been walking around the room collecting the results of duplicate bridge scores. This action on their part was as predictable as the vitamin pill phenomenon.

Food during this period was almost as dreadful as the Dark Age days, except that some greasy, vinegar-flavored chinese sardines were introduced into our diet. Tensions continued to mount and frictions built in the outside contacts with the "V" in the yard. The room leadership declared that we would go on a food strike, refusing to eat until some of our grievances were resolved. This strike was counter-productive both in morale and effect to some of the room members. Others heartily endorsed it. I was not big on self-starvation, nor were my former roommates from Heartbreak Hotel. We had been exposed to the starvation problem there. Nevertheless, I backed the food strike wholeheartedly.

The "V" reacted quickly, and violently. They immediately cut off our supply of water, and unluckily, few people had a full cup of water to sustain them for the coming period. When the "V" arrived with the food, we began to chant, "No church, no eat! No church, no eat!" After two days without food or water, the SRO felt we had made our point and called off the strike.

During this period, we began classes in Spanish, French, international relations, mathematics, beginner's bridge, etc., which received an enthusiastic reception from all. Classes were attended by many people who had a low interest level. After being deprived of anything constructive for such a long time, most of us would attend anything, both out of a desire for self-improvement, and a determination not to let anything slip by unnoticed again. I found I had developed an insatiable intellectual thirst. I wanted to know, to hear, or take part in every activity in the room. Although my voice is raspy and I have little talent for song, I even joined the choir.

One of my greatest pleasures was watching the activities of my roommates and trying to backtrack them by watching these current activities. The most painful adjustment to POW life is the transition from the high-speed, highly-interesting life of an American flyer to that of wasting an entire afternoon watching a lizard stalk and eat flies.

Categories of escape mechanisms developed. There was the memory group, who assimilated every piece of memory work possible, and walked around reciting over and over the same trivia, poetry, mathematical formulae, etc., plus attempting to add to their repertoire of material. Many spent every waking moment in this mode.

Another group was the jocks — handstanders, handwalkers, golfers. Almost, but not quite, the muscle bench crowd. The only difference was in age and coordination. Occasionally, a 47-year-old, uncoordinated, unmuscular gent would decide that the greatest pastime for a 47-year-old man was doing handstands.

The walkers were another special category, feeling the uncontrollable urge to circle the room continuously. Some would walk three or four hours at a time. I had an occasional liking for the hiking mode myself.

Others occupied themselves by going under the blanket, and like Linus, developed a fantastic attachment for that rectangular piece of cloth.

Many of the long-time solo types were extra strange, as were some of the most highly-abused tough resisters. Several of the long-time solos had been confined alone for as many as 52 or 56 months. Many of these were the old-time hard-liners; that gutsy, strong willed, pro-Uncle Sam type who, because of their "bad attitude" had seen little but hard times for their now five and a half years, or more, in confinement.

Equally strange were some of the weaker resisters, or that group who had been quite cowed, highly exploited. They had now developed guilt feelings.

Our group was composed of Navy, Marine, and Air Force officers. Most were pilots, and regular officers. An extremely high percentage were Military or Naval Academy graduates. Almost all were college graduates, and about 15% had master's degrees. I was the only lawyer in the camp, although there were several Navy officers who had attended the Naval Justice school.

Almost every one of these officers had acquired some managerial experience in his career. Many had, like me, spent hundreds of hours calculating the dead-sure, guaranteed, and easy way to become a millionaire or entrepreneur in the real estate investment field. I was a natural source for hundreds of questions on incorporation procedures, taxes, depreciation, etc.

Now, with this whole room population, an incredible variety of people, picture a Communist private standing on a ladder outside the room and looking in. Understanding not a word of English, and having a cultural deficiency that makes the Grand Canyon look like a love letter on the Waikiki sand, he is preparing a report to his seniors about the "dark schemes" in the room.

This lowly private sees men handstanding, others walking in circles. Some are playing bridge or chess, others looking at pictures from home. A few men are under a blanket. Many are either teaching or attending a class in spherical trigonometry or French. It boggled my mind, boggled the "V", and would have boggled many a head-shrinker.

I enjoyed the passing scene, the guard at the window, and snickered to myself about the chaos which was going to result from all this. The camp commander would take some action based on the information he was receiving. It occurred to me that *if* his actions were as fouled up as the guard's report, this had the makings of an incredible fiasco.

Frequently, the guard would misconstrue some action in the room. He would shout a mysterious command in Vietnamese meaning not to continue. For his trouble, he got a Bronx cheer or something worse. We began marching outside in formation, exercising in the yard by the numbers, in an effort to get a quiz with the camp commander about the status of Robbie. As usual, our efforts were unsuccessful.

Occasional packages and letters arrived. One of the real thrills for every one of us was to see a colored picture of home, family, and country.

Vietnamese guards were as curious as little children and loved to look disbelievingly at American pictures. When pictures from the U.S.A. were first distributed to the prisoners, the guards were told that the beautiful clothes, automobiles, and houses were posed propaganda. Repetition of the opulence in America in picture after picture must have given the lie to this fiction, for the guards soon stopped looking at the pictures and saying "propagandas."

Reception of the occasional letter was a real production. The Bug sent the Hawk to our front door and called my name in Vietnamese.

"Nigh," he shouted.

I went to the barred door, and he drew the back of his hand across his wrist several times, the signal to put on my long shirt. I suited up and went out to the lean-to attached to our building. It would be a "greasy" quiz.

Bug was friendly, sympathetic, and sickening. I liked him when he screamed, "Creemenal! You keeled my mother!" I was comfortable with him then, because I knew he wanted something the hard way. When he was greasy, he wanted something free.

"Ah, Nigh," he asked, "and what do you want today?"

"Nothing," I replied, hoping to cut the quiz as short as possible.

"Nigh, the camp commander, in the spirit of the 4,000-year history of the Vietnamese people, has always shown kind and humane treatment to creem-," and he stopped himself quickly before calling me a "creemenal." This was really going to be greasy!

"Nigh, the camp commander has received a letter from your family. He wants you to enjoy the letter and the good treatment of the camp."

With that, he reached into the drawer of the dilapidated table and dropped a letter on the scarred table top. The paper envelope looked starkly white against the grimy surface. He took each end of the letter and made circles on the table with it. He relished these times, knowing that my mouth was watering to have some news of the Viking and the children. This was my second letter from home in three and a half years. He knew I wanted it, and I knew he knew.

"How many family do you have, Nigh?" he asked, knowing as well as I. My three letters written home in the last three months had been addressed to Dorie and the four children.

"Four," I answered, knowing he knew there were five.

THE SHORT REUNION

He smiled knowingly, and pushed the letter across the table. My hands shook. It was not a real bright day, and my damaged eyes, now 46 years old, did not function as they had in years gone by. I tried to read the letter, but I just could not quite bring it in focus. Bug knew I had trouble trying to read without glasses. He had borrowed a pair so that I could read the last letter I had received.

"I have to have some glasses to read this letter," I announced.

"It is too bad for you, Nigh. You are old man in preeson, and now old, and you are blind. Maybe your wife will take a new husband because you are creepulled."

"I'll bet you that is what happened," I replied. "And she has probably gone to work for the CIA in the Pentagon." I thought that this would rattle the Bug's cage a little, as he hated the great triumvirate of the Pentagon, the CIA and Leendon Zhonson's War with a passion.

However, today's quiz was so greasy, he did not rise to the bait. Instead, he reached into the drawer and handed me a pair of flimsy framed glasses that would fit or be a little weak for most 45-to-48-year-old far-sighted fighter pilots.

I put them on, and Mama's strong firm hand popped through the blur. "Dearest Daddy. We are all well, happy, and waiting for you. All kids do fine in school. You be proud."

The letter was bland and sterile, for the wives had learned that only sterile letters, or bad news, got past the censors. Just as I began reading, Hack looked in on Bug, who rose from the table and walked out of the lean-to, out to the gate, and into the yard. I sat and leisurely read the remainder of the letter, re-read it, and noted that it was "only" six months old.

I had not been writing long enough to know personally, but most prisoners felt that the letters were so spaced that the POW could never really communicate with his family. He never got answers to his questions, or the news was so old that it was meaningless. I believe the camp record was a two-year-old letter received by John McCain.

Now bad news was in a different category and travelled remarkably quickly. A death in the family, an auto accident, divorce, severe sickness in the family. Those letters could get to the POW in three weeks, seldom more than five. Neither rain, nor snow, nor dark of night could stop that bad news. The mail must get through.

I re-read the letter for about the fourth time, took off the glasses and placed them on the table. I looked around. The compound was empty, except for the latrine detail. I picked up the glasses, put them on, folded the letter and left it lying on the table. I walked back to the room wearing the glasses as if I owned them. I positioned myself where I could see outside. In a few minutes, Hack entered the compound, walked to the lean-to, picked up the letter, and walked back out of the yard.

I had a small bag made from the sleeve of a castoff shirt hanging at the head of my place. I hid the glasses there. Bug did not return all day. There were no calls for the glasses on the following day, and I grew used to the idea that I had "had" the Bug. Except when our man was in the window, the glasses got a great deal of use. Happiness is a pair of glasses.

The lenses were a great aid in magnifying pictures from home. Our room was lighted by a single light bulb of about 100 watts. It was a dismal room, and for our aging group, many having suffered the beri-beri days at Briar Patch, the glasses were an absolute necessity. Men saw children in their pictures whom they had never really seen before. It was great lift to morale. I was staggered at how young and beautiful the Viking remained. Guarino and Kasler were proud that their wives, Evvie and Martha, were also vibrantly young-looking and beautiful.

Kasler put our thoughts very aptly when he asked, "Can you imagine what our wives would look like if they had to work as hard as these water buffaloes (the "V" women) outside? Can you imagine Doris looking like this if she were carrying a hod of cement every day in this cold, semi-freezing weather? She would look older than your mother." I agreed.

It was touching how much the children had grown. In one picture, Doris had posed my oldest son in his spring clothes for a fall picture. He had grown at least three or four inches during the summer. He was fast losing his little boy look, taking on the accoutrements of puberty. I was gratified not to see him with hair down to his shoulders. I associated that hair style with the beatniks and peaceniks, and was unaware that longer hair was the vogue.

It was also interesting to find in another of my nine pictures that the children were holding a couple of kittens which I had not distinguished before. One scene warmed my heart with a beautiful Peace rosebush in the background.

Roses are my favorite flower, and I had found it soothing many times in the past to tend them. I developed good "hands" with roses, and their beauty triggered my relief valve.

I developed the ability to turn off thoughts of my family. I could feel another wave of nostalgia sweeping over me. The onsurge of self-pity at not seeing my family for three-and-a-half years was near. Although signs were favorable that the military phase of the war had been pointed in the right direction, it was still obvious that my jail sentence was open-ended.

It was a frequent prisoner lament. "I would settle for a guaranteed four-year sentence . . . or five,". . . or some appropriate figure. I couldn't stand much mental speculation on this point, for while it appeared that the

THE SHORT REUNION

"V" victories were getting closer and closer to Hanoi, there was still no evidence that we were going to do anything but cool our heels for an indeterminate period of time.

My natural optimism precluded an excess of this kind of thinking. I found those who practiced it created a self-destructive weapon. There was almost *no* material reason for being an optimist. Every speculation of the past — this bombing halt, that negotiation, the 1968 elections on which so many hopes had ridden, the Paris Peace Conference, every major subject on which the POW had hung an optimistic (but unrealistic) "go home" date — had been overtaken by events. We optimists still had no convincing evidence that anything better could be intelligently predicted. In fact, the more extreme the pessimist, the more times he had been right, and the more bets he had won.

Dollar bets, bottle-of-scotch bets, room-wide pools, and even liquor-by-the-case bets had been won continually by the pessimists. Nevertheless, I preferred being a happier POW, if there were such a thing, than one of the continual doomsday soothsayers. I felt comfort in what I believed was the inevitable, that one day our country would realize they were dealing with a group of people who responded to only one thing - maximum and overwhelming military force.

Inside, I felt positive that the pure military solution would come along, but the burning question was, "When?" As the years inched past, "When?" became even more of a burning question.

The totally unreasonable and cruel face of Communism, seen nose to nose each day, did more than anything to reinforce my belief in the military solution. These "V" pawns in the cruel game of prison life were a simple extension of the hypocrisy and absolute tyranny of the Communist system. It was clear that considerations such as prolonged deprivation, high death rate of the "V" military, and military and economic losses short of near annihilation were not going to be effective against them.

The United States was firmly hung on the horns of a dilemma; either ransom the POW, or apply a military solution that would bring about a prisoner exchange. As I thought about the motto, "Millions for defense, but not one cent for tribute." I could not see ransom as a logical expectation. Neither could I see that a President of the United States, who had been elected for the purpose of ending the war, could possibly accomplish such a thing without the massive use of military power. As I saw it, this wasn't in the cards either. I hated to waste my time thinking about this subject. It was too dismal and too unrewarding.

Instead, I tried to learn something about everyone in the room, whether they interested me or not. I worked at additional bridge lessons from my old roomie, Fe, and progressed from a rotten bridge player to a lousy one.

I was surprised to find that this was a stimulating game which, like many things in the past, I had tuned out and underrated, because I refused to take time to learn what it was all about. There were several good bridge players in the room who performed yeoman service in standardizing the rules of play.

Theft of the glasses brought my contacts to a new high. I found that by showing an interest in people, they showed an interest in me. Those weak-eyed fellows particularly had a good reason for seeing more of me than would have been the case otherwise. They often brought all of their pictures, and some had many, and I obtained a lot of family information that was interesting and time consuming. After release, it was a surprise for the wives to have total strangers recognize them by name.

Unfortunately, the use of the glasses had to be covert. People had to block the guard's view or watch for him so that we would not be caught with them in our possession and lose them. Little did I know that my wife mailed me nine pairs of glasses during my imprisonment. I never received a pair. If not for the great "glasses robbery," there would have been no glasses available to the "creemenals," because this was an area in which the "people" were not "lenient and humane."

Incidents in the yard kept tensions high, and our determination to continue to demand release of our seniors, and receive treatment as provided by the Geneva Convention, kept the discontent between POWs and the camp at a high level. One of my cellmates made it a practice to bump into the guards in the courtyard for the purpose of antagonizing them. While his resistance posture had not seemed particularly high in the past, he seemed to get tougher as the days went by without any reprisals. In the perfect 20/20 vision of hindsight, it seems that someone should have talked to him and suggested backing off a little. His actions were getting more forceful as the weeks went by. He had been quite highly exploited for propaganda, and naturally, sought to even some old scores.

Very soon after pulling Colonel Risner and company from the room, a conciliatory event occurred. After the evening Hanoi Hannah news, Soft Soap Fairy began a broadcast for the camp commander. SSF solemnly announced, "It has always been the policy of the DRV to permit religious service, and religious freedom is a well known policy for all people across the DRV. Always the leadership of the DRV has supported church services, and therefore, American pilots will be permitted to have 15-minute church services. However, it cannot be used for black schemes, and it cannot be used to scheme against the camp authorities."

Such hypocrisy was a daily occurrance in our relations with the Commies. Only a Commie can mistreat churchgoers on one hand, and then announce a regard for religion on the other.

THE SHORT REUNION

This was a minor victory, but it did not get our men back, and it was the case of being thrown a crumb when a loaf of bread would barely suffice. We were able to make occasional, but good, contact with Colonel Flynn who took the reins and began operating the camp.

The results of the guard in the window began to pay off. Day by day, our more senior officers were pulled out of the room, one at a time, two by two, or three or four at a time. The yard would fill up with guards, the transfers would be accompanied by large squads armed with hand grenades and automatic weapons and an awesome show of force. The fangs began to show again!

Oblivious to the new trend, our tough guy shouted an obscene remark about Ho Chi Minh while out of doors, and was unceremoniously smashed to the ground by the "V" and jerked out of the compound. In my opinion, this put the finishing touches to a "V" plan to purge all the trouble-makers from the camp. It was the straw that broke the camel's back, according to me, and was to destine many of us to a long seige of the old way of life. The nature and timing of the remark were completely unreal in the threatening environment of the time.

Our new tough guy was dragged next door and soundly thrashed by some incensed "V" with a fan belt. His whimpering, whining, begging apologies were a long way from his tough guy act. It followed that plenty of our secrets were to be compromised when the "V" began exploitive torturing him, and this was 100% true. Pathetically, he was entirely out of step during his POW career. When the demand for strength was at its highest, he was weak. Conversely, when the demand for passive pressure was highest, he was obscenely imprudent.

CHAPTER FIFTEEN

Banished to Skid Row
(Fifth Ring of the Malebolge)

On March 17, 1971, only two days after the forcible removal of the "tough guy" from our midst, a huge group of goons assembled in the yard by our door. John McCain, Jack Fellowes and I were told to roll up our blankets and prepare to move. I left my glasses on the line for Kasler, since I knew we would be searched on arrival at the next camp.

We were blindfolded, loaded on trucks, tied, and moved out in the dark to a new unknown camp, immediately dubbed Skid Row. It was a punishment camp, geared for a total of 36 people in minimal comfort. I was senior officer.

Living conditions were very grim. We had no lights or bathing facilities. Two men were jammed into a cell, six feet by four feet. It was indescribably dirty.

The camp was a mud hole. The building was typically neglected. The shutters were falling off, paint peeling, and there was litter scattered about. All water came from a filthy, muddy well.

The pattern of harassment was similar to the fall of 1969. The rooms were not ventilated. Talking was not permitted from room to room. Communications were ordered cut off, but we ignored the order and continued to communicate.

On April 2, I was called to quiz with Soft Soap Fairy. He told me he was there to get certain information from me. He said he had been ordered by the highest authorities to get answers from me and I was ordered to give them.

I heard the whole broken record again. I was guilty of many black crimes against the people. He told me he was authorized to use any amount of force to get me to answer. He noted that, despite the fact that he personally did not have any hatred for me, he would take the steps necessary. He reminded me that I was an old man, crippled and far, far too puny to take the hard beating he was about to give me. I had noticed a set of ropes lying on the floor in the corner of the room. As my eyes adjusted, I saw a pair of portable leg irons in another corner.

"Therefore," Soft Soap Fairy advised me, "the wise thing for you to do is straight-out answer all the questions I have prepared for." If I would do so, of course, I would not be tortured.

He wasn't convincing in this role, and I didn't think I was going to be mistreated too badly. They got my attention, though, when Straps and Bars came in carrying a fanbelt. I remembered him from the Star Chamber, and the fanbelts presence was unnerving.

Soft Soap Fairy said, "Here are the questions I want you to answer. First of all, I want a complete outline of all the schemes, plans, and policies that you put into effect to resist the camp authorities, and then I want the names and positions of all men in authority back at the other camp."

I told him flatly, "I am not giving you any of that information, and I have no intention of answering those questions. I will adhere to the Code of Conduct and give name, rank, and serial number!"

He ordered me on my knees. I was on and off my knees throughout the course of the day and part of the night. My knees were scarred, but they had no open wounds. To my surprise, the kneeling was far less painful than many months ago.

Straps and Bars came in a couple of times to force me to hold my arms up. I didn't hold them up since they were still crippled from the hanging at Vinh. I would not hold them up, could not, and did not. He pounced on me, pounded me on the head and kicked me occasionally, but there was no sign of the old violent torture. There wasn't even a suggestion of using the fanbelt on me, except his carrying it for "scare" effect. There was no attempt to put me in the ropes, although he kicked them and glared at me. I realized they were not going to put max pressure on me. This inspired hope. Soft Soap Fairy continued to press me.

I told him I would be more than glad to talk to him about some of the problems and that apparently they didn't understand what was what. He desperately wanted me to talk, and he let me sit on the stool. With that, I launched into a dragged-out, time-consuming indictment of all our relationships with the Bug. I pointed out that the camp's only problem was that Bug was a miserable animal, completely unreasonable and his treatment of us was unacceptable.

I stated that if they would get rid of Bug, treat us like human beings, and give us the decent treatment that we thought the camp was trying to give us, there would be no problems. I suggested that it was very difficult to expect the POWs to cooperate with a "V" who had tortured almost every man in the room, violently and needlessly, in the past, as well as murdering several.

It was inconceivable to think that there could ever be good relationships between the POWs and the "V." I advised that what brought on all the trouble was the fact that it was impossible to look at the guards and Bug without getting angry, particularly since they still treated us with such arrogance. I felt we were going to have nothing but hatred and trouble between the "V" and the POWs as long as the situation remained unchanged.

To all this, SSF replied, "The whole problem is that every time we give you something, you curse us. We give you a letter, and you call us a son-of-a-bitch. We give you a package, and you call us thieving bastards."

I countered, "You can't cover an elephant with a basket." This was the "V's" favorite quote. "You *are* thieving bastards! Our packages arrive and you steal us blind. From a six-pound package, we get one pound. We get a Christmas package that is supposed to be twelve pounds, and we get three pounds. It's pretty obvious that you are stealing our items. We see the guards carrying and eating our package items. That's why we call you thieving bastards."

I continued, "Many of us, at this point, have had only three or four letters. It's now the spring of 1971. We have people who have been in here for more than six years who have had two or three letters from their families, and some haven't had any. We know that our families are writing every month. We have people who have now written only two or three letters. We don't know whether they got home or not, because you don't give us the letters from our families. If you expect us to have a good attitude, all you have to do is give us treatment in accordance with the Geneva Convention."

One of the most accurate and realistic comments ever made by a Commie came from Soft Soap Fairy in reply. He shook his finger at me and said, "The *Communists will never* give you treatment under the Geneva Convention. We will never give you Geneva Convention treatment!" As a matter of fact, they never did. Even after the protocols had been signed in 1973, they still did not treat us in accordance with the Geneva Convention.

I spent most of the day and evening on my knees, which I began to suspect was the limit of torture he was permitted to use on me. Then he began on a new subject. He wanted me to confirm a wide range of data that had been obtained from the "tough guy" who had been knocked down, dragged off, and tortured.

They had obtained many POW secrets — SROs' callsigns, policies, etc. This information was of little consequence, and to our man's credit, he told two POWs across the hall what info he had given. These POWs, who included the former SRO of Room Six at Camp Unity, had passed the questions and answers to us verbatim in Room Seven.

BANISHED TO SKID ROW

I found myself on the receiving end of exactly the same questions, although there was a difference! I wasn't getting stroked with the fanbelt for the answers as he had been. I stalled and evaded. Even the lights worked in my favor, twice failing for long periods during which I got off my knees.

I could have answered SSF's questions truthfully at no additional loss for the POWs, but I had grown tired of blackmailers and extortionists, and refused to give him a responsive answer to any question. While my knees ached, it was a far cry from the old days. I decided to wait them out!

At about midnight, after a 12-hour session, the "V" held a solemn court martial. Soft Soap Fairy entered and read the charges and the verdict. He had the enlisted men stand at attention and directed me to stand up as well.

He said, "You are an ex-escaper. You have always shown bad attitude to the Vietnamese people. You have always been impolite. You are the blackest criminal in the camp. You have never repented your crimes. You have killed many women, children, and old people. Now you will go back to your room and be punished.

"On Monday or Tuesday, I will be back and you will write many things and you will have time to think over your crimes. I will be back on Monday or Tuesday, and then I will see you at this time." Since none of the "V" guards could understand English, I always wondered what they thought had transpired.

I went back to the building and to a new room, finding that everyone adjacent to me had moved. The area had been cleared out so that I could not communicate. A guard was now sitting on a chair at my door. I was put into leg irons that connected to a piece of railroad track about four feet long. It weighed about 100 pounds. The steel bar on the irons ran through a hole in the piece of railroad track, and the entire device lay across my bed.

It was impossible for me to lift this iron. I was now locked onto the bed! It was bloody uncomfortable. I could not get off the bed to urinate, and I had to eat my meals on my bed in my own mess.

To my surprise, this went on only a few days. The "V" came by and removed the leg irons, telling me that I was going to be punished further. Soft Soap Fairy did not show up again and I never had the threatened quiz.

Eventually, the pressure began to ease, although I was kept in solitary 99% of the time. This gave me a fine opportunity to work on French and German vocabulary, and review poetry again.

Most of my people at Skid Row were hard-line resisters, considered by the camp to be diehards and bad-attitude cases. Soft Soap Fairy had brought the message clearly. It was, "Quiet down and settle down, or someone is going to get hurt!"

I felt it would be senseless and counter-productive to get someone injured through retaliation by the "V." We were out there to feel the full and oft-repeated pains of solitary, but, except for insulting harassment by some low foreheads, there was no severe punishment.

The inane Ho Chi Minh insult at No OK Corral was the prime reason for the "V" having moved us here, I reasoned, and it appeared to me that if we left them alone, they would generally leave us alone.

We had uselessly lost a lot of prisoner secrets and I could see no point in more needless exposure of more secrets by, in effect, forcing the "V" to torture someone. In almost every past case, whenever they went to the trouble to bend someone pretty hard, they would continue the torture for the fallout of extra information.

Discipline by my troops from the start was of poorer quality than I expected. There was a great deal of bickering with, and cursing, the guards. This was exactly what the guards were not going to tolerate, and exactly why we had been sent to this camp. I passed the word repeatedly that I didn't want anyone humiliated, but I wanted the hasseling with the guards stopped, if no good reason was involved.

It seemed impossible to get the message across. Despite whatever word I sent along, I would get a report a day or two later that some "flap" had taken place between a prisoner and a guard. The "V" solved this problem fairly quickly for me, silencing some of the newly-acquired courage and the tendency to cuss out the guards. An argument between a prisoner and guard developed over food. The end result was that the prisoner was dragged over to the small headquarters building, where a goon squad of local guards and turnkeys were permitted to administer an extremely severe beating to the man, demanding an apology.

This was exactly what my orders were intended to prevent. When the animals showed their big teeth, things settled down to a quieter pace, and there were no repetitions of the beatings, although there were a couple of sessions in irons for drilling holes through the walls and other minor violations.

I had been in Skid Row several months when I passed my fourth anniversary as a POW. My morale was not high, and I was having a hard time trying to pump up the morale of anyone else. I was plain tired of jail, of filth, of harassment, of lousy food, of rats and roaches, of dirty water, of infrequent cold baths, of not knowing how, where or what my family was doing, of the unbelievable "V" propaganda, of being hot in summer, of beds that slept like a pile of rocks, of worms, of dysentary, and I couldn't help but compare what was going on out in the real world.

I picked up my old habit of imagining that I was back in Arizona with the family at mealtime. I would use nearly an hour running through my complete prayer. I would then imagine how the kitchen looked. I'd imagine the Viking cooking breakfast. Today, it might be pancakes, bacon, sausage, Vermont maple syrup, and hot tea.

I could always tune in the voice of the Viking, but sometimes I would have to look at her picture to bring her face back. I could picture her wide smile and strong white teeth, her peaches-and-cream complexion.

I couldn't bring the children in at their present sizes. They remained frozen at the size and place where I'd left them. I wondered what kind of a car a Torino was, and what Viking did with my old Cadillac and Falcon. I pictured the wall on the right of the breakfast bar, and tried to recall my collection of jet fighter pictures and some of my memorabilia that decorated the wall.

These thoughts were seldom brought to a conclusion, since they were continually interrupted by a tap coming down the wall, a guard opening the peephole or door to the cell, another POW bringing water, the door opening to empty waste buckets, or some mundane thing that dragged me back to the stark and barren Communist jail cell.

Fridays were a particularly distressing day. Happy Hour on Friday evening all of the way through POW life was either one of my most miserable, or occasionally, the happiest period of the week. It was normally up to the POW commander to tap an "HH" on the wall, indicating that drinking time had started. If visual communications were open, orders for this or that make-believe drink would float down the sordid alleyway between our cell doors and the tall concrete wall that surrounded the camp, about four feet from our cell doors.

Sometimes, Happy Hour triggered some truly cheerful memories. As a career fighter pilot, I had travelled world wide. Some of the happiest days of my life had been the Friday evenings at Wethersfield RAF Station, England, where I had flown as a squadron pilot, a flight commander, wing gunnery officer, and the wing standardization officer.

During those days of extremely bad weather — fog, snow, icy runways, erratic navigation equipment, and first-line hot fighter-bombers to fly — the weeks were replete with "hairy" experiences. There I had experienced a bailout from a burning F-84F only to find that the parachute did not work. I sustained merely a broken leg and light injuries.

In another flight I had lost all aircraft instruments and fuel pumps in a thunderstorm and made a landing at a strange field with only two minutes of fuel remaining in the bird. On those Fridays, we relived the hairy flights of the week, and revelled in the fact that we were young, challenged by our demanding and exciting profession, and were always a little bit in awe of our nearness to death and disaster.

Doris and I had not adopted our oldest son until 1958. As a result, we didn't have any hours to keep to get home to children. I remembered well a black faille sheath dress and a brown cotton frock with painted designs which emphasized the Viking's well-rounded figure. We often stayed as late as the band played. Those fun-choked happy nights when the cup runneth over were a huge part of the paycheck for fighter flying.

When I was recalled to active duty with the Air Force, after going through flying school in 1951, I considered myself as Korean War help only. I didn't contemplate a full-time military career without some reservations. I was open-ended on the subject, but expected that I would terminate my active duty when the war was over to re-enter the practice of law or business.

After only a few years of fighter flying, I was so swept up in the profession that I eagerly accepted a Regular commission when it was offered to me. I had developed from the bud to a full-bloom fighter pilot.

My thoughts often returned to the memory of my chic and lovely Viking, the tasty cheeseburgers we polished off before we left the club, and the spooky drive of about two and a half miles from the officers' club to our home on the estate of Sir John Ruggles-Brice.

We were driving a 1935 Morris two seater, forerunner of today's sports cars. It had large wire wheels, a rag top, and the poorest set of headlights ever installed. On the nights when the fog had flattened itself firmly to the ground, we both leaned out of the open windows and inched along the road from cat's-eye to cat's-eye, which pointed the way like a glassy finger toward the nearby village of Finchingfield.

Our days in the 500-year-old farmhouse at Spains Hall, Sir John's estate, had brought some superior pheasant shooting, hare hunts, and banded pigeon shoots in the wood near the Hall. How sweet it was, but how painful to recall. When was it? Yesterday? Last century? Last millenium?

Reality . . . the dark, dank cell; no ventilation or light but for small three-inch-square holes above the door near the roof. No human to speak to for hours on end. Humiliation. Stand when the door is opened or be punished. Pumpkin soup . . . pumpkin soup . . . pumpkin soup . . .

Somewhere in the world, someone was eating cheeseburgers, filet of sole, mahi-mahi, steak and lobster, baked Idaho potatoes with sour cream. Somewhere, someone was pouring a glass of Bristol Cream Sherry for a beauty as lush and dear to him as the Viking is to me. Scotch on the rocks, a Beefeater Martini, a frozen Daiquiri. Birds, flowers, dogs, children laughing. There are such things!

Reality always called me back. A danger thump on the back wall! A "V" was coming, someone new was in camp, news was coming down the wall, a report of a quiz with Spot, all of the mundane nothings of this barren existence forged on like a juggernaut without concern for the desire of the prisoner to escape these walls in flights of fancy or preoccupation.

Back to my poetry: "Dark is the night that covers me, Black is my pit

BANISHED TO SKID ROW

from pole to pole..." My French: *Bon jour Madame. Comment allez vous? Je M'appelle Georges Jour. Permittez moi a vous introducez ma cher femme Doris Day, plus belle que tout les fleurs un jardin*... My German: *Guten morgen, Mein Herr. Wie Gehts? Ich Habe fier kindern. Ich bin fliegermann in Luftwaffe des Vereinigen Staaten.*

My French and German were showing improvement from the constant practice. Each day I received some new *Deutch* words from gutsy Marine Corps Captain Orson Swindle, written with an aluminum spoon on the back of one of our white enamel eating plates. Or new *Deutch* words were shouted down the passageway by Orson or Mike Christian.

A message was tapped out on the back wall. "A b.i.g. R.u.s.s.- t.r.a.n.s.p.o.r.t. i.s. l.a.n.dg. a.t. G.i.a.L.a.m.F.m. R.p.o.s.i.t.i.o.n. T.k.w.e. r. n.r. t. Z.o.o. H.v. s.a.m. v.u. T.k. w.e. v.e.r.y. c.l.o.s.e m.a. b.l. m.i.l.e. Translated: A big Russian transport is landing at Gia Lam Airport. From our position (the front of the building) (we) think we are near the Zoo. Have the same view (of an aircraft approaching the airport). Think we are very close (to Zoo), maybe one mile.

This was interesting! Even though we had made the trip to Skid Row blindfolded, in a sealed truck with no windows, our timing of the trip and our knowledge of previous moves had led to the concensus that our present location was approximately ten miles southwest of town on an approximate heading of 190° - 200° from the Hoa Lo prison. The Zoo was located approximately seven miles from Hoa Lo on a heading of about 200° - 210°. Thus, their view of the aircraft on final accurately proved our predictions on the location of Skid Row.

The "V" immediately went back to their old tricks of divide and conquer, and all of the front cells of the building were filled up. They opened the cell windows in the front of the building, and closed the windows in the back. This sorting process took place throughout our entire prison career. There was always the attempt to divide by giving one group of men slightly different and usually better treatment than the other. It was mostly unproductive, since the group had been moved to this or some other camp based on their attitudes. The POWs at Camp Unity affectionately dubbed us "Hell's Angels."

However, the goons did have enough success with this carrot-and-stick routine that they never stopped trying. As Ed Martin sagely observed, "If all POWs were selected down to the two most anti-V prisoners in the system, the 'V' would be trying the good guy treatment on one and the 'black creemenal' approach on the other."

In the summer of 1971 my morale got a badly-needed lift. We received very few packages and infrequent mail. But I received a package from my wife which had been mailed in a box that was previously used. The box had a printed label addressed to "Col. & Mrs. George E. Day." A careless "V" censor, who never would have told me willingly that I had been promoted, had taken a pencil and run it through the "Col. & Mrs." but failed to obliterate the printing.

Inside the box were several packages of Colonel-brand honey, an Eagle-brand item (a colonel's rank devise is called an eagle) as well as a number of objects indicating that the Viking had been on a trip to Europe and visited Geneva, Paris, Stockholm, etc. There was an unmistakable passport picture in the box. I admired my wife's intelligence in getting across to me the message that I had been promoted to full colonel, and that Vietnamese and other Communists were getting some hard questions about POW treatment and allied subjects from her. I didn't know how vocal she was allowed to be, as the role of POW wives was low profile at the time I was shot down.

The news was a shot in the arm to the entire camp, since it indicated two things. The first was that we were being promoted. The second, that if one wife was on the road working for our return, probably others were as well.

Summers in Hanoi were miserable, hot and ultra-humid. Normal summer living for us was like being in a solid brick house with a tin roof, on the banks of the Everglades in Florida. The ventilation was so minimal and room temperature so high, that we were forced to sleep nude on the concrete floor, trying to pull whatever comfort we could from the cooler concrete.

Once again, in their mercurial fashion, the "V" became convinced in 1971 that we were going home soon. They were as volatile as barometers. With almost every anti-war speech by a high-ranking Member of the U.S. Congress (and God knows there were plenty of them), by some ex-government official, or by some significant or insignificant action of the peaceniks, the "V" could fly into a frenzy of miscomprehension, and our treatment would improve a little. If the news were negative, our treatment declined. Generally the indication of their miscalculations involved little, perhaps a few more noodles mixed into the almost tasteless pumpkin soup and a useless, superficial health inspection by the "doctor." Sealed Beams became our camp medic. Though poorly trained, he got a wealth of practical experience with his captive patient group.

The "V" balloon was obviously up. There were visits to the camp by some of the Communist staff. A slight and incomplete cleanup of camp took place, followed by a personal examination by Sealed Beams. We had some shots described by a turnkey as being for flu, diarrhea, typhoid . . . and "you healthy."

These signs, while encouraging, had come and gone so many times that our situation was like that of the village to which the shepherd boy continually shouted "Wolf!" Nothing they did had any credibility. I had reached the point of numbness to minor events. I never made judgment on their actions until I had several examples, or several weeks to observe them.

The "super" rains started, providing relief from the heat. Thunderstorms, the intensity of which I have never seen equalled, built up in the Red River Valley, and the rainfall was so heavy, it defies description. A 10-or 12-inch rain in a five-hour thunderstorm was routine. The water level in our filthy well was about nine feet below the surface. After four days of rain, the well was almost ready to run over.

Rains eased for a few days and then began again. We could tell that the "V" were afraid the Red River was going to flood. As we had done at this time of the year each year before, we rolled up our meager possessions to be ready to move at a moment's notice.

In order not to break precedent, we were unceremoniously blindfolded and led to the trucks in a pouring rain at night. This move was done in a panic, and while we were tied together with ropes, the truck was not fully boarded up as it had been on our trip out to Skid Row.

By manipulating the blindfolds a little, despite some cuffing and slaps from the guards, some of the men in the front of the truck could peek out and see a little of the city. Water was deep in all of the ditches and fields, sometimes running over the roads.

On arriving in town, word filtered back from the front in a whispered voice, "You'll never believe it. The sidewalks are covered with people simply lying down under the roofs of porches, awnings, or any place out of the rain. Hundreds of people were huddled under a bridge we just passed."

I had mixed emotions. This could be a good move for us. We could very well be going back into the big rooms we had been pulled out of. It would be a nice change from Skid Row and solitary.

A whisper announced, "We're back at Hoa Lo." I crossed my fingers and hoped that we would not be going into Little Vegas and those small, cruel cells. We were not!

Instead, we were going to even smaller and crueler cells in Heartbreak Hotel. There were seven small rooms in Heartbreak, approximately six feet by six and a half feet. Two concrete slab beds ate up about three-quarters of the room. My heart fell, my spirits sank, to find that 28 of my men were going to be jammed into these seven tiny, filthy holes, joining the 29th, who was already in Room One.

When I was moved into Room One myself, I was surprised to find my friend, Navy Commander Ed Martin. He had been living in solitary in the building for some time, having shown "bad attitude." Ed's attitude never did improve.

Discount everything you have heard about crowded living. This is a "crowded" living history. The "V" moved four of us into this tiny room with Ed, totalling five men in an area slightly larger than 36 square feet. We were filthy and soaked. My newfound roommates were Commander Ned Shuman, a classmate of Ed Martin's at the Naval Academy, Ensign George McSwain, and Marine Captain Orson Swindle. This certainly cut off my complaints about not having company!

Sleeping, eating, and living became a stupendous problem. The cell was our living room, bedroom, toilet (without washing facilities), dining room, church, and recreation room. We solved the sleeping problem by putting one man on each concrete slab, since they were too narrow for two men. We put one man under each slab. Because Orson was the largest, in fact, too large for either the slab or underneath, he was to sleep on the floor between the slabs. This space was about two feet by six and a half. The mosquito nets, which had to be rigged in order to provide minimal sleeping comfort, complicated our ability to move at night, and the necessary nocturnal requirements of nature were problems of incredible proportions.

I was frustrated and angry at this new cruelty. There were several large rooms in the camp which were vacant. Some ranged from 25 feet wide by 60 feet long, to as much as 75 feet long. Suffer, suffer . . . creemenals . . . lenient and humane treatment! I was having a persistent problem keeping my temper under control, and as I look back, I believe it was the strongest discipline that I ever applied to myself.

We were immediately in contact with Room Seven, my former cell, where Larry Guarino was again senior officer. He passed us all of the current information, which sounded remarkably like the old information. We had an advisory from him and the wing commander, Colonel John Flynn, to "play it cool" for a little while. Although living conditions were very hard, this was most likely a step in the route back to a big room. If we played things low-key, there was a possibility we would be moved into larger quarters.

We were also given some performance instructions and the names of some officers who were not to command. Some sound command policies had been developed which met the realities of our problems well. We were named "The 4th Allied POW Wing."

Tempers were short, particularly as sickness began to overtake us in near epidemic proportions, with no medical response from the "V." Suffer . . . suffer . . . creemenals!

Three of my men were sick with a form of hepatitis. In spite of all my attempts to get them isolated, they were each forced into a cell with three men who were reasonably well. I came down with a painfully infected ear which burst after a few days, bringing blessed relief, since my demands for medicine were refused. POW families had mailed hundreds of pounds of wonder drugs to Hanoi.

The rains continued. The city was drowning in rain, yet in Room Eight, where we were supposed to bathe and wash our dishes, water was in short supply. We were not able to bathe with any regularity, nor adequately sanitize the dishes.

Tempers in the building were at a low boil and remained there only with difficulty. There were no incidents with the "V," and our hoped-for situation partially materialized. Several of the men, mostly junior in rank, were selected and sent to some of the large rooms. About 15 reactionaries were loaded on the trucks one evening in October. After about nine weeks of horrible living, we found ourselves back at Skid Row.

After the disgusting conditions at Heartbreak, going back to solitary at Skid Row seemed a relief. Treatment by the guards was not quite as oppressive as before, and we were put on a better bathing schedule. There was plenty of water in the well!

Food took a slight upsurge. I wondered what could be causing the improvement this time. We began getting ground fish meal, almost a coarse fish flour which I assume was a Chinese export. When fried, it was quite tasty and provided some badly-needed protein. It was "fat food" time again. The "V" were doing something for us and we all wondered why.

We were even permitted to stand in the sun in small groups for half an hour or so. Copies of Hanoi Hannah broadcasts, printed in English, were passed to the cells in front. It was then that we discovered that an aroused, enraged American citizenry was deluging the Communist delegation in Paris, all Communist embassies, and the Hanoi post office with tons and tons of mail, all protesting our cruel treatment, and demanding that the "V" act like human beings and treat us like human beings.

Hannah condemned H. Ross Perot for his "dark schemes" and referred to him as "Ross Pirate." After all, where did he get the right to demand mail, packages, and good treatment for Americans?

We also discovered that Vietnamization had been successful in the South. It was likely that if the huge force of North Vietnamese regulars were withdrawn from South Vietnam, that American troops could be withdrawn. It appeared that the tide in the South had been turned successfully by the combined U.S. and South Vietnamese forces.

For the first, absolutely the *first time*, I began feeling an almost unshakable confidence that 1972, either shortly before or after the Presidential elections, was going to be the Year of the Prisoner. Because of numerous incorrect predictions of the past, each of which had turned to ashes, it was impossible to mount ovewhelming optimism about the future. Nevertheless, for the first time in my prison days, I found that I could not tune out the family, my country, my nostalgia, and my longing for home.

Memory work on the languages suffered as I recalled the hundreds of mornings on the Wolf Creek Catch Basin, a shallow reed and cat-tail lake so beloved by the transient mallards and pintails as they hopscotched from lake to lake, traveling from Canada to Louisiana. I remembered the mornings I had been after duck on the Missouri River, North Landing River, Currituck Sound, or the Loblolly of South Dakota.

I thought of my first "double" on two Mallard drakes — beautiful, big green-headed, orange-footed Canadian ducks. I recalled the first Canadian Goose that I killed, and the day I shot three Greater Canadians out of one flock.

My thoughts would run away for hours to Iowa, South Dakota, or Nebraska pheasant shooting. I could see the face of my finest hunting dog, a well-broke English springer, named Clover. I thought of her great hunting spirit, and could see the sly look, and how her ears would flatten against her head as she "tuned in" to the pheasant smell. And how she hated a crippled pheasant.

I thought of my fine Weimaramer pup, who would have grown to become one of the strongest field dogs of his day, but who had died an early and untimely death from "hard pads." He had pointed the first pheasant he ever smelled, and he retrieved as naturally as a horse goes to drink. I remember the tears I had shed, and the agony I went through when he died after several days of sickness. I wrapped him in a rug, and buried him in a tree-sheltered grave in southern Georgia.

I imagined what it would be like, now that the children were larger, to take our white plastic ski boat for some afternoons on a lake, stopping to picnic on some magic island. Boats, water, skiis, children, soda pop, hot dogs and mustard, potato chips . . . someplace in the real world there were such things.

Sometime during these reflections, I completely stopped feeling sorry for myself, and I began to develop an inner peace that simply kept saying, "A year to go. The sentence is coming to an end next year." No more thinking, "Why me, God? Why my family? Why my children who are raised without a father? Why?"

These thoughts were interrupted with some strange and semi-interesting quizzes. Our camp officer contact was Spot, who normally called one of my junior officers to quiz, hoping to relay through them the information he wanted me to get. Their standard reply was, "Talk to the senior officer, Major Day. I am not an errand boy."

Spot called me for a greasy quiz. "How are you?" he inquired, with false, smiling curiosity. The switch was in the friendly mode today.

NATIONAL LEAGUE OF FAMILIES
OF AMERICAN PRISONERS and MISSING IN SOUTHEAST ASIA

ABOUT THE LEAGUE...

The NATIONAL LEAGUE OF FAMILIES was formed in 1969 and consists of family members only. The purpose is to assist all Americans captured or believed to be captured in Southeast Asia:

1. Securing humane treatment in accordance with the requirements of the 1949 GENEVA CONVENTION RELATIVE TO THE TREATMENT OF PRISONERS OF WAR and as recognized by general humanitarian standards for those Americans captured in Southeast Asia;

2. By obtaining identification of all those who are being held captive by the NORTH VIETNAMESE, the VIET CONG, the PATHET LAO, and any other hostile forces;

3. By obtaining proper medical care for all;

4. By making the American people and the people of the world aware of the unconscionable plight of those Americans who are missing or captured in Southeast Asia and their families;

5. By facilitating and promoting communication of information of mutual interest among all families of missing and captured Americans;

6. By facilitating and developing activities with other private or public groups or organizations and governmental agencies which are working to achieve the same humanitarian objectives;

7. By maintaining and supporting the morale of all captured and missing Americans and their families; and above all,

8. By obtaining at the earliest possible time the release of and complete accounting for all captured and missing Americans in Southeast Asia.

The League does not engage in activities that are inconsistent with the qualification of a charitable, humanitarian, non-profit, non-partisan corporation.

Belgium	Ethiopia	Liechtenstein	Portugal
Bolivia	Finland	Luxemborg	Rumania
Brazil	France	Mexico	England
Bulgaria	Greece	Monaco	Holy See
Canada	Guatemala	Nicaragua	El Salvador
Ceylon	Hungary	Norway	Sweden
Chile	India	New Zealand	Switzerland
Columbia	Venezuela	Pakistan	Syria
Uruguay	Yugoslavia	Turkey	Czechoslovakia

4. Express your concern to elected officials to avoid an apathetic approach to beneficial legislation for POW/MIA's.

5. Urge the support of your local news media to show TV and print in newspapers and magazines the Ad Council ads.

6. Contact the churches in your community and ask them to include the POW/MIA's and their families in prayer each Sunday until the men are returned safely.

7. It costs money to keep this issue before the public eye. The League needs and appreciates all contributions.

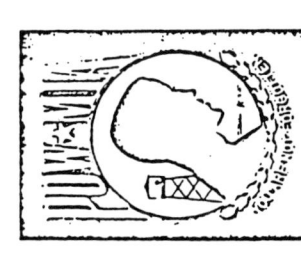

National League of Families
of
American Prisoners and Missing in Southeast Asia
1608 "K" Street, N.W.
Washington, D.C. 20006

Telephone: Area Code (202) 628-6811

THE ISSUE:

Over 1600 Americans are missing or imprisoned in Southeast Asia. NORTH VIETNAM admits to holding Americans; the VIET CONG and PATHET LAO admit they hold American POW's; but refuse to release a list of any kind, leaving unaccounted for, over 1200 United States servicemen.

The NORTH VIETNAMESE GOVERNMENT signed the 1949 GENEVA CONVENTION RELATIVE TO THE TREATMENT OF PRISONERS OF WAR on 28 June 1957, but refuses to accord American POW's even the most basic requirements.

VIOLATIONS OF THE GENEVA CONVENTION

REQUIREMENT	DRV PERFORMANCE
Account promptly names of all POW's held, notification of known dead.	Never released complete list; rare assertion of deaths.
POW's must be humanely treated, protected; reprisals against POW's prohibited.	Paraded in streets, forced to make statement, some torture; many held in solitary confinement for years.
Provide sufficient food to prevent weight loss.	All POW's underweight and suffer from malnutrition. Standard fare – pumpkin soup, rice, bread, pig fat.
Adequate medical care.	Much evidence to the contrary.
Minimum of 2 letters and 4 cards per month.	Average of 2 - 3 letters per year. (None at all for some).
Immediate repatriation of seriously sick and wounded. Release of POW's long held in captivity.	First prisoner taken in 1964. Few ever released, health or duration were not factors in those.
Neutral inspection of all camps; interview of POW's without witnesses.	No inspection; propaganda interviews only.
Free receipt of parcels.	DRV said POW's could have 1 parcel every 2 months; evidence indicates delivery irregular, many are returned.
Write to family within 1 week of capture	Some have not been permitted to write for 5 years.

WHO IS HE?

HE'S A MAN OF MANY FACES, OF EVERY CREED AND COLOR

HE'S AN AMERICAN !

HE NEEDS YOUR HELP !

DON'T LET APATHY KEEP HIM IMPRISONED !

There have been many tangible results since began to express their concern to leaders in other countries. Although the country leaders in other countries. Although the country sible for our men being detained may not publicly, they are extremely sensitive to the growing aimed at gaining relief for, and the release Americans being held in Southeast Asia. Your concern, however small you feel it to be, is important becomes an integral part of a massive "collective being expressed nationwide.

1. **Get Involved!** Speak packets are available League of Families so that you can be totally informed. Inform others. Work with local family members local POW/MIA groups.

2. Express your concern to North Vietnam and urging compliance with the Geneva Convention.

NORTH VIETNAM
Premier Pham Van Dong
Democratic Republic of Vietnam
Hanoi, North Vietnam (21¢ postage)

DRV
Minister Xuan Thuy
Delegation of the DRV
8 Avenue General LeClerc
Choisy-LeRoc
Paris, France (21¢ postage)

SOUTH VIETNAM VIET CONG
Madam Nguyen Thi Binh
National Liberation Front of VN
49 Avenue Cambaceres
Verrieres LeBuisson
91 Essone, France (21¢ postage)

3. Express your concern to other foreign government signators of the Geneva Convention; urging the their influence on behalf of American POW's e:

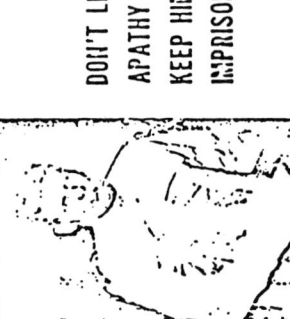

CHINA
Mr. Chiang Kuan-Hua
Hotel Roosevelt 14th Fl.
Madison & East 45th Street
New York, N.Y. 10017

RUSSIA
His Excellency
Anatoliy F. Dobryn
Embassy of the U.S.S
Washington, D.C. 20(

also —

Afghanistan	Cuba	Iran	Paragu
Albania	Denmark	Ireland	Nether
Argentina	Egypt	Israel	Peru
Australia	Ecuador	Italy	Phillip
Austria	Spain	Lebanon	Poland

"OK," I stated.

"I have for you good news, Jorgeday," he said. As did Soft Soap Fairy, Spot always ran my two names together. He went on. "Your wife . . . she works for peace." Working for peace in Communist dialect means that she was working against my country and for the "V."

To that I replied, "Baloney! If my wife is working, she is working for me, and to see that I am treated according to the Geneva Convention agreements. My country knows how you have treated me, and my wife knows about you."

"Jorgeday, you are a diehard, but soon you will know the truth," was his reply.

My wife was working for peace, with honor. As the Arizona Coordinator of the National League of Families, she was speaking, writing, and traveling Arizona, Iowa, California, Washington, D.C., Florida and Europe, in an effort to get the "V" to treat us in compliance with the Geneva Convention, to receive and send mail and packages, to identify all captured airmen, for inspection of the camps by international agencies, for a complete list of prisoners with a report on their condition, and for the immediate release of the sick and injured. Her reasons for working were well founded. From my date of shootdown until she received the first letter from me in the late fall of 1970, my name and five other known POWs had never been reported on any of the lists that were put out, ordinarily through some peacenik organization.

She knew I was alive. The early returnees knew that I was alive. My country knew that I was alive. The "V" knew that everyone else knew that I was alive. The Viking cited this fact continuously to demonstrate the cruel and inhumane tactics that the "V" applied to the families of missing airmen. She felt very strongly that if my name was not on the list of POWs held, I could not come back.

She had known from her contacts with my "nurse," Major Norris Overly, that I was alive in February 1968, for he had seen me on the 16th of that month. It was her hard work, along with the actions of many other families, Mr. H. Ross Perot, patriotic organizations, the Air Force Association, the *Reader's Digest*, and our government that resulted in my greasy quiz with the Bug and permitted me to write that all-important letter of October 1970, that became an official acknowledgement by the "V" that I was a prisoner. A nice job by other "diehards."

My first letter home was carried back by one of the Peacenik, anti-war types. Viking received a phone call from the pro-Communist Cora Weiss who wanted to impress on her how wonderful it was that the Communists had acknowledged I was alive and a prisoner, after only three years of hiding it.

Doris made it clear that she already knew that I was alive and a prisoner. She did not need help from any Communist sympathizers or fellow travellers. Every pro-Communist delegation to Hanoi somehow hurt the POW. They carried back propaganda for the Communists, detrimental to the POW. The propaganda diluted the reasoning power of the public, confused the issue of how bad the Communists were, and supported the claims of the peaceniks and pro-Commie anti-war groups. During rational times in other wars, such people would have been hanging from telephone poles. A pity that these were irrational times.

During our tenure at Skid Row, the "V" solicited us heavily to write letters, which I favored doing. It was interesting to find out through later letters from our families that this mail had been interfered with by the peaceniks. Our letters were accumulated and delivered in one bundle to wives and families by some louse on Christmas Eve. Another cheap "V" publicity stunt, assisted by some equally cheap anti-war types.

Little wonder that we could never get any meaningful exchange going with our families, or direct answers to many questions about the children, living conditions, and those matters of ordinary family concern. It is my belief that none of our mail went through normal international channels, most being funneled through the pro-Commie Cora Weiss "Committee of Liason." She was no friend of the POW or of America.

In order to get to write a letter, one had to take a piece of toilet paper and "rough" the letter, which was limited to six or seven lines. Then the "V" would take it, read it and re-read it, then censor it, frequently leaving nothing more than the greeting and sometimes changing even that. With my short fuse, these session of writing the "ruffs," and the harassment that went with it, were so overbearing that I frequently could not get past the rough stage. The "V" were looking for an excuse to claim that we were "impolite" and therefore disqualified from writing during that month.

"Bad attitude" cases did not get to write often, another club used to do us out of as many letters as possible. At this time, late 1971, a fair generality was that many, perhaps most men, had written about six or seven letters in an average of four and a half years of imprisonment, and received about the same number. Some had received only one or two, and some had received none. Most or all of the letters had been received in the previous 18 months!

My window was now left open most of the time, although I was still on the backside of Skid Row. I was occasionally moved adjacent to the three or four other men on the backside. We still had our front side and our back side group. It was a great morale boost to be able to lean against the bars of the door and talk to the POWs in the adjoining cells, and it was a great improvement over ordinary solitary where one never heard a friendly voice.

Suddenly, again during a black fall evening, the "V" ordered the men in front to roll up their belongings. Another move. Happily, this was back to Hoa Lo, and we all heaved a sigh of relief as we passed Heartbreak Hotel gate and headed into the yard of Camp Unity, or No OK Corral.

We assembled en mass in Room Two of the block of buildings that in general formed a rectangle, making up the camp. We were on the north side, next to Room One which was being used as a theatre. Next door in Room Three were a number of ex-Son Tay people, headed by Navy Commander Doug Clower.

How sweet it was! Morale bounced off the roof.

A message of "Welcome!" and "Well done!" came from Colonel Flynn, who advised us of the composition of the group into an Air Force wing structure. We also received a nice greeting from the director of operations, Colonel Robbie Risner, and a stirring message from the chaplain, Commander Charles Gillespie.

Togetherness . . . how sweet it was!

Christmas was coming, and the holiday spirit was upon us. The birthday of the Navy and the Marine Corps were close at hand. It was time for celebration . . . but quietly. There was no enthusiasm for a return to Skid Row.

CAMP UNITY
(Inside Hoa Lo Prison)

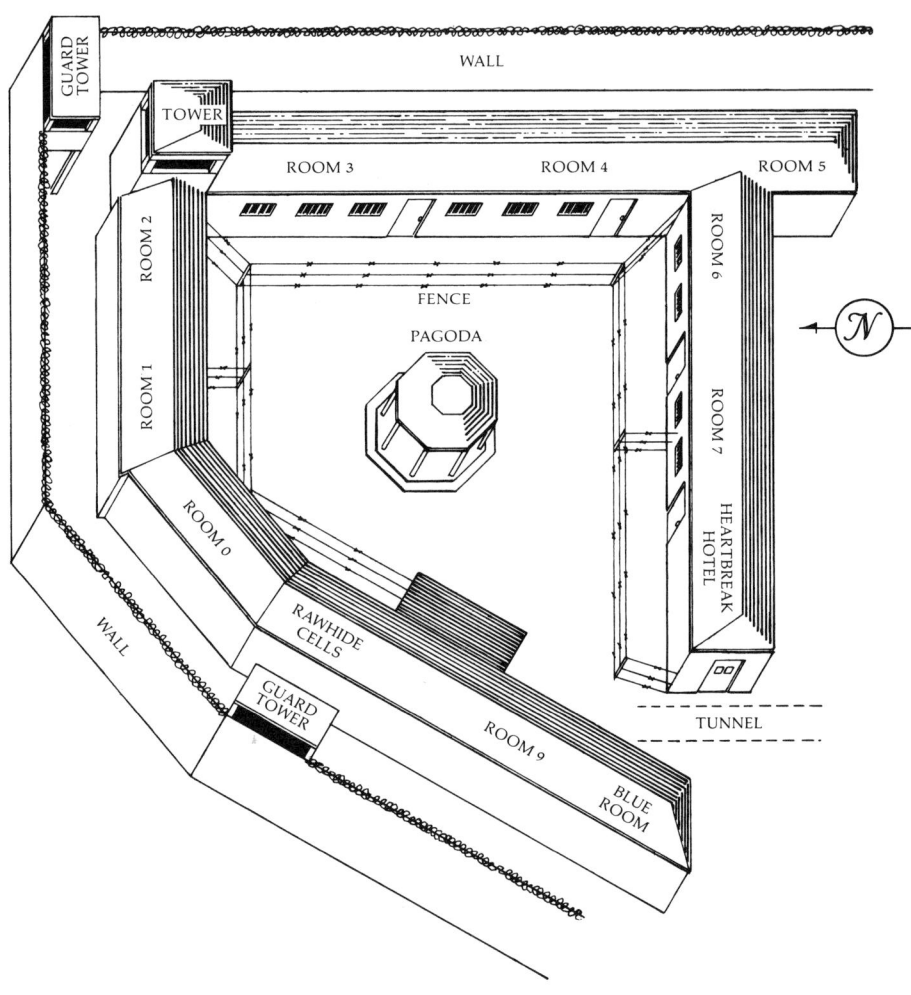

CHAPTER SIXTEEN

No O.K. Corral
(Sixth Ring of the Malebolge)

Our first priority was to organize flights and chain of command. My deputy was Navy Lieutenant Commander Moon Mullen; cool, effective, and gentlemanly. It was exhilarating, warm and exciting to have a large group of people to associate with once more.

Several men volunteered as chaplains, and our recreation and education officers took off at high speed. In only a few days, bridge classes, card games, acey-deucey contests, church and choir, history, law, Spanish, and German lessons were under way.

As Christmas approached, we were able to steal some thin discarded blankets that the "V" negligently left unwatched. These increased our comfort as we slept on cold concrete which chilled us to the bone. There was little mail for Christmas, and the scattered packages were barren. By popular assent, all packages went into a common pool, and were drawn by my sterling commissary officer, Air Force Captain John Fer.

Navy Day (October 27) and Marine Corps birthday (November 10) were whopping successes. We had cakes manufactured from bread dough, complete with Marine Corps globe and anchor, covered with various mixes from the packages of Kool-Aid, sugar, chocolate, etc. The group demonstrated all of the ingenuity that had made America so great in the past, and there was little that could be manufactured, stolen, or created that we did not have.

Christmas was sheer delight. John McCain, Orson Swindle, Bob "Daddy" Waggoner, John Fer, Jim Hivner, and others starred in the Hanoi Players' version of Charles Dickens' masterpiece on Christmas. Scrooge was meaner than a barrel of snakes. Tiny Tim and Bob Cratchett, the poor overworked bookkeeper, were more pathetic than ever. Tim was sick from worms, diarrhea, and beri-beri. Ghosts flittered about in white mosquito nets, and the POW dialogue was the greatest shot in the arm I had during confinement. It was the *first* time I had laughed hard, long, and loud in more than four years. Dickens might not have recognized the story, but every man in the room did!

The Christmas food was good. An exchange of presents was made by swapping promises of a future gift to the person whose name was drawn from the hat. Christmas, 1971 — great step up from past days.

The "V" clearly wanted to keep tight control and avoid more of the incidents that had caused us to get moved to Skid Row. This put the guards in a difficult position. They had been so overtrained in the "max hate" position, that they had a difficult time not lapsing back into their old arrogant ways.

Moon and my competent staff of flight commanders made strong efforts to keep a lid on the simmering pot and avoid any hard confrontations that would get our people put back into solo, without giving the enemy anything or accepting any unnecessary humiliation. This was a delicate balance to maintain. They had stopped seeking propaganda from us, but they continually tried to degrade and humiliate us.

In early spring new men arrived, bringing our total to 43. It was very crowded, but delightful to have new faces and diversified talents. We fully integrated the communications net, and brought Colonel Risner and the Rawhide crew on line with flash communications. Robbie and his group had communication with Sky and Blue, our senior officer group, consisting of our boss, Colonel John Peter Flynn, and all the senior officers in the command group. Operations went smoothly. The entire prisoner population was united as the 4th Combined Allied Wing, which included our South Vietnamese friend, Max (Nguyen Dat), and three Thai prisoners.

We received clarification from Colonel Flynn regarding standards of conduct, standards for command qualification, and removal from command for malperformance. We were delighted to find that Commander Walter Wilber and Colonel Edison Miller were prohibited from command because of their cooperation with the "V." It was heartening to hear that our commander prohibited any early release except in the case of simple expulsion from the country.

As the new year began, the big news was an announcement by the "V" of a visit to China by Henry Kissinger. Then we heard that President Nixon would also be visiting China. We were prepared to hear from the "V" of the great victory for the socialist cause of China, as well as the great victory for North Vietnam over the U.S.

Days passed and no mention was ever made again of the trip. We believed this meant that Nixon and Kissinger had explained to the Chinese that the Vietnam War was going to come to a halt this year, 1972.

Two of my most astute thinkers, John McCain and Ed Martin, advanced

NO O.K. CORRAL

the theory that China had been made to understand that it would not be wise to make mistakes about U.S. intentions. Since China was not going to intervene and smash the U.S., the North Vietnamese had no great news to announce.

Emotions in our group were widely divided. Some men in the room were close to seven years in confinement. Some were crippled badly, some very long-time solos. They ranged from the most extreme optimist to some of the most incredibly pessimistic people I have had the misfortune to live with. The latter were a drain on group morale. Some men were instant crowd dissolvers. As soon as one of them approached a group, it departed for other places.

One unusual situation was the ultra-glutton group. They had developed an irrational attachment for food. They went to some disgusting lengths to obtain either more food, or special food, or would handle the food received in some highly abnormal ways. I decided we would attempt to re-humanize these folks, and issued orders that any weird food "acts" would be stopped. Social pressure was a great correctional device, but I was not completely successful.

In early April, after Hanoi's spring offensive, President Nixon resumed the bombing of Hanoi, and our morale went sky high. As the bombs began to fall, many of the men in my group leaped up on the beds, shouting and cheering. Thank God for the bombing! The moves required for our honorable release included bombing. It seemed to me that this was a follow-up to the President's visit to China.

The "V" became angry about our cheering as bombs were falling, and climbed into the windows with automatic weapons. I ordered everyone to sit on the beds to avoid the disaster of having a man shot by a trigger-happy guard at this late stage of the game.

On Saturday of the same week, we had another morale boost. After dark, our front door sprung open and four POWs entered with their bed rolls. We leaped up to greet them. They were Navy Lieutenant Commander Jerry Coffee and Lieutenant Dave Carey, with Air Force Captains Mike Brazelton and John Borling. They had come from the Zoo and had unbelievable news. They had been exposed to some of the December 1971, and January 1972, shootdowns and had a wealth of news from the States.

The Zoo was now an easy treatment camp. There were two groups there. One small group was not resisting the "V" propaganda efforts and was cooperating with the "V." The second group of POWs was not cooperating and was trying to influence the first group to stop cooperating.

The cooperators were isolated from the main group of POWs by the "V," who hoped that the actions of the few would influence the larger group. Two of the group, Lieutenant Colonel Miller and Commander Wilber, had been relieved of all military duties because of their misconduct, but it was difficult for a new shootdown to know this. Only the mass of old shootdowns were aware of it. According to the *Des Moines Register* of October 7, 1973, Miller "in 1970 and 1971, was heard frequently in radio propaganda broadcasts by North Vietnam."

For their conduct, according to our sources, one group had an open-door policy in the prison. This meant their doors were opened early in the morning, and they had the run of the camp during the day. Other rooms and groups were on restricted outside time. We were to hear their names on an anti-war tape appeal to the United States Congress, in a tape with Ramsey Clark, Jane Fonda, and other anti-war sympathizers who were despised by the rank and file POW.

The good news from the states was mixed. We learned of the terrible inflation (bad news) and our pay scales (good news). Miniskirts, double-knits, square-toed shoes, wide neckties, long collars, and long hair were greeted with mixed surprise and dismay.

Expressions of widespread support by people across the nation for the POW cause, POW-MIA bracelets, the flood of mail to the Paris conference, criticism of the "V" by the International Red Cross, the fantastic efforts of H. Ross Perot, efforts by Bob Hope to get into Hanoi to put on a Christmas show, missing-man formations, bumper stickers, billboards proclaiming the plight of the POW . . . all were music to our ears. Our happiness, morale, and respect for our great people and country rose in a crescendo of appreciation that we had not been forgotten.

The senior officer of our new group believed that he and his three friends had been thrown out of the Zoo. Jerry Coffee had contacted Wilber at the Zoo and asked him to stop shutting the gates for the Vietnamese, since the gates blocked off communications between prisoners when they were closed. The next day they were transferred out of the camp and told by Rabbit that they had "bad attitude."

They also gave us the full story of the 1968 election. We had been very curious and had many questions. They told us the recent U.S. bombing efforts had been far more effective and devastating than any previous period in the war, and many high-value targets had been destroyed. This gave us much satisfaction and hope. These events were our ticket home!

Our thrill over the renewed bombing was set back on April 24, 1972, when the goon squad appeared at the door. They called out Lieutenant Mike Christian, a fine, hard resister, who had already taken much mistreatment and conducted himself so well for many years.

As soon as he stepped out of the door, he was smashed to the ground and stomped and beaten by the goons. They dragged him across the courtyard, pounding and beating him as they went. In all, he took a total of seven hard beatings that evening and the next morning. He returned the next day, bruised and bloody, with a black eye and cracked or broken ribs. The animals showed their fangs again.

"Sweat Pea," the officer in charge, made it clear that this was because of the cheering during the bombing. I believed that it was also connected with the fact that Mike had been caught with an American Flag sewed inside his shirt. It had been discovered during an inspection a few days earlier. Mike and Air Force Captain Jim Hivner had manufactured the beautiful flag, which was sewn inside Mike's shirt to avoid detection.

Every afternoon, as soon as the door closed and the guards cleared the yard, Mike hung the flag on the line. We all stood and pledged our allegiance to the flag. I'm quite convinced that he was beaten for possession of the flag. He and Jim immediately made another one.

We were both appalled and delighted with the news of the invasion of South Vietnam by the North Vietnam Regulars. We were appalled at the stupidity of such a move on their part, and delighted with what was going to happen to them when the U.S. air power got a shot at massed tanks, vehicles, and personnel in one area. It was bound to be a turkey shoot, and all of us ached for the opportunity to fly against this ground force and help turn it into hamburger.

This invasion ripped the facade off the so called "uprising" and "civil war" in the South. It exposed the war for what it was and always had been — a pure, naked invasion from North Vietnam by Communist troops. Only such rabid apologists as Tom, Jane, and Cora could label it as anything other than a Communist invasion.

What heartened me most was the way this clarified the position of the Commies to the U.S. public and to Congress, who had problems for years identifying fact from fiction about the war. It also gave President Nixon a clear-cut reason, which any decent and loyal American could understand, for bombing the North Vietnamese until they decided they had enough. In so doing, our honorable release could be secured. Our morale climbed again!

Another plus for our four new arrivals was that Dave Carey was a French course just waiting to land on someone. Both Coffee and Borling were fluent also. French boomed! Carey was extremely well qualified, with a masterful background. He recently had access to a dictionary and possessed great recall for rules and details that were unavailable before.

My German practice had to take a back seat to French, because we had learned to seize any opportunity and milk it dry as rapidly as possible. Things changed too quickly. This was a good decision because within six weeks, Mike, John and Dave were moved out of the room and sent north to a camp on the Chinese border. It was called Dog Patch. The "V" had us ready to go also, but the move was cancelled at the last moment, even though our dishes had already been moved out.

That move wreaked havoc with our communication system. It took great ingenuity to develop new links, and to re-establish old ones. The "V" began some renovation work around the camp, and the bombing continued.

About the end of June another new man came into my room. He was senior to me and had been a full colonel for years. Normally, he would have taken over. However, he had been taken out of the chain of command, so I continued as commander. He had been in solitary confinement for an exceedingly long period and had some very different ideas on resistance than I did. He had not concurred with the high resistance posture of the group he previously lived with.

My policy was that we did not speak to the "V," that we had no conversation except in the course of business. We would not accept treatment from the "V" which we considered harassment or degrading. The officer group which he came from were living in hard conditions like those we had at Skid Row. Moving into our room was a step up for him, and we truly hoped that this was the first step in an improvement of conditions for all our seniors. He was welcomed into the room and well received.

I explained that I would continue operating the room and that neither Moon nor I would consult him on policy decisions. Initially, this seemed not to pose any problems, but things changed. He was friendly with the guards, calling the enlisted guards, "Sir." He socialized with them in a manner that was disgusting both to me and to my troops. My young officers began to complain about his conduct. I was reluctant to talk to him about it, hoping that example and social pressure would bring him around.

We had a confrontation in the yard one day when an arrogant and insolent guard named Gap was harassing my black supply officer, Colonel Tom Madison. Commander Mullen told me that Tom was being harassed for no reason over cigarettes. The problem was racially motivated. Most of the "V" hated Tom, hated him for being black and a good, tough resister. They talked about nondiscrimination as if they practiced it. They discriminated against him continually in all ways.

I advised Moon, "We are not putting up with that. We're either getting equal treatment for everybody, and from all the guards, or we're going to protest it." I directed Moon to tell the men to go into the room as a passive objection to this act, which he did. When we got inside, everyone had obeyed my order, with the exception of the colonel, who would not come in.

NO O.K. CORRAL

This provoked me. It was the first time I had ever been exposed to a POW who would not back other POWs, most particularly at a time when torture was not occurring. I refrained from talking with him that evening because I knew that I was emotional. I would have a great deal of difficulty discussing it with him without getting angry.

I understood very quickly why he had been relieved of command. I was unsuccessful in my efforts to get him to conform, so I asked the wing commander for a direct order demanding revised and improved performance. I never had another problem, and we never exchanged another word.

The fall of 1972 was a mixture of good and bad news. We had contact with some new 1971 and 1972 shootdowns, notably the well-known Air Force balloonist, Joe Kittinger. His group were agressive performers and good resisters, which is why they were in Camp Unity instead of the Zoo.

They began writing long newsgrams and sketching comprehensive diagrams on every subject they thought we would have an interest in. They asked that we tell them what we wanted to hear about and they would write every scrap of information they had on that subject.

The group smuggled comprehensive notes and sketches to us of the Boeing 747 Jumbo Jet, the F-14 and F-15 fighters, the construction of the moon rocket and all of its details, automobile sketches and data, motorcycles, quadrasonic radio, light aircraft information, recent targets destroyed, everything a "hungry for news" POW could want. They were superb, kind and sympathetic beyond description.

One of the new shootdowns, Major Paul K. Robinson, was an ex-Misty. The Mistys had organized themselves into generations, I discovered, and had achieved considerable success. They were a legend in Southeast Asia, and a unit of high stature in the history of the Air Force. I was informed that they were still using tactics I had developed. He told me they held a "practice reunion" each year, awaiting my release and that every reunion began with a toast to "Bud Day, Misty One." It was a great boost to the Viking's morale as she was always an invited guest to these reunions. On my release, we would have our first real reunion!

While these strong, young, new POWs were toughing it out in the tradition that we had established, Miller, Wilber, and the boys at the Zoo were bleating an appeal to Congress to end the war, on the "V" terms. A copy of their appeal appeared in Issue 69 of *Vietnam Magazine,* their signature clearly visible. We had the misfortune to have to listen to their cowardly broadcast over the "V" radio.

In September 1972, a pattern of treatment change began to emerge slowly, almost imperceptably. It was part of a pattern aimed at a 1972 release. Hooches were built in front of most of the rooms to accomodate a ping-pong table, although we were not permitted to use it. Some of the ugly tarpaper fencing was taken down or moved. Slightly permissive contact between rooms began when we were out-of-doors. Not free, easy, and open exchange, but halfway permissive.

I went to a quiz with Sweet Pea who informed me that I could ask for some small notebooks and pencils for languages, if I would give the name of the instructors and submit to inspections of the books.

I had strong reservations about his offer, because they had pulled this sneaky trick before. In the fall of 1970, they asked a number of men living in solo or small rooms in Little Vegas whether or not they wanted some notebooks to make their own dictionaries. Of course they did! The "V" supplied them with a notebook, required them to write their names on the books, gave them a dictionary, and let them start writing.

As soon as the notebooks were full, the "V" came around and collected them, put them on display for the visiting delegations to show how kind and decent the "V" Commies are, and the POWs never saw the books again.

I knew it could easily happen again. I told Sweet Pea that I knew what had happened before, and that if it happened again, I would not be responsible for the actions of the men in my room. He was aghast that I could think that the "people" would do such a thing. His viewpoint was that the "people" wanted us to enjoy good treatment.

Gap, an obnoxious guard, did not get the word that the "people" could hardly do enough for the old Air Pirates. At afternoon muster, he began some harassment which resulted in my dismissing the men before he had completed his improperly slow head count. The "V" could not let an insult of this high proportion go without retaliation.

On the following Saturday afternoon, I was unceremoniously jerked out of the room and roughed up by Gap, Pimples, and another guard. My crippled arm was forced up behind my back and I was beaten and pushed out of the yard into Sweet Pea's office.

Sweet Pea told me I had commited a serious "crime" against the camp and that I would be severely punished. They put me into a set of figure eight manacles, screwed them down until they cut the flesh deeply, and pounded me along the route into the "Tower," a solitary confinement cell between Rooms Two and Three. It was dismal, filthy beyond description, with some pooled water at the foot of the bed.

A monstrous cloud of mosquitoes roared into the air as I stepped over the water. Rat droppings covered the bed. A large pile of rat-chewed cartons from POW packages littered the left end of the pedestal. An iron bar that was designed to hold one leg of each of five prisoners leaned against the wall.

NO O.K. CORRAL

The "V" orderd me down onto the pedestal in the prone position and tried to force me into the stocks. The bar was so rusty and disused, they could not close it. They were unable to lock me into the stocks. Happiness is a rusty set of torture stocks!

The door smashed shut, and I was back in filthy solitary again. The manacles pained me severely, and my hands and fingers began the characteristic swelling that accompanies this torture. Within an hour, my fingers looked like huge sausages, and my hands were turning blue.

At 9:00 p.m. the door suddenly opened, and a different guard appeared and unscrewed the manacles, handed me a cup of water, two small bananas, and departed. I was ignored completely the next day, except to receive a full cup of water, and a fairly decent-sized meal.

Sleeping without a mosquito net in this room reminded me of my days on the bank of the Ben Hai. My right hand again became totally paralyzed.

The following day, about noon, I was taken out of the room, punched and banged into the fencing with my arm again twisted up behind my back. I was pushed into the quiz shack. My quizzer was now the Rat. It was a greasy quiz, very low key, and I got the message.

They had made another mistake in pulling me out of the room without clearing the action with the Communists at their downtown headquarters. They had pulled me out, expecting to have authority to give me the mistreatment they had given Mike Christian. When they told the story to headquarters, they were ordered to back off. This explained why Rat was conducting the quiz. Sweet Pea could not admit that he had exceeded his authority, or "lose much face." Rat was smoothing things over. I was glad!

Without much feeling, Rat told me that I would be severely punished if I ever tried to run the room again, emphasizing that I was not in charge, only the camp authorities (who were as will-o'the-wisp as "the people") could be in charge. Because the camp wanted me to enjoy good treatment, I was permitted to return to my room. This was the last roughing up of any of the old shootdowns.

The "V" propaganda machinery went into perpetual motion early in the fall. We began getting censored pieces of the *Communist Daily Worker*, *The Soviet Union*, *China* and *Vietnam Magazine*. All were a poor imitation of *Life* magazine. Same format, same layout, a crude imitation.

The "V" actually delivered on the notebooks and approved them for French and Spanish. Several propaganda pamphlets published in French became available. The books went into the French program, directed and supervised by Jerry Coffee.

Wednesday and Saturday night at the movies was conducted by anyone who could remember and tell a movie as he recalled it. There was no premium or penalty for accuracy. The novel came into popularity, starting with its historical perspective, and carried through to the present. Since the course involved some telling of the stories, it became extremely popular.

In September, part of another group of early releasees (Gartley, Charles, and Elias) were taken home by their mothers and wives. I posed this question to myself. "How did you get home from the war, Daddy?" Answer: "My mother came and got me!" Wow! That should impress the kids.

In one of the *Daily Workers* I saw that Gartley had been presented with a red, white, and blue automobile by his home town in Maine. I always wondered why. A POW had penciled in under the picture, "Needs a yellow stripe down the back to match."

The theatre next door had been abandoned, and Larry Guarino and the remainder from Room Seven moved in. The rest of the tarpaper fences were dismantled, and a slight bit of mixing was permitted in the yard. But only a little, and for a short time.

There was some concern by the "V" about the old Air Pirates' eyes and whether we could see well enough. Some large bulbs, perhaps 300 watts, replaced the small bulbs, and made it possible to study in the room at night. How sweet it was!

The radio, printed matter, and massive propagandization concerning the "uprising" in the South, the great victories at Quang Tri and Hue, seemed to take on a desperate note, as if they were trying harder to convince themselves than to convince us.

Pro-communist Americans began to rain on Hanoi. Jane Fonda cavorted with the enemy antiaircraft gunners, and bleated lies about Air Pirates bombing the dikes. Ramsey Clark was quoted in "V" propaganda tapes as denouncing the U.S. role in the war, and repeating many of the Communist propaganda distortions about South Vietnam. His gullibility and naivete sounded childishly foolish.

These disgusting attempts to help the enemy had been very effective in the past in their prolongation of the war by building "V" morale, and by clouding the issues with their lying testimony in America. However, this time it was a wasted effort on their part.

We were elated to hear of the heavy bombing of Haiphong by B-52s, and super-delighted to hear that Haiphong port had been mined. Other fine news was that the Thanh Hoa Bridge had been cut and dropped. This was a dreadful blow to Vietnamese morale, as the bridge was a symbol of national resistance. The Doumer bridge in Hanoi, crossing from downtown Hanoi to the Gia Lam Airport marshalling yard and railroad intersection was sliced. The floods began and the "V" panicked that the U.S. was going to cut all the dike complexes. This brought a hail of pre-emptive announcements that the U.S. had already proceeded with this program, coming from all Communist countries and Hanoi's foul-mouthed friend, Jane.

The "V" laid all their bets on the Democratic contender from South Dakota. We were read repeatedly every plank in his platform, every favorable comment on anything from the Democratic side, with never a mention of the platform of the incumbent. We were drowned with rhetoric, persuasion, and distortion.

The "V" were solidly behind the proposal of candidate George McGovern to crawl on his knees to Hanoi to obtain the release of prisoners. I, as one of many, would not have returned with him, had such a thing come to pass. Had he been elected and crawled to Hanoi, I fully intended to kick him in his misdirected ass and walk over him on my way out.

The Democratic platform was referred to as the "peace" program, as opposed to the Republican "illegal war" program. Several POWs became quite emotional about the possibility of a Democratic victory, and threats of emigrating to Australia, England or Canada began to mount. The POW concensus was that we wanted to go home, but not at that price. Even though we had been gone from America for a long time, very few POWs were so far out of contact with the realities of American politics as to believe that the Democratic party had a prayer of winning the election. Most predicted a whopping defeat for McGovern.

The "V" were finally faced with the facts of life of a real war. Haiphong was mined by carrier aircraft and heavily bombed by B-52's and reduced to rubble in many places. There was no unrestricted port where all the fuel, oversized cargoes, such as missiles, aircraft, and guns, could be freely delivered. The munitions ships and supply ships were not queued up in a huge line waiting to discharge the war materiel that made this war go.

More and more Communist sympathizers arrived to buck up "the people" in August of 1972. It is interesting that the International Red Cross and other impartial groups never were permitted to make one visit to Hanoi.

I always wondered why group after group seemed to say how wonderful the Communists were and how bad the United States was. I wondered how they could determine those facts in just a few days, when our experience over many years had shown that everything was just the opposite.

It did not surprise us when we learned from new shootdowns that these groups returned to the U.S. and faithfully reported that our treatment was good, and in keeping with the Geneva Convention. I always wondered what POWs they had talked with, for none of the hard-line tough guys that I knew had ever met one of these delegations. I had never known of any open visits conducted by visitors in an average camp and a meeting with just ordinary prisoners.

In a closed society such as North Vietnam, it is both incredible and unthinkable that any free, unguided, unarranged tour of the country or prisons could have taken place. These delegations got into Hanoi only by agreeing to return to the States speaking well of the Communists and badly of U.S. conduct. In my view, Article III, Section 3 of the U.S. Constitution, and the highest law of our land, applies. "Treason against the United States, shall consist only in levying war against them, or in adhering to their enemies, giving them aid and comfort."

Different generations, with other dispositions, have done such things as tar and feather and try for treason those groups who have aided and assisted the enemies of this country. In spite of the efforts of these fall visitors, the Democrats lost the election.

With all of the tarpaper dividers in the courtyard removed, the bamboo mats which blocked the air and our view came down. We were permitted to play basketball or volleyball with another room. Only the senior group of officers, Colonel Flynn and his staff, were held in hard living. "Magic lines" were drawn on the cement that a man from Room Two could not cross, for instance. He could stand on one side of the line and talk across, but the "V" scurried about sending men back to their room for "crossing violations." Many stools were brought into camp, not for torture this time, but because the "people" wanted the old Air Pirates to be comfortable, to have something to sit on. Packages arrived and more pictures and package goods were distributed. A fairly large amount of clothing from old packages was delivered. Much of it was mouldy and chewed by rats, but it was a good supplement for the coming winter.

The "V" sprang a surprise on us, telling us before elections that our government had signed some agreements to end the war, but then had reneged on them. They put a guard in our window to observe and record our reaction to this and similar radio programs. We were of course deeply interested, but showed a bland disbelief.

The ploy was so crudely done, that it was impossible for anyone to fully accept it, but it contained enough truth that it held the seed for some great speculation. We eagerly anticipated the elections, for we were unanimous in our feelings that with the combination of defeat on the Quang Tri front, the bashing of Haiphong, and the selective destruction of targets of real significance around Hanoi, the "V" were seriously negotiating, expecting the same results that we did. Our beliefs were reinforced by the first semi-professional dental care that had ever occurred in the camp. Even the bad attitude cases could get a tooth filled or pulled. This was without precedent.

Even more unbelievable were campwide chest x-rays taken in a portable East German machine. There probably was no film in the machine, but it made good propaganda. I almost expected Spot or Soft Soap Fairy to pop out and swat me on the back and say, "Hi, there! Nigh, old buddy, how's it going?"

Suddenly, it was election day. Tensions were high in early November 1972. We wondered how soon we would hear the results. A message came through the wall that Soft Soap Fairy had commented that the "V" had been studying the news and did not think the new president would be McGovern. This was typical of SSF, always leaving himself an out.

The election returns came quickly. A smashing defeat for the man who was going to crawl to Hanoi to bring us home! Some rejoiced; others were sad as they saw him as their messiah. Those who had expected immediate action by the president were plunged into despair, and there was that group who direly began predicting, "Another four years."

I was able to get in touch with Jim Kasler at this time and get back the pair of glasses I had stolen from the Bug a year and a half before. Kasler had carefully guarded the lenses, getting them safely through a raft of room and shakedown inspections. Several men in that room needed glasses, and shared them. Since the frame was nearly worn out, they tied it together with some lightweight wire. I have the glasses now as a souvenir.

We were given a French-to-Russian textbook, *Manuel de Francais*. It was of great value, even though it was totally Communist propaganda. It gave us something to read, examples of construction, idioms and usage that we needed badly.

There didn't seem to be too much that the "people" could do for the Air Priates. A word has to be said about the Communist dialectic. Being old-line revolutionists, the party verbiage is replete with archaic Communist expressions long out of vogue in the more civilized Commie countries. The "V" radio continually talked about "the people," that mythical group existing only as a facade for the Communist Party. If, for example, "The Vietnamese people protest," that meant the Communist Party protested.

Many Western concepts are corrupted in the same way. According to the Communist, for example, all wars of revolution are just wars. Therefore, any resistance to a Communist revolution is unjust. Any government, including the U.S., which resists revolution is, therefore, fighting an unjust war, according to "V" logic.

By the same line of logic, Communists always seek peace, by killing non-Communists. But if the intended victim resists getting killed, he becomes a fascist war monger, reactionary, or criminal.

From the Communist publications carried into the camp by the anti-war visitors, we learned of the Watergate burglarizing (many speculating that theft of political secrets must truly be *petty* larceny), and of the bizarre story of Senator Edward Kennedy and Mary Jo Kopechne. It was a small world when news of such happenings travelled 10,000 miles around the world into the Stone Age.

CHAPTER SEVENTEEN

The End Cometh
(Seventh Ring of the Malebolge)

On the evening of December 18, 1972, the normal evening routine drew to a close. Mosquito nets were strung, elaborate bedrolls were laid out to ward off the cold, and the bridge games and reading groups began to close off their activities. At 9:00 p.m., the normal time for taps, the air raid siren began to shriek.

The turnkeys and guards, whose off-duty jobs were self-defense and prisoner control, joked and lollygagged around noisily as they went to their defense positions. Loud laughter from the guards rent the evening air just as some of the lights were extinguished. A silence set in as POWs searched for their beds and attempted to get under their nets.

Suddenly the bark of anti-aircraft guns, rifle fire, and the *blam! whoosh!* of surface-to-air missiles sliced through the evening quiet. Bombs began to fall in an awesome thundering pattern in every direction around the camp. Nervous, frightened oohs and aahs rose from the guards outside. Out of the east window of the room, we could see enormous explosions as an area near the Doumer Bridge and Gia Lam Airport brightened the sky with the explosion of fuel, ammunition, and supplies.

Every man in the room was on his feet and whispered voices were heard. "Great Scott! Look at that!" A huge fire ignited behind and southwest of Colonel Flynn's and Robbie Risner's cells. The attacks were hard to fathom.

The "V" privates were wildly firing their rifles at unseen aircraft four to five miles away, and gun positions seemed to be firing at each other. Hanoi had been surprised, and it was clear that this was no ordinary attack. Missiles were fired in salvos of two, three, or four. Shock waves from the firing guns and launched missiles blasted through our open windows, rattling the roof and causing small pieces of plaster to fall from the ceiling.

Aircraft engines roared, guns fired, bombs continued to fall in no clear pattern, and the earth groaned in agony as it vibrated, rippled, and twisted. At about 9:12, a brief silence fell. Something was burning in every direction from the prison, like waves emanating outward from a pebble dropped into the water. The pebble was Hoa Lo Prison, and all around it, and outward from it, death and destruction rained with more intensity than the summer torrents.

On the heels of this brief silence, out to the east, came that unmistakable noise that I had heard during my escape. That delightful, beautiful shrieking roar of a long, extended stick of bombs from a B-52! Those bombs had scarcely stopped exploding when from the west, than the northeast came the same sound. Gasps of fright, awe, terror and despair slipped from the mouths of the guards as they watched whole sections of Hanoi rise from the ground as solids, to become flying pebbles several hundred feet in the air.

A muffled, suppressed cheer of relief and joy rippled quietly through the building. The wellsprings of cheer boiled within me as I realized that I was *now* a free man. No one was going to have to crawl to Hanoi to secure my release. After a few days, hours, or minutes of this, the Communist hierarchy would be begging to release the POWs.

"I'll bet it takes less than a week to fold their knees," my brain asserted. I could scarcely restrain myself from cheering, shrieking the news. I'm free!! After all those years, our president has finally applied the correct solution. Let us hope it will be remembered by future presidents . . .

The feeling was electric, and roared through the room like a locomotive. We were filled with an ecstatic air of happiness, and men stumbled over each other in the darkness, congratulating one another upon their emancipation, viewing the rain of fire with rapt awe. It was the first time most of us had seen real air power from the target point of view.

The night passed slowly for us, but it was an agonizing eternity for the "V." The raids continued until daylight. There was never a period of more than a few minutes between huge bomb clusters smashing the ground, wave after wave, ripple after ripple.

Early in the morning, a B-52 was hit by a missile, and its enormous fuel load torched off like a giant searchlight in the sky, illuminating the earth from horizon to horizon with an orange-white glow. Gasping noises of disbelief rose from the guards. I did not sleep a wink during the night, and my thoughts free-wheeled between bomb bursts, fires, and the future. This was the day. For five years and three months, I had waited for it. Soon, very soon, I would hear the contralto voice of the Viking in something besides my dreams. I would be back with her, with the children, back to the evening red-burned clouds at sunset as they scalloped Camelback Mountain in Phoenix, back to America. The thought was so delicious that it was fearsome.

Even the most serious, dead-to-the-world sleepers did not sleep. Almost

THE END COMETH

every man was up all night. Every few minutes, one of the guards would come to the Judas hole and shout, "Kipsillent!" There was little persistence to this harassment, and many "V" realized that the war was just about over.

At about 4:30 a.m., the bombing halted as abruptly as it had begun. The air raid siren did not sound the all-clear for quite some time. The attitude of the "V" was to act as if the raids had not occurred, as if by not thinking about them or mentioning them, that somehow they would just go away.

Sirens sounded. They did not go away! All day . . . all night . . . the planes came. B-52s, A-6s, F-111s, F-4s, F-105s. The city shook, vibrated, cowered, pained, and bled.

As our morale climbed, the "V" sagged. The camp radio announced defiantly that the U.S. aggressors could never cow, never blackmail the "people" into submission. The people, it said, would fight to the last drop of Vietnamese blood.

Like locusts, the bombers came, sowing destruction, terror, fire and annihilation.

Vietnamese who had claimed that they had defeated U.S. air power now came to understand that they had never *seen* air power. The puny raids of the past had been only the most token of gestures. The real world of air power was now being displayed on the stage of the Hanoi streets, and it was a real "hit." The arrogance so characteristic of the prison managers melted and ran into the sewers as they speculated that perhaps George Day, or one of the POWs, might soon be the new prison commandant, and they might soon be behind the bars. Sweet Pea went from arrogant to sickeningly servile with the attack.

Days passed at a snail's pace. A number of ranking Communist Party members who had been around POWs for years began to show up in Hoa Lo prison. The prison was the aiming point for the bombers. The bombs were falling outside a one-mile circle around the camp. It was clear that the safest place in Hanoi, in fact, the *only* safe place in Hanoi, was the POW camp. I believe that Heartbreak, NGV, and the courtyard became a haven for those brave leaders of the "people." We could see that the last drop of Vietnamese blood they fought to . . . *was not going to be their own!*

I thoroughly enjoyed the notion that many of these cruel animals were cringing for protection in the same areas where they had mistreated us. I was like a drunk at the peak of an alcoholic jag. My spirits were buoyant, bubbling, and anxious. Did I dare set some magic date? Did I dare speculate that on January 9, or on February 12, I would be walking out the front door of Hoa Lo, heading for the airport, or the port of Haiphong?

The multitude of disappointments from the past exercised a restraining hand on my runaway dreams, and I had to tune out anything as positive as a date. My experience with the "V" instinctively told me that I could not be certain of leaving at a particular time. I would not be certain when I walked out the gate, not when I boarded a truck for this or that destination. I would be certain of leaving only when I was in international waters, or international airspace, and well away from North Vietnam.

I realized that I was but one of many minute actors in the show of international diplomacy. While my exact date was unknown to me, someone in my government knew, and knew firmly, that I was a free man. Perhaps Henry Kissinger or President Nixon. When? That was the nitty-gritty!

The bombs fell day and night, night and day, and the targets burned. By late December, the supply of SAMs had been used up, and shortly after Christmas the attacks of the bombers were met with only token resistance from guns or missiles. There were few missiles to fire, the anti-aircraft guns were silent because of a shortage of ammunition, and Hanoi lay prostrate, bleeding, helplesss, frightened. Its aircraft, guns, missiles, railroad yards, etc., were in shambles. President Nixon's air power had creamed them.

The myth of invincibility of the "people" had been squashed like a ripe grape under the tread of an elephant. The pathetic claims of great victories over the capitol by Hanoi Hannah could not stir even the most rabid and deranged Communist. America's air forces had defeated North Vietnam.

Everyone who saw or heard the destruction knew that the Communists, not the attackers, had been smashed. All the giant had to do was step on the Communist worm and the head would die. On December 29th, much to my disappointment, the bombers did not return. What a pity!

Just before the bombing halt, Guarino and I were moved out of our squadrons, and into the Rawhide area, commanded by Colonel Risner. This group was composed entirely of commanders and lieutenant colonels, so LG and I were the junior men in the group as majors. It was a wonderful reunion, enthralling to see some new faces. After almost five years of harassment for leadership, it was great simply to melt back into the crowd.

The bombs had stopped and did not start again. The "V" regained some of their despotic arrogance and living conditions improved slightly. We began to get some letters. I received one from Doris which was a direct response to some coded hints I had given her only a few months before. I had written, "Buy the twins pink elephants. Don't buy Steve a donkey, as they are unreliable and can't be trusted."

Her letter replied, "Steve's donkey (the Democrats) is dying." I was to receive more letters in January and February 1973, than in all of my previous months of confinement.

On the evening of January 27, 1973, the "V" announced the terms of the Paris protocols, promising that we would receive a copy of them the

THE END COMETH

following day.

This was a positive step forward, after all the rhetoric. The "V" handed a copy of the protocols through the door, specifying the conditions of the bombing halt, and the prisoner release procedures. It was an historic moment, and I promptly asked all of my roommates to sign my copy.

That evening the radio offered the following warning. "Many detainees (a step up from Air Pirates) have done some very bad things against their country while in detention. If anyone slanders the DRVN, these black deeds will be exposed."

A roar of laughter rose at this crude blackmail attempt. It was accompanied by loud and numerous Bronx cheers across the camp. How, and in what words, could anyone slander North Vietnam?

We were to be released by order of shootdown, subject to priority for the sick and wounded. This release order was generally followed by the "V," except that Navy Captain Wilber and Marine Colonel Miller from the Zoo were released early and out of sequence, on the first release. One month of freedom was a small paycheck for three or four years of treachery.

CHAPTER EIGHTEEN

Out of the Darkness
(Eighth Ring of the Malebolge)

On February 3, 1973, I was ordered to roll up my belongings, then moved with a number of men in my shootdown group to the Plantation. I was moved into Room Four of the Warehouse with Colonel John P. Flynn, commander of the 4th Allied POW Wing, and David Winn, the vice commander.

We knew from the protocols that our release date had to be about March 15, 1973, if the "V" carried out their part of the bargain. None of us had much confidence that they would. The "V" did hold up the second release for what must have been the longest pair of days in the lives of the men waiting.

It was a great pleasure to meet John Flynn and Dave Winn. I knew of John from the 20th Wing at Wethersfield, where he had preceded me slightly, and where he had enjoyed a fine reputation among his fellow pilots. This was his third war as a combat fighter pilot. Although quite crippled in body, he had lost nothing in mind, in spite of the long days of isolation.

Dave possessed a quick, calculating mind, and was also a long-time, salty fighter pilot. Quiet, keen and bright, he was a pleasure to live with. I enjoyed hearing their views, since I had been on the bottom, middle and top in some of my isolated commands. Their approaches to our problems were sound and rational.

"Bushy," the former commander at Son Tay, was camp commander at the Plantation. He stuck to the foolish policies of the past, refusing to deal with Colonel Flynn, and attempting unsuccessfully to deal with us through the junior officers. One could logically have expected the immediate pre-release treatment of the prisoners to improve, in order that the departure would end on a less sour note. One would have expected a rash of high-calorie food, improved medical care, and morale and comfort items. Not so! East is east. "V" are "V." Leopards do not change their spots, and perhaps they realized the irreparable cannot be patched.

OUT OF THE DARKNESS

In the course of some afternoon time in the sun, where I leisurely studied my German and French, I took the time to do some introspection and reflection. There is a time to sow and a time to reap. What had we, as POWs, sown, or reaped?

We had sown good leadership, good example, ethical conduct, concern for our fellow man, love of country, obedience to national and international law, and to our Code of Conduct. We had sown loyalty and allegiance to our fellow man and country, as well as love of God. The general feeling among the POW population was high regard for each other, and high satisfaction of a job well done under difficult circumstances.

Some possessed guilt feelings at not having been men of iron. Some were appalled at their weaknesses. Still others marvelled in their strength. Senior and junior officers alike had tried to keep all Americans in the fold, and when some slipped out, tried desperately to bring them back into the group with amnesty and forgiveness.

What had we reaped? In opposition to the Korean War prisoners, we had not thrown anyone out into the snow to die. Instead, we had pulled some poor performers back into fellowship when they strayed. Willful and intentional misconduct had been held to the lowest level possible. Misconduct had been pointed out to the wrongdoer, and he was urged to improve or desist in his actions.

Men had become charged with a regard for country and its institutions, a regard forged in the fire of adversity. Men now fully understood the true meaning of words such as freedom, democracy, and self-government. Men had grown close to God, to His ways and truths.

Men who had light convictions in the past now held fixed views on virtue, loyalty, decency, valor, honesty, and malfeasance. For those to whom America had been the horn of plenty, lavishing wealth and luxuries on its citizens for minimal performance, a true appreciation for this Colossus of goodness had been formed.

Many understood for the first time the practical meaning of tyranny, and viewed America through the eyes of the struggling immigrant from the alleys of Naples or the ghettoes of Warsaw. They saw it as the seat of the most responsive democracy yet designed. Few of us saw it as the perfect solution to government, but none of us doubted that it was the best around. Not only did we see its many plusses, but we could now articulate them without fear of inaccuracy!

An understanding of Communism, gained through first-hand experience by a large sampling of Americans over a long period of time, was another part of the harvest. We not only knew what Commies said, we knew that there was little relationship between what they said and what they did. The shabby nature of treason, and the practical conduct required for its success, were no mystery to us who had seen it, or experienced its demoralizing effects.

The decency behind the U.S. Code of Conduct had become understandable and was endorsed by all but a tiny minority. The POW knew what the persecuted Pilgrims knew — the sweetness of freedom from tyranny.

Furthermore, we knew what "national decency" was all about, and what kind of men it took to obtain it. We knew the kind of people and acts required to keep it. We no longer wondered about the nature of patriots like Nathan Hale, Thomas Paine, Daniel Webster, Thomas Jefferson, George Washington, Abraham Lincoln, or Harry Truman. They had, in a sense, sometimes slept next to us on a stone pallet.

The rank and file POW, nearly to a man, spoke well of fellow men and country, and understood and praised the virtues of America and its institutions. Many Americans were surprised when Commander Jeremiah Denton stepped off the first aircraft at Clark AFB and said, "God Bless America." We were not surprised. He spoke for all of us.

Big times were ahead. On March 10, 1973, four days before release, I was issued my first Red Cross package, chock full of goodies, as only American gifts can be. I found a razor, *sharp* blades, my first comb, my first shaving cream, playing cards, and most important of all, some good paperback books to read — also a first.

On Monday, the 12th, we saw some pictures posted of the first group of POWs departing Gia Lam Airport. They were dressed in light windbreakers, cheap button-front trousers, and similar quality shoes. It was a great sight!

One of the books in my Red Cross package was Alexander Solzeneitsin's *One Day in the Life of Ivan Denisovich*. I couldn't believe my good fortune! A day in Ivan's life was exactly like a day in George Day's life, except Ivan's tormentor was white, mine yellow. Everything else was the same. Same kind of thinking, same kind of actions, like robots off a production line. I hope every free man in the world reads about Ivan.

Incredible as it sounds, Bug brought a group of Communists through the camp to demonstrate our pre-release treatment. He was roundly booed and hissed! Shouts of "torturer!" were heard.

Another Commie group tried to exploit us with photographs, but tough, quick-thinking Ray Horenik seized the photographer's unit and stomped it on the ground. Never the twain shall meet, especially when the mice have become lions!

Word was circulated through camp that we would depart Wednesday, March 14th. We waited apprehensively, but happily, devouring our American books. I read six paperbacks during that period, starved for the beautiful, unslanted word.

OUT OF THE DARKNESS

Wednesday morning dawned. We picked up our issued clothes and turned in most of our prison clothes. We were permitted to carry out our cups, spoons, Red Cross package items, and one suit of prison clothes. We fell straight into line by date of shootdown, loaded on busses, and drove to the airport across the Doumer Bridge. The big bridge had been badly damaged by precision bombing.

Crowds of people lined the streets curiously, many smiling and waving. The "V" tried some photographic propaganda, but Colonel Flynn had anticipated this and turned it off by passive resistance efforts, directing all officers to be alert for exploitation and to turn their backs on the cameras. Obscene gestures were prohibited!

All the way to the airport, I wondered if this were real. It had to be! The stark nakedness of action was hard to dismiss, and pessimistic as I was about the "V" intentions, the tails of U.S. aircraft on the airdrome at Gia Lam were unmistakable. The bomb damage around the airport was incredible, and it was little wonder that President Nixon had buckled their knees with ten days of bombing. It was what every POW had known would happen.

I was soon in line behind my ex-neighbor from the Zoo, Major Chuck Tyler, a fellow Arizonan. The spiteful and widely-hated Rabbit was designated to call our names to step forward from the line and report to the American representative. I was tense and apprehensive until Rabbit read "Major Jorgeday." I stepped forward with a feeling of having hurdled some high object, and saluted Brigadier General Ogan, USAF, the most welcome American face I had seen in 67 months.

Minutes later, I was aboard a U.S. Air Force C-141, airborne, and winging my way toward Clark Air Base, in the Phillipines. A slight cheer went up as the aircraft broke ground, but there was not a prisoner on the airplane who was sure he was going to get out of Vietnam.

When the pilot announced that we had crossed into international airspace, a huge roar went up, a disbelieving release of joy, hope, and anticipation. We hugged each other and danced with joy. Commander Chuck Gillespie, our erudite and Christian chaplain, led us in a deep and moving prayer of thanks to our God, our families, our country, and our president.

I couldn't wait to get to a telephone and hear what the Viking had to say.

CHAPTER NINETEEN

Out of the Malebolge

PARADISO XVIII

*106 and lo! when settled into place each flier,
I saw an Eagle as to head and breast
delineated by that patterned fire.
124 O heavenly host on whom I gaze, implore
for them who are here on earth, each one
misled by ill example! War of yore
127 Was waged by dint of sword, but now 'tis done.*
— Dante's *Inferno*

Our arrival at Clark Air Base would have melted a heart of stone. American flags, children, parents, civilian and military, all packed the ramp near our aircraft. Signs expressing support for every POW on the plane were waved by children and adults.

As I marched down to salute the Commander of the United States Forces in the Pacific, the Commander of 13th Air Force, and the United States Ambassador, the sight of Old Glory and the crowd overwhelmed me. With tears brimming from my eyes, I happily saluted and wished that I could seize my flag in a dignified way and give it the kiss of relief and love that I felt in my heart.

We had been briefed on the aircraft that our release was being viewed back in the United States via satellite television. The response from the crowd was marvelous and heartwarming. As I looked toward a group displaying a "WELCOME HOME, COL. DAY," sign, I saw slightly beyond them, a man standing on a yellow-painted metal stand used to work on a large aircraft. In disbelief, I realized it was my dear friend, flight surgeon Colonel Hap Hansen. It was Hap who had picked me out of the trees following my "no chute" bailout, and administered my first medical assistance at that time. How sweet it was, and how perfect! Like my guardian angel, he stood erect and tossed me a "highball" of welcome. The

OUT OF THE MALEBOLGE

score: Nigh - 1,000; "V" - 0!

In a few minutes I was debriefing an intelligence officer on everything I knew about other American POWs, particularly anyone who had been reported as deceased by the "V," and many about whom our government was seeking information.

An efficient production line served our medical and dental needs, and within hours, I had two badly-infected and painful teeth extracted, all of my shots brought up to date, and I was fitted for glasses which would soon arrive from Okinawa, 1,000 miles away.

An Air Force chaplain appeared and gave me the dreadful news that my half-sister, Verna Collins from Chicago, had passed away. So had my half-brother, Orval Dowell. This news was a knife thrust, because my sister was most dear and had been exceedingly kind to me. Our relationship had grown stronger over the years. Since my children had no grandma on my side of the family, I had plans for establishing better contacts with her in the future, that they might know her and love her as I did.

An especially beautiful letter from the Viking was waiting, complete with pictures of the family, and even sketches of our new house. Colonel Al Davis, POW project officer at Clark, and an old friend of 20 years, was a natural to welcome me.

Telephone calls to the family were available, and I eagerly anticipated my first talk with the Viking. My own special escort officer, Colonel Al Beckner, had made arrangements for the call, and he handed me the phone. When I heard my wife's voice, I felt as if I might melt into the phone.

All those years of waiting welled up in me like the pressure of a tornado. Although I had many things I wanted to ask her, most of all I wanted to hear her saying things. The words didn't matter, as long as it was her voice. She came through strong and clear. She was well. The children were well. They were as anxious to see me as I was to see them. All of the important things in my existence were in order.

Her parting words were, "I love you, Bud. Hurry home." That became my first order of business.

CHAPTER TWENTY

California, Here I Come

Our reception at Clark was only the first of several inspiring welcomes. Our release from Hanoi clearly had the blessings of the majority of Americans. They were happy that we did not return at any price. They, as we, were cheered and bouyed by the realization that the agony was ended, and happy that we came home united, and speaking well of flag and country.

They were thrilled, as we, that we had not disgraced ourselves as a group, but instead, came home proud, with our heads high, as Americans had done in the past, and should do in the future.

Our reception at Honolulu and March Air Force Base were equally impressive. A debt of love from country to eagle, and from eagle to country, was being satisfied in the court of common pleas.

As I stepped to the doorway of the Starlifter jet that carried me from Honolulu to March AFB, California, my eyes misted and my throat choked as I surveyed the crowd. Hundreds of Americans stood on the ramp in a gesture of welcome to their own. Fathers, mothers, families, friends. There was not a stranger in the crowd, for every person knew or loved some returning warrior.

I scanned the crowd for the Viking and children, but I saw only a blurred sea of faces. No more time, I must step down! At the foot of the steps were Major General William Pitts and Brigadier General Robin Olds. I saluted them, shook hands, and thrilled to the solid happiness that my feet were on United States soil.

Old Glory waved welcome in red and white stripes, and a guide pointed me to the microphone, where, as senior officer, I was expected to briefly address the crowd. I stated warmly my thanks to my God, my country, my people, and my president for their support of us.

From my left, I heard the familiar clicking of a woman's running heels, and I intinctively knew it was her. My head jerked sideways to look across the new eagle on my shoulder at the hurrying figure of the Viking, a huge smile of welcome on her face.

Her hair was perfect, done in the same style as her pictures where she'd worn the green dress. Now in a powder-blue suit, she looked like an angel. As I kissed and squeezed her, her contralto voice spoke shakily. "Welcome home, Daddy! I love you! It has been sooooo long!"

Over her shoulder, I could see four handsome children charging us. My Steve, now taller than me. George, Jr., dark-haired and erectly serious. The twins, nearly dancing with joy.

"Dear God, finally, I'm home. It's real. I'm here." All of my anxieties and apprehension were washed into oblivion as I looked into the happy faces of my family. Their goodness and love lighted my spirit as the rising sun glorifies the morning flowers. I basked in an overwhelming joy. "All those prayers are answered, God. Thank you!"

One of the children shyly handed me a crudely-scrawled note. Twelve words said it all.

"Welcome home, Dad. We love you very much. We have been waiting."

Tears poured from my eyes. Deep in my throat, words silently formed, "Dear God, it was the trial of trials, but thankfully I can look them in the eye and hold my head high. Perhaps that makes it worth while."

EPILOGUE

1989

The Viking and I resumed our love affair and renewed our marriage vows in a quiet family ceremony. My children were clones of their mother and we blended together like a good song. I had to take exhaustive daily physical therapy ("civilized torture") to enable me to return to flying fighters.

It was thrilling to confirm my wife's incredible efforts to secure humane treatment for the POWs, and to know of her unflagging support of bombing Hanoi. We travelled extensively, and incorporated the NAM-POW group. We met and were recognized by President Richard Nixon, Secretary of State Henry Kissinger, Secretary of Defense Melvin Laird, and numerous other politicians and senior military officers. After being "the blackest criminal," it was great to have someone speaking well of me for a change.

Within weeks of my return, Misty One and Two (Bill Douglass and Bud Day), were back flying a two-seat Hun. Both discovered, surprisingly, that I could still fly the jet. I was returned to flying status in July 1974, and checked out in the F-4 Phantom. I was assigned to Eglin Air Force Base, Florida, as vice commander of the 33rd Tactical Fighter Wing.

Letters, cards, telegrams, and gifts of welcome rained on us. Invitations to speak, travel, and vacation were so generous, many could not be answered.

My hero H. Ross Perot (plus the EDS gang) feted us in San Francisco, and introduced us to Colonel Bull Simon and the entire group of Son Tay rescuers. I conveyed my heartfelt thanks to those heros.

In December 1974 I was invited back to South Vietnam and awarded its highest medal by President Thieu, along with several other decorations. On March 14, 1976, I was awarded the Medal of Honor by President Gerald Ford. Since President Richard Nixon had caused the bombing of Hanoi that obtained my release, I requested my medal be re-presented by him . . . which was done in 1977.

This medal, in addition to my Air Force Cross, made me the nation's most highly-decorated hero. I possessed every significant combat medal and approximately 50 combat awards. The anti-U.S. bias of the press made me think about the meaning of the word "hero." Dorie and I became actively involved in politics and highly critical of the press.

Despite my extensive fighter experience and years of combat leadership, I was not offered the type of top military leadership position I felt I deserved. Instead, I was offered a non-promotable, non-flying job. Rather than accept it, I retired early from the Air Force in 1977 to return to the legal profession.

Having been a lawyer since 1949, I took the Florida exam and was admitted to the Florida Bar in 1977, and today I am a trial lawyer in Fort Walton Beach. Viking and I lecture frequently on the war and POW experiences to both military and civilian audiences. Dorie runs my law office efficiently, and we celebrated our 40th wedding anniversary in 1989. Our love affair goes on.

All of my children are doing well. Steve, the oldest, has his 200-ton master's license as a boat captain. Captain George Day, Jr., flew F-4s overseas as a Wild Weasel missile killer, and is now in the Air Forces UPT Program (Undergraduate Pilot's Training Program). Sonja operates a computer business, and Sandra is married to a Navy helicopter pilot. I recently flew the F-4E in a Weasel mission with my son, George. I still have the "right stuff" and if he lacks any of it, he is well on his way to getting it. My recent flights in the F-15 and F-16 assure me that for several years in the future the United States Air Force will be the most lethal in the world.

My reflections on almost 40 years of flying jet fighters and six years as a POW cause me to ask God to reincarnate me as a 26-year-old captain, flying the Advanced Tactical Fighter. When I die, I want to come back doing about 2,000 miles per hour.

The thing that people wonder about most, perhaps, is whether, after all this time, I feel it was worth it. Was the suffering, the pain, the deprivation, the lack of support from some segments of the population and the press, and even the occasional lack of respect, worth it?

I must answer with a resounding "Yes!" All of the splendid thoughts I have had about my country have proven themselves to be 100% correct. My expectations of the "good life" after my return have been fulfilled.

Our system may not be perfect, but in light of recent events in Europe and other parts of the world, it has proven over and over again that it is far out in front of whatever is in second place.

Most importantly, I did not let myself down. I lived up to the code of ethics I believe in, and I was able to return with honor.

ABOUT THE AUTHOR

Colonel George "Bud" Day

Every war has produced some legendary heroes. WW I gave us Eddie Rickenbacker and Frank Luke. WW II produced Audie Murphy, Dick Bong, and Pappy Boyington. Naturally, the long Vietnam war would produce its own legends. "Bud" Day is one of them.

As an Air Force jet fighter pilot, Day lived through history's first "no chute" bailout from a burning jet fighter, as well as surviving a fire on takeoff in another jet.

He achieved world-wide recognition in the military aviation community for his technical writings on delivery of nuclear weapons from fighter air-craft, and for his development of fuel data for maximum-range flights of jet fighters. Few equalled his bombing and gunnery skills.

Bud held every job in the fighter field, and flew almost every fighter, including the F-80, F-84, F-100, F-101, F-104, F-105, F-106, FB-111, A-4, A-7, F-15, and F-16, and the workhorse of tactical fighters, the F-4C, D, and E. He has flown worldwide. At shootdown in 1967, Bud was one of the nation's top fighter pilots with 4,500 hours of single-engine jet time, and more than 5,000 hours total time. He now flies civil aircraft.

He was the only POW of the Vietnam war to escape from North Vietnam and to make his way to South Vietnam. He is the nation's most highly decorated hero, holding more than 50 combat decorations and awards, including the Medal of Honor, Air Force Cross, Distinguished Service Medal, Silver Star, Distinguished Flying Cross, Bronze Star, Air Medal, and several Purple Hearts and a dozen battle stars. Of foreign decorations he holds South Vietnam's highest medal — the National Order of Vietnam, and the Gallantry Cross with Palm . . . both presented by President Thieu in Saigon in 1974.

Acquiring a law degree in 1949 and an M.A. in political science in 1964, Day combined his remarkable flying and intellectual skills to become one of America's stand-out combat leaders of the Vietnam war.

He is now a practicing trial lawyer, writer, and lecturer on politics and war.